SUPER LEAGUE '96
Same game. New attitude.

Graham Clay
Tim Butcher

All the best Gordon,
Here's to Doncaster in '97

Tim Butcher

League Publications Limited

First published in Great Britain 1996 by
League Publications Limited
The T&A Building
Hall Ings
Bradford BD1 1JR

A CIP catalogue record for this book is available from The British Library
ISBN 1 901347 00 1

Designed and Typeset by League Publications Limited
Printed by Stanley Press, Dewsbury, West Yorkshire

Project Editors	Graham Clay
	Tim Butcher
Design	Tony Hannan
Contributors	Martyn Sadler
	Malcolm Andrews
	Daniel Spencer
Photographers	Andrew Varley
	Simon Wilkinson
	Vicky Matthers
	Andy Howard
	Martin Robson
	Sig Kasatkin
	Paul Cooper

CONTENTS

ACKNOWLEDGMENTS

The decision to launch what is intended to become an annual reflection on each Super League campaign was taken, in publishing terms, extremely late.

It took a great deal of effort by many people to bring the project to fruition and the publishers gratefully acknowledge the following.

Malcolm Andrews, whose Sydney apartment became home for the authors en-route to linking up with the Great Britain tour squad. It was here the majority of the book was written during a frantic couple of weeks in September.

Tony Hannan, who held the fort back in Bradford and prepared the book for printing.

Danny Spencer, who compiled the statistics with great care and attention to detail.

The *Rugby League Express* and *Super League Week* writers, who reported on the games and dug out the news all year long. Special thanks go to John Huxley, Andy Wilson, Trevor Hunt, Phil Caplan, Mike Latham, Mike Rylance, Tony Beattie and Raymond Fletcher.

The majority of the pictures are from the files of photographers Andrew Varley, Simon Wilkinson and Vicky Matthers at the Varley/Wilkinson Agency (Leeds).

Additional pictures by Graham Clay, Andy Howard, Martin Robson, Sig Kasatkin and Paul Cooper (Paris).

FOREWORD

Super League!

A new idea born in 1996. Rugby League by another name, but taken away from the mud, wind, fog and rain of winter.

Suddenly the game played under grey skies in Northern England became the sunshine sport, giving its supporters the chance to take a boat trip down the Seine or the Thames to watch their local club playing in Paris or London.

After years of hiding under a bush, the greatest game of all suddenly began to discard that lack of confidence that has seen it accept its undeserved second class status as a sport that no one outside the north would be able to appreciate.

For years those of us who love Rugby League have wanted to take it to a wider audience.

Suddenly Super League gave us that opportunity.

Super League had a wonderful launch in late March in Paris's Charlety Stadium.

The new Paris St Germain club surprised everyone - first, by drawing more than 17,000 fans for that first televised game, and second, by defeating the Sheffield Eagles in a wonderful Super League encounter that was to set the tone for the remainder of that memorable season.

There were so many wonderful matches, great tries and superb performances during that first season that you may, like me, have struggled to remember all the highlights.

There were ups and downs, and it wasn't all plain sailing, especially for those clubs that had been leaders in the old game and found difficulty in adjusting to the new. Everyone had to come to terms with a new order in Rugby League.

As the season neared its end the editorial team at Rugby League Express, the country's leading Rugby League weekly newspaper, put our heads together and decided that we would record all the excitement of this first season.

We thought it would be easy to do, given that every week in the pages of our newspaper we had recorded all the events that had marked this new phase in Rugby League's noble history.

But little did we realise how difficult it would be to do justice to this extraordinary season.

To select the highlights when there were so many was a major operation in itself.

But finally we have done it.

We have produced the first major record of Super League - the matches, the personalities, the international events, the statistics, the celebrations and the tears.

It's a gripping story.

We hope you will enjoy reading this book as much as we enjoyed producing it.

Martyn Sadler, Managing Editor, Rugby League Express

INTRODUCTION
Super League - The Beginning

The two and a half year period from March 1994 to October 1996 comprised the most dramatic months in the history of Rugby League, since its very formation a century before.

Wigan won the World Club Championship in Brisbane. Great Britain beat the Kangaroos at Wembley before sinking to yet another series defeat.

The game approached its Centenary and prepared many grand plans to celebrate the 100th year since that meeting at The George Hotel in Huddersfield, culminating in the Centenary World Cup.

But behind the scenes, far more dramatic events were unfolding.

In Australia, the Australian Rugby League (ARL) had begun negotiations with Rupert Murdoch's News Limited for Ansett Airlines to take over sponsorship of its competition from 1996.

Part of the deal was that the number of clubs in the Sydney area would have to be rationalised. The ARL rejected this idea, but News Limited found support from Brisbane Broncos and Canberra Raiders and the first murmurs of Super League were heard.

In November, ARL chairman Ken Arthurson threatened to kick the rebel Brisbane club out, and flew home from the Kangaroo tour of Britain for urgent talks.

But the day he arrived in Sydney, news broke that Murdoch was already planning a $500million Super League.

Arthurson, realising the concept of Super League was fast gathering momentum, asked the clubs to sign five-year ARL "loyalty" agreements. All 20 clubs did, but some later claimed they had been threatened with expulsion from the 1995 competition had they not signed.

In February 1995, talks between the ARL, News Limited and the 20 clubs broke down. The following month, News Limited confirmed they would press ahead with plans for a Super League, and began legal action to challenge the ARL's loyalty agreements.

News Limited appointed Brisbane Broncos chief executive John Ribot to head the Super League operation, and his first task was to sign up players for the new competition.

The ARL responded by doing the same, backed by finance from Murdoch's rivals - Optus Vision and Channel Nine.

Murdoch drew first blood, and the Canberra, Brisbane and Perth clubs agreed to align themselves with Super League.

Then, on April 6th 1995, Great Britain and New Zealand delivered a stunning blow

Introduction

to the ARL by also signing up en-bloc for Super League. But the ARL had already raided British shores and secured the services of, among others, Gary Connolly, Jason Robinson and Ellery Hanley. Huge sums of money were offered to even the most ordinary of players as each camp battled to secure enough players for their respective competitions.

Down under, leading players and referees continued to defect from the ARL. Another club, Penrith, joined up and the flow was only stemmed when four Canterbury players had second thoughts and rejoined the ARL.

Super League shrugged off the brief setback, and launched a club in Newcastle, the Hunter Valley Mariners to rival the Knights, and another in Adelaide. They paraded sportswear giant Nike as the major multi-million pound sponsor of Super League.

Immediately after the World Cup in Britain, the RFL officially launched European Super League, and unveiled a new team in Paris.

The World Super League Board was formed, with Maurice Lindsay as its chairman, and plans for a World Nines tournament in Fiji were revealed.

But in February 1996, on the second day of that World Nines event, news came from Sydney that the ARL had been successful in gaining Federal Court orders to prevent Super League starting in Australia.

The ARL were powerless to stop Britain going ahead with their original plans, and in March the European Super League kicked off in Paris.

In Australia, the battles raged on as the ARL competition, under the new guise of Optus Cup, started. Some players, reluctantly, returned to honour their ARL contracts. Others sought spells in Britain.

The News Limited appeal lasted right the way through till early October. Then, the week after the ARL had ended its season, the judges handed down their verdict.

Super League had won an overwhelming victory. Worldwide Super League could begin.

It capped an amazing 30-month period, and one that is hard for observers in the northern hemisphere to fully understand. After all, apart from switching to summer, the British game continued pretty much unaffected.

But the global vision for this great game - the sporting world's best kept secret - has now been mapped out.

This book records in detail the exciting inaugural European Super League season and its associated tournaments. It was published at a time when many exciting new initiatives were being discussed, including world club championships, tours, and expansion plans.

Super League has arrived.

1
THE SUPER LEAGUE SEASON

A month by month review

MARCH
Paris in the Springtime

It was almost surreal. Just weeks after celebrating 100 years as a winter sport, Rugby League's much debated switch to summer and the birth of European Super League were about to take place on a cold late-March night in Paris.

The desire for quality rather than quantity, in the desperate quest to reach and then surpass the standards set by the Australians, had led to revolutionary proposals to drag the game kicking and screaming into the future.

The traditionalists were outraged, but the visionaries could see the long overdue need for a bright modern image. A game played on firm grounds in decent stadia before big crowds was the vision of what League could be like.

At last, the game's administrators were acknowledging that all was not well. Sport around the world was charging relentlessly ahead toward intercity, interstate and even international competition fought out before a world-wide television audience thanks to the advent of Pay TV. Even the RFU, after a century of ostracising its rival code, were making plans to go professional. In the southern hemisphere an off-shoot of union, Super 12's, was about to bring together Australia, New Zealand and South Africa into a truly international competition. Soccer was enjoying its highest attendances for years, and new sports such as ice-hockey and basketball were fast gaining a foothold in major British cities.

At the same time some Rugby League clubs were financially insolvent, and if the game was to survive in this much changed environment drastic action had to be taken. No longer could a nine-month long winter league involving teams in places that no-one south of Sheffield had ever heard of be put forward as a serious rival for the public's hard earned cash and leisure time.

Perhaps the furious pace at which the changes took place shocked everyone, but when the knight in shining armour came galloping into town in April of 1995 with an offer of £87 million, few hesitated in accepting Rupert Murdoch's generosity. From the moment Murdoch's offer was accepted it was less than 11 months before Super League exploded onto the scene.

To set the ball rolling, the RFL produced 'Framing the Future', a 51 page document which would have far reaching effects on every club. Suddenly, minimum standards had to be attained and strictly adhered to. Some clubs reacted positively, and went about appointing the necessary personnel and improving their facilities. Others complained and sought sympathy rather than rolling their sleeves up.

Radical changes were made on the field too. In a desire to speed up the game the authorities moved scrums further in-field and allowed the scoring side to re-start from

First night celebrations at the Charlety Stadium,
home of Paris Saint-Germain

the centre spot. The idea of four substitutes, trialled during the Centenary Season, was adopted permanently, and referees received help during televised games from a big screen replay.

The clubs also came to the party. Marketing nicknames such as Bulls, Bears, Tigers, Reds - even Blue Sox - were introduced to hype up the likes of Bradford, Oldham and Castleford, along with glitzy new kits and promises of themed pre-match entertainment.

Paris Saint-Germain became the 'European' involvement, and there was much excitement about possible teams at Newcastle, Cardiff, Dublin and even Barcelona and Milan.

Every month or so, the RFL invited the media to witness the historic changes. Even Mal Meninga, Australia's Super League ambassador, jetted in to help promote the new global vision.

The theory couldn't be faulted. A 12-team Euro Super League would play from March to August, with a live televised game each Friday and Saturday evening. Academy games would be curtain-raisers, and clubs would provide a full afternoon of entertainment, including live bands and dancers.

The European Championship, featuring England, Wales and France, would be staged in June, and Scotland and Ireland would be encouraged to eventually form a Five Nations series.

Aussie legend Mal Meninga *(right)* jetted in
to help Maurice Lindsay promote the new global vision

The climax was to be the World Club Championship, with the top four in Europe meeting their counterparts from the Southern Hemisphere. The games would be played before huge crowds at prestigious venues such as Wembley and Old Trafford, with the final in Sydney. Unfortunately, the Australian Rugby League's success in halting the launch of Super League down under aborted that plan.

And so, on March 29, the theory was put into practice. The doubters were still numerous, but 18,000 people witnessed a thrilling game between Paris, packed with French internationals, and Sheffield Eagles who had had their best ever league campaign during the Centenary Season. Paris, against the odds, defeated the Eagles 30-24 to leave RFL chief executive Maurice Lindsay hailing the advent of Super League as an "outstanding success."

"Some reporters came for a funeral and had to write about a party," he beamed afterwards. "This is what Super League is all about. Just imagine, within a short time we could have Brisbane playing Paris."

The opening weekend also saw the re-birth of Bradford, by now called the Bulls and heading for Wembley after a semi-final success over arch-rivals Leeds. Their 30-18 home win against Castleford was played out before over 10,000, more than double the previous season's average. The Bulls were nearing the end of a massive rebuilding programme that coach Brian Smith had instigated six months earlier, and the club's vigorous marketing policy had paid immediate dividends. Some things remained normal however, with a sprinkling of snow falling across the huge Odsal expanse to welcome the new summer season!

Big Aussie Jeremy Donougher, recruited from South Sydney, had been the man-of-

Phil Clarke recovers in his Sydney apartment
after suffering a horrific career-threatening spinal injury

the-match in the semi, and again starred with a hat-trick of tries. James Lowes and Glen Tomlinson debuted for the Bulls, and Frano Botica made his bow for the Tigers in his first game since breaking a leg playing for Auckland Warriors almost a year earlier.

London Broncos, under new coach Tony Currie, came away from Halifax with a 24-22 win. Halifax had finished third in the Centenary campaign and big things were expected of Steve Simms side. But a controversial late penalty awarded against Paul Rowley for reefing the ball out in a two-man tackle gave the Broncos good field position for Darren Shaw to score the winning try. After the game, Currie predicted his side would finish in the top six. His captain, Terry Matterson, was more ambitious and claimed a definite fourth spot. He was to be proved right.

Phil Clarke in critical condition after suffering spinal injury playing for Sydney City....Neil Harmon delays in signing new contract at Leeds....Welsh international Daio Powell cleared of manslaughter in Perth....Huddersfield thwarted in attempt to sign Graham Steadman from Castleford.....South Wales sign Andy Currier but have a bid for Salford's Mike Gregory rejected....Leeds fail in bid to sign Noel Goldthorpe from St George.....RFL stop Keighley making any signings until financial dispute settled.....Wigan are priced 1/3 favourites to take the first Super League title, St Helens 100/30, and Leeds third favourites at 10/1........

At Headingley, Iestyn Harris inspired Warrington to upset Leeds 22-18 to gain revenge for their Challenge Cup defeat a few weeks earlier. Harris was in sparkling form, and scored a terrific try in helping his side sweep to a 22-6 lead. The Loiners

March

were without a recognised half-back pairing, a problem that would hinder them for much of the season, but they eventually clicked into gear and stormed back in the final quarter. Only superb scrambling defence denied Leeds.

Coach Dean Bell pointed out: "Warrington's desperation defence was great at crucial times. It's extremely disappointing but I remain optimistic."

The big winners were, as expected, Wigan, who thrashed Oldham in the first Saturday night TV game, and St Helens who gave notice of their intentions under Shaun McRae with a 62-0 romp at Workington.

At Boundary Park, the champs were 36-0 up at the break, with a Gary Connolly hat-trick the highlight of a clinical display. They eased off in the second half and the Bears gained a little respectability in the final score of 56-16. Oldham coach Andy Goodway hinted that the choice of venue was a major contributing factor to his side's poor show, saying the wide open spaces and flat surface handed the initiative to Wigan and negated "home" advantage.

In Cumbria, Saints winger Danny Arnold grabbed four tries, Paul Newlove charged in for three, and Bobbie Goulding pulled the strings as Town, still recovering from horrendous off-field problems, were simply outclassed.

APRIL
A tale of two Cities

April began with a bang and the evocative round two opener between London Broncos and Paris Saint-Germain on the Easter Thursday evening. Earlier fears about the timing of the game on the eve of the bank holiday weekend in the capital were dispelled when a crowd of almost ten thousand Londoners flocked to The Valley to see the "Tale of Two Cities - Rugby League style".

TV satellite viewers were treated for the first time to the superb skills of former Souths stand-off Duncan McRae, who scored a brace of tries as the Broncos made it two wins out of two games with a 38-22 victory.

Players to make their bow on a national stage who would become household names over the season were Greg Barwick, Tulsen Tollet - who was subsequently uncovered as a bona-fide Englishman with an Aussie accent - and prop Tony Mestrov, who went on to be one of the most effective forwards in Super League.

Mestrov replaced State of Origin player Gavin Allen, one of the Broncos' most high profile signings, who broke an arm in only the second minute of the game.

The game, or at least its aftermath, earned London coach Tony Currie the title of "League's Mr Grumpy" in Super League Week after he described his team's performance in a TV interview as "crap".

Good Friday produced one of the pivotal games of Super League 1996 with the local derby at Knowsley Road.

After half an hour, the match had gone as predicted, Wigan had raced into a 16-4 lead through tries to Terry O'Connor, Va'aiga Tuigamala and Henry Paul against one to Danny Arnold.

But, inspired by captain Bobbie Goulding and former Balmain forward Derek McVey, and roared on by a near 16,000 crowd, Saints fought back brilliantly either side of half-time. Arnold and Keiron Cunningham - a Super League star throughout 1996 - started the comeback with tries; Arnold went on to complete his second successive hat-trick to take him to the top of the try-scoring charts; and Ian Pickavance demonstrated the impact that replacement players were to make under the new interchange laws, when he bumped off Paul for the try that gave St Helens the lead four minutes into the second half.

Wigan pulled it back to 29-26 through tries to Rob Smyth and Hall, his second, before Goulding steadied the ship with a teasing kick that baffled Kris Radlinski before Tommy Martyn took advantage to score the four-pointer. Andy Northey's try at the death merely rubbed salt in Wigan's wounds, and the scores finished at 41-26.

It was a game that illustrated the speed and quality of summer football. Saints' coach Shaun McRae put the game into context. "It was a hell of a game," he said. "The intensity matches any Brisbane Broncos v Canberra Raiders clash: high scoring matches with the ball going from one end to the other. But the defences were pretty sound - you couldn't say either side was poor defensively - the teams got some lucky breaks and took the opportunities. There were some brilliant athletes out there on both sides.

"We've not got to get carried away - there will be a get square later in the year, but there's plenty of games left before that."

Elsewhere, the poor starts to the season by West Yorkshire hopefuls Leeds and Halifax Blue Sox were slowly turning into nightmares.

Leeds travelled a few miles down the road to Castleford Tigers and looked to be on course for their first win of the season when Anthony Gibbons dropped a 75th minute goal. But in a sensational finish, starman Frano Botica created a last minute try for Jason Flowers, to the utter disgust of Leeds coach Dean Bell.

"We lacked desperation and the will to win," he said, a sentiment he was to repeat often during the summer.

The Blue Sox, lacking John Bentley and John Schuster - dropped by coach Steve Simms after the defeat by London - also bombed for the second round running, this time away to unfancied Oldham Bears, playing, controversially, at the ramshackle Watersheddings ground. Less than four thousand turned out to see another nail-biter. Despite the loss of Paul Anderson, sent off for a high tackle on Dave Bradbury on the stroke of half-time, the Blue Sox clawed their way back to 22-all thanks to two tries from young half-back Craig Dean.

But, led by Welsh international full-back Paul Atcheson, the Bears scored twice in the last eight minutes, Darren Abram and Martin Crompton getting the tries that gave them their first win by 34-22.

Down the road at Wilderspool, Warrington kept up their 100% record against most people's favourites for relegation, Workington Town. The Cumbrians, who new coach Ross O'Reilly confessed had an "inferiority complex", were still in the game for an hour, but gifted Wire two interceptions as the game finished with a flurry of seven tries in the last twenty minutes.

Warrington were once again grateful to Iestyn Harris, this time his boot doing the trick. The youngster ended the game with eight goals from nine attempts, with a drop-goal thrown in for good measure.

The crowd of four and a half thousand was a disappointment, with football manager Alex Murphy calling for more support from the people of Warrington.

"You've got to support the club," said Murphy, before somewhat perversely adding, "but we're not good enough."

Over the Pennines in Sheffield, the Eagles kick-started their season with a 40-24 success over the Bulls.

Mark Aston, returned to the Don Valley Stadium after a spell at Featherstone Rovers, and his place under pressure from the young gun half-backs of the Eagles, Dean Lawford and Ryan Sheridan, masterminded the win.

But the victory was founded as much on Bradford's indiscipline, as Karl Fairbank

Halifax Blue Sox' John Schuster - dropped by Coach Steve Simms
after a poor display against London Broncos

was dismissed for a high tackle on Andy Hay after half an hour, and Graeme "The Penguin" Bradley was sin-binned twice, once in each half.

During his second ten minute absence Sheffield rattled up 18 points to wrap up the match, with tries from Sheridan, Keith Senior - another find of the season - and Hay. Aston scored a try himself two minutes from time to add to his eight goals.

"It would have been almost a mistake if we had won the game tonight," admitted Bulls mentor Brian Smith.

In division one Salford stated their intention of winning a promotion place to Super League with a 46-14 defeat of fancied Widnes at the Willows, and in two, South Wales recorded their first victory, a 24-22 win at Prescot Panthers, the re-named Highfield club.

Despite the principle of only one game per week for Super League, the clubs found it hard to resist the allure of traditional bank holiday money-spinning games and crammed in two rounds over the Easter weekend.

On the Monday, Saints kept up their winning habit with a 46-24 win at Headingley, and Danny Arnold continued his try-scoring record with two more to put him at the top of the try-scoring chart with nine in three games - four players were in second spot with four each!

April

The second of his efforts against Leeds showed he wasn't just the kind of winger who was in the right place at the right time, as he went in from dummy half from 70 metres out.

Leeds again started brightly and held a 14-6 lead at quarter time through tries to Francis Cummins and Phil Hassan. But the Saints' attacking machine proved irresistible, as Alan Hunte and Andy Northey gave them a half-time lead, and Paul Newlove, Keiron Cunningham and Tommy Martyn finished off the Loiners, orchestrated of course by the ebullient Bobbie Goulding.

RFL boss Maurice Lindsay, energised by the start of Super League reveals he is aiming for clubs in Spain and Italy.....South Africa announces it is to to launch a new 12 team competition under new administration.....Castleford Tigers sign sign Newport and Wales 'A' rugby union player Diccon Edwards....Super League Week exclusively reveals that Leeds have signed former New Zealand Test player Dean Clark....listed Warrington half-back Mike Ford signs for first division Wakefield Trinity and the Wire replace him with Auckland reserve grade player Willie Swann...

"It's been a very tough weekend," admitted Shaun McRae.

Wigan meanwhile got back in the winning groove against Warrington at Central Park. Henry Paul opened the scoring with a typically elusive try from 45 metres out. Andy Farrell starred as Wigan ran into a 16-6 half-time lead and then, after the break, Shaun Edwards charged down a Iestyn Harris kick to score the first of his two tries and seal the victory, Wigan eventually running out 42-12 winners.

London Broncos' coach Tony Currie was again in the news as his side fell to its first defeat of the season at Odsal against the Bulls by 31-24.

Broncos were 24-18 to the good after a Kevin Langer try when the Bulls got back on terms in controversial fashion. Karl Fairbank scored the try after the ball had ricocheted off Graeme Bradley. Everyone except referee Alan Bates thought there'd been a knock on but the score stood. Paul Cook converted and then dropped a goal to snatch the lead, before Robbie Paul darted over from 20 metres out to finish the scoring.

"Rupert Murdoch is putting £80 million into this league and we get blatantly bad decisions which are costing a team like us, who are trying to establish ourselves a niche in London, both supporters and money," blasted Currie.

"I could talk about swings and roundabouts," retorted his opposite Brian Smith.

The other big city club fared slightly better, as Paris Saint-Germain came from behind to snatch a late draw against Oldham Bears at the Charlety Stadium. The class of Martin Crompton had given the Bears a 14-4 half-time lead, the Irish international putting on tries for Aussie back-rower Matt Munro and centre Darren Abram.

Francis Maloney's dash down the blind-side seven minutes into the second half, plus his conversion, made it 18-4. After Didier Cabestany's reply, another Aussie, centre Andrew Patmore, restored the 14 point margin. But the French fought back superbly. In the last minute, with Oldham's star turn, loose-forward Howard Hill, in the sin-bin, Patrick Entat, who had scored a try himself 17 minutes earlier, put in a hopeful kick. Paul Atcheson fumbled, and Pascal Bomati pounced to go under the sticks for

Patrick Torreilles to snatch the 24-24 draw.

Up on the west coast of Cumbria Workington were on the end of another 50-point hammering, this time at the hands of Sheffield Eagles. But the 54-22 final scoreline hid the true story of the game. Town were well in the hunt until the hour mark, when they bombed a gilt-edged try-scoring chance to take the lead. The Eagles replied with 20 more points in the final ten minutes, with tries from Mick Cook, Anthony Farrell and Andy Hay, plus four goals from Mark Aston.

On Easter Tuesday Castleford Tigers produced their second comeback of the week when they shocked Halifax Blue Sox at Thrum Hall with a 34-30 win.

"We've been written off in many quarters," said Tigers coach John Joyner, "but there's a lot of character in this Castleford side. They never give up."

At 24-6 down, with Wayne Parker creating the openings for the Blue Sox, in a fast and furious opening, Cas looked dead and buried. But Brendon Tuuta and Tony Smith battled them back into the game, and tries either side of half-time from sub Ian Smales got them level. Jason Flowers and Tuuta added two more before Paul

Auckland reserve grade player Willie Swann wings his way to Warrington

Oldham Bears' Afi Leuila gets it in the neck from Greg Kacala
during their 24-24 draw with Paris St-Germain

Anderson pulled Halifax back to within four points. But the Tigers weathered a thrilling last ten minutes to move into sixth spot in the table.

With some pundits bemoaning the glut of points-scoring in the drier conditions, Round Four turned up the kind of conditions more reminiscent of the winter season, at least in Friday night's live TV game, when Warrington inflicted a fourth straight defeat on the Blue Sox after eighty minutes of non-stop sleet.

Ankle deep mud and 26 predominantly scrappy points led League Express reporter Tony Beattie to ask "Doesn't it make you feel nostalgic for the old days?" He answered himself, "no, actually it doesn't."

The two teams served up a creditable game in the most trying of conditions, with a Mark Forster interception swinging the game Wire's way, and winger Richard Henare getting their other try seven minutes later to complete a 16-10 win.

St Helens won the Wembley rehearsal against Bradford Bulls at Knowsley Road by 26-20.

The league leaders looked to be coasting at half-time, with a 24-8 lead. But Matt Calland, the form centre of Super League in the early part of the season, scored two more tries to complete his hat-trick, and the Bulls spurned plenty of other try-scoring chances as the Saints held on for the last ten minutes, despite having Samoan Vila Matautia dismissed for an elbow on Simon Knox. The game was the signal for the start of the Bulls' phenomenon despite the failure to collect the points.

"They were absolutely outstanding," beamed Brian Smith. "I am excited about coaching a team that can show that sort of character away from home."

Wigan kept in touch with a 28-10 win at Wheldon Road.

The Tigers shocked the reigning champs, taking an 8-0 lead. Tony Smith was in outstanding form again at scrum-half, scoring a 25th minute try from his own kick through. 10-6 down at the break, Wigan coach Graeme West took remedial action by withdrawing half-back Craig Murdock, moving Shaun Edwards to scrum-half, and Henry Paul from full-back to stand off. It worked. Andy Farrell revelled in the new found

Bradford Bulls Coach Brian Smith was left beaming after his side's narrow defeat at St Helens

freedom, creating tries for Rob Smyth - when Cas' prop Nathan Sykes was in the sin-bin for deliberate off-side - and Gary Connolly, with an individual effort by Paul in between.

Sheffield Eagles moved into third position with a 34-18 home win over London Broncos. Sheffield back-rower Paul Carr described the opening 20 minutes as "the toughest, most intense period of football this season. Both teams were at it hammer and tongs."

Keith Senior made another huge contribution to the Eagles' cause, scoring two tries in a fine all-round display.

Leeds' woes continued, and only Workington's inferior scoring record kept them off the bottom of the table. They slipped to a 25-16 defeat at Watersheddings in the Saturday night game in front of a paltry crowd of just over three and a half thousand.

Former Wigan teammates Dean Bell and Andy Goodway squared up as head coaches for the first time, and it was the Englishman who came out trumps. "We stuck to our game plan superbly," he said after the match.

Dean Bell's comments reflected a sense of exasperation. He said: "It's vital we get that first win soon. We are playing like a desperate team, but tonight we were not desperate enough for victory."

Oldham's opening salvo was too much for Leeds and they rattled up a 17-0 lead

Champions Wigan are hit by a shock transfer request
from flying winger Jason Robinson

after half an hour. But after the introduction of former Roughyed Barrie McDermott from the bench, they managed to claw themselves back to 17-16 before a Crompton penalty, awarded after referee John Connolly had sin-binned Leeds full-back Anthony Gibbons for ball-stealing in what looked like a one-on-one tackle, stirred the Bears to a big finish.

A deal to take Wigan prop Kelvin Skerrett to Wilderspool fell through....Castleford sign Western Samoan union international Junior Paramore......Wigan are hit by a shock transfer request from 21-year-old Great Britain winger Jason Robinson....and are fuming that Aussie club Perth Western Reds have played England World Cup centre Barrie-Jon Mather without completing a transfer deal.....Workington Town import Australians Tony Smith and Brad Nairn...Sheffield Eagles sign Adelaide Rams centre Danny Grimley

Crompton added a try and conversion to end the contest.

To compound Leeds' woes, George Mann was subsequently suspended for three matches after the RFL executive committee viewed a video of his challenge on Bears' hooker John Clarke.

Workington remained pointless despite Mark Wallace giving them the lead at the Charlety Stadium. Paris skipper Pierre Chamorin scored a try hat-trick in a 34-12 victory.

Already the writing seemed to be firmly on the wall for Town. Even the usually optimistic coach Ross O'Reilly, four weeks into a role that had been described as "the coaching job from hell", lapsed into despondency. "In all the previous games I have been able to draw out something positive, but not tonight," he reflected.

Meanwhile in division one Dewsbury pulled off the shock off the season, beating Hull 12-10 at New Crown Flatt and Keighley Cougars won a nail-biter at Huddersfield Giants by 12-10.

Round Five almost saw the winning run of St Helens brought to an end - for the second successive week - when they escaped by two points against the Blue Sox.

Many were expecting them to falter with Wembley only a week away. Shaun McRae blasted after the final whistle: "I'm tired of players who are not prepared to work unless they have the ball in their hands."

A Paul Newlove hat-trick was the cornerstone of the 30-28 win, with John Schuster's try and goal five minutes from time providing another nervous finish for the Saints.

Five fruitless games left Steve Simms sanguine: "All we need is a little bit of luck," the Halifax coach said.

On the Friday night, Wigan and Bradford Bulls produced one of the outstanding games of Super League 1996. Wigan showed their resolve to emerge 22-6 winners against a Bulls side that threw the ball around with no regard for ball security.

Shaun Edwards remarked after the game that he felt 105 years old, such was the pace of the game.

Error strewn it was, and thoroughly entertaining, as Bradford created chance after chance - without being able to score until the 60th minute, when Paul Loughlin finally got over the goal-line.

Before that, Henry Paul, Andy Craig and Simon Haughton had scored tries for Wigan, and their two biggest stars, Paul and Va'aiga Tuigamala, created a brilliant final score for Craig Murdock.

Leeds at last got off the mark at Headingley, with a 36-22 win over Sheffield Eagles. Graham Holroyd starred with two tries that proved crucial, as Dean Bell confessed: "I was desperate for the points." Kiwi import Nathan Picchi played his one and only game for the Loiners, dislocating his shoulder seven minutes from the end of his debut.

It left Workington Town looking increasingly isolated after their 58-0 humbling at London Broncos. The Workington team bus was stuck in traffic caused by the London Marathon which delayed the kick-off for 20 minutes, hardly ideal preparation. The Broncos took full advantage, running in nine tries, with Terry Matterson kicking eleven goals. "We were totally outdone today," admitted Ross O'Reilly.

25

April

Oldham Bears moved into fourth spot with their third win to add to their draw in Paris, this time pulling off an against the odds win in a spiteful match at Castleford.

Against the odds, because of the loss through injury of inspiration Martin Crompton. But half-back partner Francis Maloney filled the gap admirably, having a hand in all the points. Two tries in four minutes from Paul Atcheson just after the break did the damage for the Bears.

Castleford centre Grant Anderson was sent-off for a high tackle and copped a three match ban, while the Bears' Jason Temu was suspended for two games after being put on report. Bears' winger Scott Ranson was also handed a three match ban, for an elbow that left Cas' prop Nathan Sykes nursing a broken jaw, after the RFL executive viewed a video of the game.

Warrington took over third spot from Sheffield with a ruthless 48-24 win over Paris at Wilderspool. Paris were looking increasingly jaded as the season wore on, though they never threw in the towel.

Kiwi teenager Toa Kohe-Love was the Wire gamestar with two tries, but Paris utility Regis Pastre-Courtine outscored him with a hat-trick for the losing side.

TABLES AT END OF APRIL

STONES SUPER LEAGUE

	P	W	D	L	For	Agst	Diff	PTS
St Helens	5	5	0	0	205	98	107	10
Wigan	5	4	0	1	174	85	89	8
Warrington	5	4	0	1	143	124	19	8
Oldham Bears	5	3	1	1	123	138	-15	7
London Broncos	5	3	0	2	162	109	53	6
Sheffield Eagles	5	3	0	2	174	130	44	6
Paris St Germain	5	2	1	2	134	146	-12	5
Bradford Bulls	5	2	0	3	111	130	-19	4
Castleford Tigers	5	2	0	3	108	135	-27	4
Leeds	5	1	0	4	117	141	-24	2
Halifax Blue Sox	5	0	0	5	112	138	-26	0
Workington Town	5	0	0	5	64	253	-189	0

DIVISION ONE

	P	W	D	L	For	Agst	Diff	PTS
Featherstone Rovers	5	4	0	1	147	75	72	8
Salford Reds	4	4	0	0	142	75	67	8
Keighley Cougars	4	4	0	0	114	54	60	8
Huddersfield Giants	5	3	0	2	119	68	51	6
Dewsbury	5	2	1	2	56	144	-88	5
Hull	4	2	0	2	114	66	48	4
Widnes	4	2	0	2	97	84	13	4
Batley Bulldogs	5	1	2	2	58	86	-28	4
Wakefield Trinity	4	1	0	3	64	112	-48	2
Rochdale Hornets	5	0	1	4	90	115	-25	1
Whitehaven	5	0	0	5	45	167	-122	0

DIVISION TWO

	P	W	D	L	For	Agst	Diff	PTS
Hull KR	5	5	0	0	296	63	233	10
Swinton Lions	5	4	0	1	182	71	111	8
Carlisle	5	4	0	1	178	82	96	8
Doncaster Dragons	5	4	0	1	181	96	85	8
Hunslet Hawks	5	4	0	1	155	74	81	8
Bramley	5	2	0	3	102	103	-1	4
York	5	2	0	3	87	163	-76	4
South Wales	5	2	0	3	70	148	-78	4
Leigh Centurions	5	1	0	4	137	135	2	2
Barrow Braves	5	1	0	4	60	150	-90	2
Prescot Panthers	5	1	0	4	76	167	-91	2
Chorley	5	0	0	5	64	336	-272	0

CHALLENGE CUP FINAL

BRADFORD BULLS.........32
ST HELENS.....................40

"SENSATIONAL" was the front page headline of League Express on Monday 29th April.

And sensational it was.

Commentators were already describing the 1996 Challenge Cup Final as the greatest well before the final curtain was drawn on a match that displayed the quality of Super League to a far wider domestic audience than satellite TV could deliver.

Robbie Paul picked up the Lance Todd Trophy as the man of the match and a cheque for £10,000 as the first scorer of a hat-trick at Wembley. His second try in the 53rd minute, which stretched the Bulls lead to 26-12, will go down as one of the best tries ever scored on this stage.

Incredibly, Saints, with Bobbie Goulding coming up trumps again to stake his own

Chris Joynt barges through the attentions of ex-Saints team-mate Sonny Nickle

claim to the Lance Todd, had the resolve to fight back and lift the Cup.

Bulls' full-back Nathan Graham will also be remembered for the part he played. In the space of seven minutes St Helens had scored three tries from Goulding bombs, the first when Graham let the kick bounce in the in-goal for Keiron Cunningham to score.

Brian Smith refused to let Graham shoulder the blame. "All those who'd like to be at the back to catch those balls, with people coming through with baseballs bats and hand grenades, should form a queue outside my office on Monday morning," he said.

It was a record aggregate score at a Wembley Cup final, and the biggest scores for the winning and losing teams.

And it did the cause of both clubs considerable good. Bradford and Saints both went on to be the most improved clubs in Super League, both on and off the field.

Nathan Graham spills the ball
and St Helens' comeback begins

CHALLENGE CUP FINAL RUNDOWN

03 - **STEVE PRESCOTT** try after Gibbs shakes off Loughlin in the right corner   0-4
17 - **STEVE PRESCOTT** volleys ahead Goulding kickthrough for spectacular score   0-8
24 - **JON SCALES** rounds Prescott after being released by Loughlin on 40 metre line,
     PAUL COOK conversion   6-8
31 - **COOK** penalty   8-8
33 - **DANNY ARNOLD** sidesteps and dummies the cover after Newlove bust   8-12
38 - **ROBBIE PAUL** try under the posts after Graham breaks from his own quarter,
     COOK conversion   14-12
47 - **BERNARD DWYER** dummies and goes over near the posts, **COOK** converts   20-12
53 - **PAUL** scores miracle try from dummy half, **COOK** converts   26-12
57 - **KEIRON CUNNINGHAM** leaps for Goulding's bouncing bomb over the line,
     GOULDING converts   26-18
60 - **SIMON BOOTH** scoops up another Goulding bomb, **GOULDING** adds goal   26-24
64 - **IAN PICKAVANCE** dives on a third Goulding bomb, **GOULDING** kick   26-30
67 - **ARNOLD** backs up Hammond after setting him on his way to score in right corner   26-34
71 - **PAUL** mesmerises the Saints' defence to register his hat-trick, **COOK** converts   32-34
75 - **APOLLO PERELINI** settles it, crashing over from a Goulding drop-off,
     GOULDING kicks the last points   32-40

MAY
Moving in the right direction

A week after Wembley, Bradford Bulls picked themselves up and got back to the bread and butter of the league by defeating Warrington 36-14, while the victorious Saints celebrated with a thumping of Oldham Bears.

For the Bulls, it confirmed they were gathering pace as real title challengers, and illustrated to Brian Smith just what his new team could be capable of. "You've always got to be a bit worried and wonder how players will react after losing at Wembley," he said. "But I think we are moving in the right direction, and will put up a good show in Super League."

Smith's prediction would eventually be proved correct, as the Bulls began a glorious run that saw them take the points in 15 of their remaining 17 games. There were several outstanding displays in the defeat of Warrington, but stand-off Graeme Bradley was the major threat, with a powerful exhibition of forceful running. He created Paul Loughlin's opening try after just three minutes, and went on to dictate play as the disappointing Wire were totally outplayed.

It proved to be the perfect game for Nathan Graham to recover from his nightmare Wembley outing. The full-back was never put under any pressure thanks to the inexplicable absence of a kicking game by his opponents, despite threats during the build-up to the game from Alex Murphy that Graham and his team-mate Jon Scales would be subjected to an aerial bombardment.

The defeat was a massive setback for Warrington, whose only previous loss had been to Wigan. This was the year the Wire fans fully expected their team to emerge as serious contenders for top honours, but they trudged away from Odsal disconsolate.

Saints fans on the other hand basked in the glory of the Wembley win, as the sun shone at Knowsley Road for the homecoming party. Poor Oldham were merely bystanders as Paul Newlove paved the way to a 66-18 victory with a hat-trick in front of over 10,000 adoring fans, still hungover from the week long party. In all, Saints ran in 13 tries against an understrength Bears side. The win stretched Saints unbeaten run to six games, but coach Shaun McRae, like Smith, had been worried about his team's reaction to the previous week.

"I was happy to be playing at home straight after Wembley," he said. "There's nothing like playing in front of a vocal crowd, and I'm thankful to them for the way they lifted the players. It wasn't difficult to motivate the players - we're top of the league and that's motivation in itself. But it would be very easy to go off the rails. We must make sure that doesn't happen to us."

Second placed Wigan were hurting to see their arch-rivals at the top of the ladder.

May

Saints as league leaders and Wembley winners was almost unbearable for the Centenary Champions, and they were determined not to hand over the Championship crown without a fight.

Paris Saint-Germain arrived at Wigan with a pretty impressive record for a new team. Two wins and a draw from their opening five games was more than even the most optimistic had dared predict. But the cracks were beginning to show. The PSG players were suffering the effects of playing mid-week domestic games in competitions organised by the French Federation. Inevitably, they were given a harsh lesson in the finer points of the game, as Wigan's class and experience shone through in a 76-6 mauling.

Afterwards, Paris coach Michel Mazare tried to be philosophical: "We knew it would be hard and Wigan did not surprise us. It is difficult for us, because this is the fourth game of the week for some of my players."

It was an explanation that would be much repeated as the summer progressed, but his opposite number Graeme West was sympathetic. "The League should ensure that they can concentrate on Super League," he said. "They need to be able to prepare and get themselves fit. They are playing at a much higher level and need time to adjust. If they keep playing two or three games a week back home, their form will nosedive."

Wigan release Scott Quinnell to Richmond RU club....London cut Keiron Meyer, Shaun Keating and Danny Smith for missing training....Robbie Paul is acclaimed the "best player in the world" by Broncos chief Barry Maranta....Hull knock back a merger with Hull KR....Huddersfield sign Phil Veivers from St Helens....Wigan fail in bid to sign Auckland Warriors forward Bryan Henare.

Wigan collected 14 tries, the first from Andy Farrell after just 44 seconds. Rob Smyth and Henry Paul claimed hat-tricks, and Simon Haughton and Gary Connolly grabbed a brace each. But perhaps the biggest cheer of the afternoon was for busy Paris substitute Vincent Wulf's last minute effort.

Sheffield Eagles, back at Fortress Don Valley after the disappointing loss to Leeds, got their show back on the road with an unconvincing win against Castleford. Nearly 6,000 fans were entertained by a clutch of local stars from stage and screen, including Prince Naseem Hamed, who rolled up in a stretched limo. But the Eagles found the pre-match extravaganza a tough act to follow, and couldn't string more than two passes together. Thankfully for them, a top defensive effort was enough to blunt the Tigers attack and take them into third spot.

Skipper Paul Broadbent reflected after the game: "We lost the script after 20 minutes and never picked it up again. We were indisciplined in attack, but we did keep going forward with the ball."

The Eagles had new Aussie centre Danny Grimley on the field for the first time, and he contributed much to a solid back line that only Frano Botica seemed capable of breaking. It was the New Zealander's kicking game that created most of the worries for

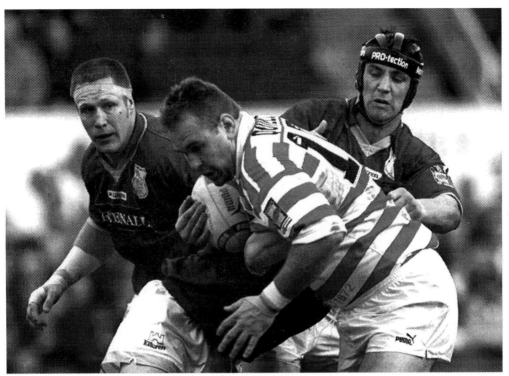

Wigan said goodbye to
giant forward Scott Quinell

Sheffield, and he appeared to have scored after a thrilling chip and chase. But Stuart Cummings, unsighted and unsure, called for the replay and subsequently ruled out the effort after the video ref deliberated for over two minutes. Minutes later, with the Tigers clearly annoyed at the decision, the Eagles went ahead through Anthony Farrell.

Cas launched wave after wave of attack, with new signing Richard Gay to the fore, but the Eagles stood firm, and wrapped the game up when substitute Darren Turner scored within a minute of coming on.

A few miles up the M1 at Headingley, it was the clash of the big cities, Leeds and London. For Broncos coach Tony Currie it was a triumphant return to his old club, as his charges returned south with a famous 27-20 victory that had looked highly unlikely when they approached the break 18-0 in arrears, and were reduced to 12 men for the final 30 minutes following the dismissal of Terry Matterson.

The delighted Currie said afterwards: "I felt at 18-0 it was a false reflection of the game, and even when Terry went off I was pleased with our ball control and tackling. We went back to a basic game plan. I make sure the guys are fit and disciplined, give them a structure to follow, and leave the rest to talent."

But for Leeds, the optimism of their first victory two weeks earlier quickly

31

evaporated with a woeful second half display. "We lost the desire and commitment," sighed Dean Bell. "Full credit to the Broncos, they wanted it more than us and stuck to their task."

The final game of the round was played out before Sky's cameras at Workington on a Monday evening. Halifax Blue Sox were the visitors, and they battled out a thrilling 18-18 draw that had fans on the edge of their seats. Town coach Ross O'Reilly was looking for a cigarette with ten minutes to go "and I haven't smoked for 12 months," he laughed afterwards.

It was a classic game of two halves, Town leading 18-4 at the break before Fax hit back to tie the game with a late, late Michael Jackson try. The shared points didn't really do either side much good, and they remained locked together at the foot of the table with just one point each from a possible twelve.

One of the most memorable games of the year was St Helens amazing last gasp 24-22 win against London Broncos in Round Seven.

"Beware the Broncos," was Tony Currie's message after his side squandered a 22-8 lead in the last 30 minutes to allow Saints to continue their unbeaten run. Out for the count and totally lacking in cohesion and ideas, McRae's marvels pulled themselves together to get a roll on that stunned their own support, let alone the Broncos. "We were very, very lucky today," the Saints coach said with a huge sigh of relief, after Bobbie Goulding inspired his side to two tries in four minutes to turn the game on its head.

Currie saw it differently. "I really blew my top after the game. Our kick and chase was good, our defence was good. I thought they were there for the picking. But we

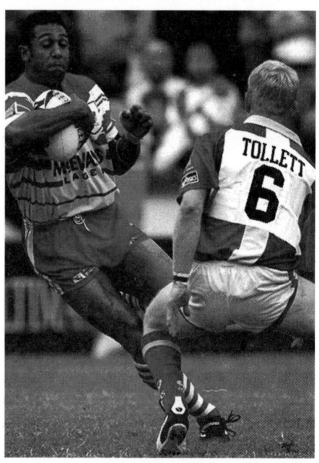

Alan Hunte tries to round Tulsen Tollett in Saints' narrow defeat of London Broncos

constantly made the same error - giving Saints the ball 20 metres from their line."

It was the 69th minute before Goulding's conversion, following Tommy Martyn's try put Saints ahead for the first time. But the Broncos could still have snatched it back. It took a great tackle by Scott Gibbs on Junior Paul to deny them in a thrilling finale.

Though disappointed, Currie warned: "We can play this game. People will start taking notice of London Broncos. We'll only get stronger and stronger."

Troubled Leeds' next port of call in their search for points was Paris, and they returned back across the channel having become the first team to win at Charlety. The Loiners had Kiwi signing Dean Clark on debut, but it was second rower Adrian Morley, on his nineteenth birthday, who inspired the 40-14 victory. He timed his runs to perfection and was rewarded with two tries, his first virtually sealing the win by putting his side 20-4 ahead, killing the game as a contest after a positive opening quarter from the French.

Paris were much improved on their previous outing at Wigan, and the crowd of over 15,000 were suitably impressed with a performance full of pride and passion. But the continuing problem of too many games in the domestic competition was still haunting PSG as chief executive Tas Baitieri admitted.

"Our guys were lethargic because of the number of games they have had to play," he said. "We came alive in the second half and showed what we could do. The positive thing for us is that we got another big crowd, and that impressed the PSG top bosses."

Bradford Bulls continued their surge up the table with a 30-10 win at Oldham.

Sheffield take the bold step of switching their home game with St Helens to Cardiff Arms Park....Bradford sign Fijian winger Joe Tamani....Leeds prop Barrie McDermott is arrested at Manchester Airport on a criminal damage charge....Halifax winger Mark Preston moves on loan to Widnes....Leeds rumoured to be ready to swap Graham Holroyd for Halifax's Paul Rowley....Featherstone sign Bulls' utility back Neil Summers.....Saints' Scott Gibbs ruled out for six weeks with shoulder injury....Bobbie Goulding starts negotiations with Saints after interest from ARL and RU.

They sealed the points with what was fast becoming the Bulls trademark - a blistering opening quarter. Bears coach Andy Goodway fielded a side weakened by injury and suspension, and suffered the loss of influential trio Dave Bradbury, Francis Maloney and Darren Abram during the game. He watched helplessly as the Bulls ripped into his side, with Paul Loughlin producing possibly his best game of the year.

Over at Wilderspool, Iestyn Harris ended Alex Murphy's search for a world-class stand-off with a scorching performance in the 36-26 defeat of Sheffield. A week earlier Murphy had revealed the club were scouring the world for a new stand-off, but the 19 year-old Welsh international responded by bagging 24 points. It may have been a masterful piece of psychology, but Murph couldn't resist a wry smile when he said:

May

"I've always known Iestyn is a world-class player......"

Eagles boss Gary Hetherington agreed. "We are two evenly matched teams but Iestyn's contribution was exceptional. He was a significant factor in the result," he reflected.

Castleford entertained Workington on the back of three successive defeats, and the 50-16 success brought much needed relief to Wheldon Road.

Scrum-half Tony Smith inspired the Tigers by involving himself in almost every move. Adrian Flynn benefited with two tries, and Frano Botica kicked nine goals from nine attempts to help relieve the pressure on coach John Joyner.

"It's the first time that everything they've done in training was done right in the match," he said of his players. "We scored some excellent tries and didn't ease off. Hopefully this is the turning point."

Wigan and Halifax completed the round in midweek, following Wigan's involvement in the first match of the Clash of the Codes against Bath at Maine Road. It was business as usual for the champs, who romped to a 50-4 win at Thrum Hall.

The game will be remembered not for the superb tries, but for the controversial dismissal of Blue Sox forward Michael Jackson. Referee Stuart Cummings clearly picked out the wrong man after Asa Amone felled a Wigan player, and despite protests from Halifax players backed up by Amone himself and several Wigan players, Cummings insisted on walking Jackson. The incident occurred after just nine minutes, and Halifax never had a chance. As coach Steve Simms noted: "It's difficult beating Wigan with 13 men, impossible with 12."

A week after suffering the heartache of a narrow, late defeat, London Broncos endured another thriller at Castleford, but this time emerged winners 21-20.

The victory put the Broncos third, and brought much praise from Tony Currie, who claimed his side's last three games (Cas, Saints and Leeds) had proved the Broncos could mix it with the best.

Fullback Greg Barwick was the star of the show, scoring one try, setting up another and then clinching the points with a 72nd minute drop goal. He also pulled off a tremendous try-saving tackle on Simon Middleton, when the Tigers winger appeared almost certain to score what would have been a match-winning try.

Castleford, who lost Graham Steadman, Richard Goddard and Frano Botica early on, had their chances but, as John Joyner admitted, they shot themselves in the foot. "It was a match we should have won, but we took the wrong options," he sighed afterwards.

The gloom also deepened at Headingley, where Halifax gained their first win of the season on a cold and wet day. A try blitz at the beginning of the second half did the damage, as Leeds again infuriated their support by failing to build on that win in Paris with another woeful performance.

Dean Bell stormed: "I'm embarrassed to coach a side that puts up a performance like that. It was totally amateurish, and if I could make changes I would. The fans have every right to have a go at us."

Paul Rowley skips past Leeds' Neil Harmon
in Halifax Blue Sox' first win of the season

The star for Halifax was hooker Paul Rowley who, after a relatively quiet first thirty minutes, exploded into life to dominate the crucial midfield area and score the gamebreaking try.

Oldham's problems continued too, this time at Don Valley, where Sheffield won a scrappy game 23-10 in which Ryan Sheridan starred with an outstanding display.

The Bears frustration spilled over in the final minutes and led to the dismissal of Martin Crompton and Joe Faimalo. Added to yet more injuries, this time to winger Scott Ranson and prop Ian Gildart, coach Andy Goodway had sound reason for looking despondent.

Bradford ran up 60 points against Paris, but were disappointed to concede 32. Coach Brian Smith blasted his side for the way they eased off after the break and allowed PSG to score four tries to three. Once again, PSG had been caught cold by falling behind inside the first minute, and trailed 44-12 at the break. The Bulls paraded new signing Joe Tamani, who instantly won over the Odsal crowd with a series of block-busting runs.

Warrington list Kelly Shelford at £15,000....Bradford Bulls sign fullback Stuart Spruce from Widnes...Maurice Lindsay reveals a new format for the Challenge Cup, including a supplementary competition for lower division clubs....Regal Trophy is officially dumped....Two French clubs invited to join division one....Plans to expand Super League to fifteen clubs announced.....Great Britain's tour of Fiji, Papua New Guinea and New Zealand confirmed

The game of the round was another tight win for Saints, this time a 25-24 effort at Warrington. As against the Broncos just five days earlier, Saints managed to snatch the points from the jaws of defeat when, with 10 minutes to go and seven points adrift, they hauled themselves off the canvas to deliver a stunning knockout blow.

Wire appeared to have done enough to end Saints' winning run, but when Alan Hunte headed purposefully towards the line Lee Penny flung out a loose arm and caught the winger with as clear a high tackle as you'd ever see. Penny walked, Goulding popped over the penalty, and Saints launched an all out attack that led to Derek McVey making the incisive break for Ian Pickavance's crucial try. Goulding stepped up to kick the winning goal, but Wire could still have snatched it when Chris Rudd had a last minute shot at goal from a penalty on the half way line. He was well short, and Wire slipped to their third defeat of the season, while Saints remained unbeaten.

Their main challengers, Wigan, kept up the pressure with a predictable thrashing of Workington. The writing was on the wall for Town when Jason Palmada knocked on from the start. Andy Farrell was outstanding and contributed 24 points.

Bradford Bulls ended the month in fine style with a 54-8 thrashing of Leeds. The defeat was made worse for the Loiners by the dismissal of Adrian Morley, and coach Dean Bell afterwards made a formal plea to the Headingley board for cash to rebuild his sorry side.

But he was quick to reject suggestions he may be ready to quit.

"I'm here for the duration, they'll have to kick me out." he declared. "I need some

Leeds went to Widnes for David Hulme *(above)*
whilst brother Paul found himself at Warrington

money to buy new players. Everyone else is strengthening around us and we're doing nothing, so we're going backwards."

Stuart Spruce scored two tries on his debut, as did former Loiner James Lowes. But the star for the Bulls was Steve McNamara, with a 22 point haul and an outstanding display of handling skills. The win took Bradford to third place, a position they wouldn't relinquish.

Warrington and London produced a thriller at Wilderspool, with the Wire eventually emerging 28-24 winners. Before the match, both sides were level on 10 points, and had each suffered a last minute defeat to St Helens. It was therefore always going to be a real humdinger, and the fans weren't disappointed.

With the scores locked at 24-24 with two minutes to go, it looked like a draw was the only outcome. But Jon Roper stunned the Broncos with a great last ditch effort, sprinting down the touchline to charge over for the winner.

Warrington move in for Paul Hulme, while Leeds check out his brother David....Maurice Lindsay shocks everyone by saying the Challenge Cup could move to Twickenham....Wigan announce plans to make an off season tour of New Zealand

Broncos coach Tony Currie was furious, particularly when his side had survived so long with twelve men, following Evan Cochrane's 24th minute dismissal.

There was another late, late show at Watersheddings, where Workington gained their first win of the season thanks to a last minute penalty goal by Wayne Kitchin. At half time Oldham had been 14 points clear, but Town stormed back to send their large travelling support delirious with joy. Two games were played on the Monday, including Halifax's trip to Paris. Their 38-10 win saw them jump two places up the ladder, and it relieved mounting pressure on Steve Simms. It was by no means a classic - "absolutely terrible" was how Simms described the game - but it was at least the Blue Sox' second win of the season.

Paris were still suffering from burn-out, and they did well to make a game of it in the first half. But when Asa Amone completed a hat-trick within minutes of the re-start, the game was over.

Castleford continued to bewilder everyone with their form. A 62-24 thumping at Saints was probably their worst display of the year, as Steve Prescott reminded the watching England coach Phil Larder that he deserved a place in the European Championship squad. He crowned a marvellous performance with a stunning 90 yard solo try to add to his first half touchdown. It was also a good day for Tommy Martyn, who celebrated making the starting line-up for the first time with a well taken try in the 25th minute that broke the Tigers' resistance.

The round was split thanks to Wigan's sojourn to Twickenham for the return match in the Clash of the Codes. They returned to league action in midweek with a big win over Sheffield Eagles, who continued to suffer from travel sickness. Wigan made several surprising changes, moving Jason Robinson to stand-off with Henry Paul dropping back to loose forward. They took a while to adjust, but still managed a half century of points with Martin Offiah bagging a hat-trick.

TABLES AT END OF MAY

STONES SUPER LEAGUE

	P	W	D	L	For	Agst	Diff	PTS
St Helens	9	9	0	0	382	186	196	18
Wigan	9	8	0	1	414	119	295	16
Bradford Bulls	9	6	0	3	291	194	97	12
Warrington	9	6	0	3	245	235	10	12
London Broncos	9	5	0	4	256	201	55	10
Sheffield Eagles	9	5	0	4	249	238	11	10
Oldham Bears	9	3	1	5	188	286	-98	7
Castleford Tigers	9	3	0	6	214	254	-40	6
Halifax Blue Sox	9	2	1	6	204	234	-30	5
Paris St Germain	9	2	1	6	198	360	-162	5
Leeds	9	2	0	7	203	268	-65	4
Workington Town	9	1	1	7	143	412	-269	3

DIVISION ONE

	P	W	D	L	For	Agst	Diff	PTS
Keighley Cougars	8	7	1	0	238	104	134	15
Salford Reds	8	7	0	1	292	131	161	14
Featherstone Rovers	9	6	1	2	258	161	97	13
Huddersfield Giants	10	6	0	4	257	152	105	12
Widnes	8	6	0	2	207	140	67	12
Hull	8	5	0	3	212	163	49	10
Dewsbury	8	2	1	5	94	250	-156	5
Wakefield Trinity	8	2	0	6	146	217	-71	4
Batley Bulldogs	8	1	2	5	88	198	-110	4
Whitehaven	9	1	0	8	96	281	-185	2
Rochdale Hornets	8	0	1	7	130	221	-91	1

DIVISION TWO

	P	W	D	L	For	Agst	Diff	PTS
Hull KR	9	9	0	0	466	129	337	18
Hunslet Hawks	9	8	0	1	292	147	145	16
Swinton Lions	9	7	0	2	322	152	170	14
Carlisle	9	6	0	3	295	156	139	12
York	9	5	0	4	209	243	-34	10
Doncaster Dragons	9	4	0	5	237	242	-5	8
South Wales	9	4	0	5	196	248	-52	8
Leigh Centurions	9	3	0	6	238	201	37	6
Bramley	9	3	0	6	178	258	-80	6
Barrow Braves	9	2	0	7	124	270	-146	4
Prescot Panthers	9	2	0	7	137	285	-148	4
Chorley	9	1	0	8	107	470	-363	2

JUNE
Video replays rule, OK?

June kicked off with one of the most controversial games of the season, a Friday night TV clash between Castleford and Warrington at Wheldon Road.

There were many heated discussions after the game, which the Tigers lost 17-22, and all were centred around the use of the big screen video replay. John Joyner was furious after seeing three out of four debatable touchdowns go against his side, to send them spinning to a sixth defeat in seven games.

But it was referee Stuart Cummings' decision not to call for electronic help after Richard Henare's 26th minute try for Warrington that really had Joyner fuming. "Everyone could see he had put a foot in touch before scoring," blasted Joyner. "Four times the referee called for replays of other scores, so why not that one? It's a joke."

He was also upset at the decision to rule out what appeared to be a perfectly good Chris Smith try. Cummings, who had been ordered to take a weekend off by Greg McCallum after dismissing a wrong payer at Halifax earlier in the season, was this time fully backed up by the referees' boss.

But McCallum did apologise to Castleford for the Henare incident. "I was bitterly disappointed that the touch judge failed to inform the referee that Henare had put his foot on the touchline," he said, and then later demoted Billy Blunden, the touch judge concerned.

Not surprisingly, Warrington coach John Dorahy was full of praise for the TV replays. "I think they are certainly showing their worth," he said.

Castleford could be considered desperately unlucky, especially having appeared to have clinched a much needed win when Frano Botica's 73rd minute drop goal put them 17-16 ahead. But Paul Sculthorpe squeezed out a pass for Paul Barrow to charge clear and send Chris Rudd under the posts in a stunning 70 yard raid.

It was a good night for Wire hooker Andy Bennett. He had a terrific hour before being replaced by Aussie Kris Watson who had only stepped off the plane twelve hours earlier. Bennett was rewarded by being taken off the transfer list.

There was another fast and furious game at Thrum Hall, where Halifax secured their first home win with a 33-30 success over a Sheffield side still leaving their best form behind at Don Valley.

In a game that swung one way and then the other, Blue Sox winger Abi Ekoku finally sealed the win with a 65th minute try that opened up an eight point gap. A mighty defensive effort, especially from Carl Gillespie, in the final quarter secured the points, despite the superb prompting of Mark Aston and strong running of Fijian fullback Waisale Sovatabua.

June

Eagles' coach Gary Hetherington was annoyed at his sides' inability to win away from home. "Some of our players let us down badly with an unprofessional performance," he said. "We had a lot of chances and should have had the game wrapped up by half time."

Steve Simms was happier. "Three wins on the trot and moving up two places for the second week running is very pleasing," he smiled.

While Halifax were moving up rapidly, Leeds were sinking fast. But their 40-20 loss to Wigan was a much improved display.

Stunned by the mounting criticism, the Loiners showed much more pride and passion. But it wasn't enough to stop a rampant Wigan side which ruthlessly punished every small error and eventually overwhelmed Leeds in the final quarter.

Yet at the break Leeds were only two points adrift, after a performance highlighted by Barrie McDermott's tough tackling, Tony Kemp's organisational skills, and the enthusiasm of youngsters Terry Newton and Lee Maher.

"That performance gave me heart, and I've at last got something to build on," said Dean Bell. "At least we showed a bit of commitment for a change. In fact, we showed more in 60 minutes than we have all season."

Jason Robinson again played at stand-off for Wigan, and he had a huge influence on the game, looking dangerous every time he touched the ball. It was his searing break that led to Craig Murdock's try that finally killed off Leeds' hopes of a shock win.

Unsettled St Helens hooker Keiron Cunningham asks for a new improved contract....Bobbie Goulding pulls out of the Euro Championship, allowing Shaun Edwards a recall....More talks on Humberside about a possible merger....Salford attempt to sign Kelly Shelford from Warrington

Coach Graeme West was pleased with side's effort. "We've had a hard month and I'm relieved we've picked up maximum points," he confessed. "The players have really put their noses to the grindstone. I played Jason at stand-off because he can really create havoc there. And a big plus is that the wingers are still scoring tries."

The problem for Wigan was that St Helens were also claiming maximum points. Such had been their fine form that a 52-10 win at home against Paris Saint-Germain had critics asking: "Is that all....?"

"It's the great expectation," suggested coach Shaun McRae. "Everybody now expects us to rattle up the points every week, but it's a lot easier to say it than go out and do it."

Skipper Bobbie Goulding sat out the game, and in his absence Saints did look disjointed in attack and fragmented in defence. Derek McVey opened the account after just three minutes, but the remaining 77 were frustrating for the Saints fans. Chance after chance went begging as they took the wrong option or spilled the ball.

Third place Bradford kept up the pressure on the big two by rattling up over 50 points for the third consecutive match. The Bulls were bang in form and coasted to a ten try victory against Workington that visibly upset Town coach Ross O'Reilly.

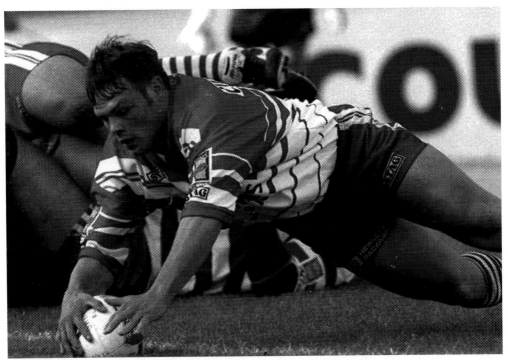

Unsettled hooker Keiron Cunningham asked St Helens for an improved contract
but still put in some outstanding performances

Once again, it was that trademark frantic opening quarter that did the damage for the Bulls. Four tries in sixteen minutes left Town with a mountain to climb at 22-0 down, but they regathered well to stem the flow. A measure of the Bulls rising prominence in the game was reflected in a crowd of 8,658.

The beginning of June was an important time for the London Broncos, when for the first time in six weeks they actually staged a home game!

They had been forced onto the road by Charlton Athletic's involvement in the soccer play-offs. Tony Currie had earlier suggested if they could remain in the top half while on their travels, they would return home with a real chance of pushing for his pre-season target of a top four spot.

Sure enough, they arrived back in the capital lying sixth, and to celebrate they defeated Oldham Bears 28-22. But it was a lacklustre game, and the final score flattered the Bears, who gained respectability with two late efforts. It was probably the Broncos poorest performance of the season, but Currie was philosophical.

"For the first time I've been here, we actually won a penalty count," he said with a hint of a smile. "But we were off our game. Everyone raises their game against us, almost as if it were an international. It's more than north against south - it's a real battle."

June

The win was marred by serious injuries to key players. Scott Roskell, Tony Mestrov and John Minto all suffered breaks of some kind to add to the loss of Gavin Allen and Peter Gill, leaving the Broncos squad seriously depleted.

The game also saw the Super League debut of Australian referee Bill Harrigan, a victim of the ARL war down under who had travelled around the world to continue his career.

The battle for a place in Super League intensified in that first weekend of June when Keighley Cougars entertained Salford Reds. The two were beginning to pull away from the chasing pack of Featherstone, Huddersfield and Hull, and the Reds won the battle with ease 45-8. Steve Blakeley was the star of the show, appearing to be a level above the rest with fast thinking and incisive breaks.

London Broncos hit the road again in Round Eleven, this time to Wigan for what would turn out to be the major turning point of the year.

The Broncos fought their way back from 18-4 down to snatch a hard-earned draw, with a last minute penalty goal by skipper Terry Matterson. But the Wigan faithful were furious with the Broncos tactics, and Tony Currie was accused of deliberately slowing down the game. He didn't disagree.

French cities Bordeaux and Toulouse bid to join Super League....Steve Prescott gets late England call-up for Euro Championships....RFL chairman Rodney Walker voices concern at some clubs' low crowds....South Wales get the Super League nod, subject to meeting certain criteria....Clubs upset at being told to release overseas stars for the Oceania Cup

"We reckoned there are 20 scrums in a game. If we took 30 seconds to walk to each scrum, that's 10 minutes gone - ten minutes where Wigan can't score. Add on time for goal kicks and questioning referee's decisions, and that's even more time gone," he admitted.

"But we are a good team, and we should get the respect we deserve. Wigan had one hell of a tough game and they know it."

The dropped point was to prove crucial to the Championship race. But London thoroughly deserved their share. The Broncos pack continually made more yardage than the Wigan six, fullback Duncan McRae was in fine form at the back, and stand-off Tulsen Tollett "wouldn't look out of place in a Great Britain shirt," claimed Currie.

Only Va'aiga Tuigamala prevented a complete loss as the Broncos gathered steam in the second half, and it was his rampaging runs and rock solid defence that kept Wigan hopes alive. The Broncos almost snatched both points, but Shaun Edwards charged down McRae's drop goal attempt almost on full time.

The result meant Saints had now opened up a three point lead thanks to a 43-32 victory against Sheffield Eagles at Cardiff Arms Park.

The match was a home fixture for Sheffield, but the unavailability of Don Valley,

London Broncos stand-off Tulsen Tollett "wouldn't look out of place in a Great Britain shirt" said his coach Tony Currie

and the RFL's desire to promote the game in South Wales saw Super League hit the road.

It proved a success all round, as an estimated 4,500 locals made up the bulk of a 7,000 crowd.

They had plenty to enthuse about, but Saints weren't at their best.

Handicapped by the loss through injury of Goulding, Martyn and Gibbs they did just enough to keep the Eagles at bay. For an hour Sheffield refused to buckle, and continually threatened to shock the Saints, but Paul Newlove's try in the 61st minute finally created a bit of daylight. Despite a final late flurry the Eagles were beaten.

At the other end of the table Workington and Leeds battled it out at Derwent Park. It was a crunch game for the Headingley giants, and they returned to Yorkshire victorious by 48-18 to leap frog over Paris Saint-Germain to the relative safety of third bottom.

At the same time Town were cast adrift with just three points from a possible 22, and a massive negative scoring record.

But the Loiners were made to work hard for their spoils. It took a Graham Holroyd interception just before the break, which led to a try for Tony Kemp, to put Leeds 18-8 ahead and allow them to turn around with confidence.

Over in Paris, Castleford Tigers dished out an expected mauling in searing heat. Day-time temperatures were approaching

43

June

100 degrees, and by kick-off it was still in the high eighties. John Joyner decided against a training run-out on the morning of the match, after taking advice from his medical staff, who were concerned about the effects of dehydration and heat exhaustion. Summer rugby had arrived with a vengeance.

The Tigers led 42-6 at the break, but were out on their legs. The French pulled back to outscore Cas 16-12 in the second half, but Joyner's team held on for only their second away win of the season.

The battle-weary Paris players had been looking ragged in recent games thanks to their dual commitments, and now had to endure even more games with the approach of the European Championships. Behind the scenes, officials were expressing grave concern for the club's future unless drastic action was taken.

A crowd of 7,000 turned out - including a sizable contingent from Castleford - an impressive figure considering PSG had gone seven games without a win. But their problems extended beyond the playing field. As one PSG official said: "Jack Gibson said, a successful sports club starts at the front office. Well, we don't even have a front office."

At Thrum Hall, the West Yorkshire derby between Halifax Blue Sox and Bradford Bulls was a rip-roaring affair. It was a game that silenced the critics of summer rugby, who had claimed that the new rules had eradicated bruising, physical games. The power and ferocity on show was of the highest quality, and the game had everything, as Bulls' coach Brian Smith noted.

"The intensity was very high," he said after his side triumphed 22-20. "It's the best game we've had in a while, and it took a really strong performance from my side, particularly in defence, to come up with the points. From a neutral point of view it was a first class game of rugby league."

Wigan announce plans to leave Central Park for a shared super stadium with Orrell RU and Wigan Athletic....Wigan legend Billy Boston receives the MBE and Rodney Walker is knighted....Maurice Lindsay tells clubs to frame up or face expulsion from Super League....Paris chief executive Tas Baitieri quits to take up a position with the ARL....Parramatta show interest in Bulls' coach Brian Smith....Struggling Workington receive transfer requests from Colin Armstrong and Jason Palmada

His opposite number Steve Simms agreed. "Nobody can fault the commitment of the players."

The shock of the round was at Watersheddings, where Oldham stormed to a 35-24 win against Warrington that effectively ended Wire hopes of a Championship for another year.

The Bears scored four first half tries to establish an unlikely 26-4 lead, but Warrington hit back after the break. They soon got a roll on and scored three quick tries, including two in as many minutes by Richard Henare. Suddenly, it appeared Oldham would be washed away, and at 26-20 the Bears began to panic.

But a penalty mid way through the half stopped the rot and gave them new heart.

Jason Palmada stunned struggling Workington Town by putting in a transfer request
along with team-mate Colin Armstrong

The Bears pack reasserted their authority and took control of the game once again,
allowing Adrian Belle to grab the clinching try.

As the temperatures rose throughout June, so did the heat in the race for the inaugural
Super League crown.

With the big Saints-Wigan showdown just a week away, both sides prepared with
runaway wins. St Helens ran up 60 against hapless Workington, while Wigan enjoyed
a spree against Oldham.

Saints were inspired by the return of Bobbie Goulding, and the scrum half kicked
eight goals to earn his place in the record books for the fastest century of goals after
just seventeen games. He also broke the 800 point barrier for Saints, a remarkable
achievement in less than three seasons at the club.

Goulding took a huge gamble in playing against medical advice, but he was desperate to prove himself fit for the upcoming Wigan clash. "I knew I had to have at least 20 minutes before the Wigan game, and the record was also at the back of my mind," he reflected.

Saints had built up a commanding 32-2 lead by the break, having scored six tries, the best coming from Steve Prescott, who defused a bomb on his own 20 and sprinted back toward the other end to score. Workington improved slightly after the turnaround, and earned praise from Shaun McRae for their resolve.

But the Saints boss wasn't too impressed with his own team: "The way we're playing you'd have to say Wigan are the favourites," he said, looking ahead to the big one. "Teams very rarely get a result at Central Park, although they are probably under more pressure than us."

The bad news for Saints was the loss for a month of rampaging centre Vila Matautia, who limped off with ankle ligament trouble.

Wigan had a slightly sterner test against Oldham Bears, managing just 44 points. Jason Robinson was the hero, back on the wing after several outings in the middle at stand-off, but he proved just as devastating with a superb hat-trick. Oldham clung on for half an hour until the half back pairing of Shaun Edwards and Craig Murdock began to boss the show. The Wigan team had a strange look about it - no Offiah, Radlinski, Hall or Skerrett - but it made little difference. What was more worrying for the Wigan board was the missing fans. Just over 7,000 turned out, well down on

Huddersfield Giants launch bid for Super League....Former Wigan prop Andy Platt says he will quit Auckland at the end of the season and starts a clamour for his signature....The controversial Oceania Cup is postponed....Bradford say they will demand huge compensation if Brian Smith quits for Parramatta

the twelve and fourteen thousand that had become the norm in recent years. Those who did attend were again furious with the visiting teams' tactics, as the Bears followed the Broncos' lead and used every trick in the book to slow the game down.

Bradford Bulls, unbeaten since Wembley, were emerging as serious contenders to the crown. They travelled to Castleford hoping to create space between themselves and fourth placed Warrington. But the Tigers withstood the heat of the jungle to come out on top at white hot Wheldon Road.

"This compares with Townsville and Cairns in Queensland," said Lee Crooks as he cooled off in a tub. "And it was hotter than Paris, which is saying something. Full credit to every player out there today, especially those who played the full eighty."

Ironically, it was the first Cas game with a mid-afternoon kick-off, following the club's decision to move back from an evening start in the hope of increased gates.

The Cas fans amongst the 6,500 crowd feared the worst when the Bulls roared to a 16-8 lead just after the re-start. But Frano Botica injected himself into the game when those around him were tiring, to spark a terrific fightback. Once again, it was a kicking game that brought down the Bulls, as Botica hoisted two towering kicks which had Bradford reliving their Wembley nightmare. His first led to a flip-down from Diccon Edwards for Adrian Flynn to score, and he followed up to collect his second and put

Nigel Wright made his long-awaited return after injury for Wigan, coming on as substitute in their 21-0 win at Warrington

David Chapman over. Cas had the upper hand, and went on to record a 26-23 win, much to the delight of John Joyner. "We seemed to have learned from past lessons," he smiled.

Down in London, Halifax came up with their performance of the year in completely outplaying the Broncos to win 52-24 before the TV cameras. John Bentley grabbed the glory with four tries (he had another two disallowed!), but John Schuster was instrumental in everything the Blue Sox did.

Before the game, Steve Simms thought he had spotted a weakness down the Broncos left, and sure enough John Minto and Mark Maguire were cruelly exposed. The Broncos could point to a lengthy injury list, but coach Currie offered no excuse for his side's display. "I'm not making excuses, we were beaten fair and square," he said, before blaming an M-People concert in Hyde Park for disrupting his preparation.

Bentley joked: "I was very surprised with London. Did they have a midweek game....?"

Leeds' problems continued at Warrington, where prop Mark Hilton had his coach John Dorahy drooling. The young forward was outstanding in the 36-12 win, and Dorahy beamed: "If I was the Great Britain coach I'd be booking a seat on the plane to New Zealand right now. He's gotta be the best young prop in the country."

Not for the first time it was a poor second half that let Leeds down, for they had still been in the hunt at 18-6. But Adrian Morley's second dismissal of the season, this time for a high shot on Hilton, was too much for them, as three tries after he had walked wrapped up a convincing Wire win.

Paris, too, were struggling, and Sheffield Eagles gained revenge for their opening day defeat with a comfortable 52-18 victory. It was an optimistic night for Super League, as over 5,000 flocked to Don Valley, despite the counter attraction of Euro '96, thanks to some imaginative promotion by the Eagles.

Round Thirteen was dominated by the much anticipated Wigan-Saints encounter. Over 20,000 crammed into Central Park to see if Saints could repeat their impressive early season victory over their arch-rivals.

They couldn't, and Wigan thrashed them 35-19. "One point behind when it could have been five," was how Graeme West summed it up afterwards.

"If we had lost, the title race would have been over," added Craig Murdock.

Saints coach Shaun McRae was remarkably relaxed about the stunning loss, his first since arriving at Knowsley Road four months earlier.

"On the day we were beaten by a better side," he said. "They played exceptionally well, and we'll learn from this. After all, between us it's only one-all. You don't budget for losses, but coming to Central Park is always a tough task. And London didn't do us any favours when they grabbed a point here."

That final comment seemed strange, but McRae felt Wigan had been stung into action by dropping that point, and it had stirred a collective sense of resolve amongst their players.

The game itself began sensationally, when Danny Arnold raced clear down the right wing. Bobbie Goulding was on Arnold's inside to take the scoring pass, and he added the conversion and then tagged on a drop-goal.

"We didn't get the best of starts, it was lacklustre," said Graeme West. "But in the game at Saints we built up a lead and then died."

When Wigan did recover from a nervy start, a superb try-scoring flurry realised 16 points in nine minutes, and effectively sealed the game.

Saints were 22-7 down at the break but, briefly, spied the chance of a famous comeback as they began the second half as well as they had the first.

But an amazing try, initiated by Robinson, settled matters.

Straight from dummy-half, the winger broke clear from well inside his own half. Though Andy Northey collared him, the supporting Murdock galloped in by the posts.

Tuigamala left a heap of bodies littering the floor and gave Simon Haughton a walk in to complete Wigan's try-scoring, and Robinson tagged on a drop goal, cool as you like, from 37 metres.

"It might be the wake-up call we need," said Northey afterwards. "The title is still in our hands, but tonight we ran into individuals like Tuigamala, Robinson and Connolly in top form."

It was a game which more than lived up to its billing, and was best summed up by a weary Tuigamala making his way up the tunnel past the assembled press corps. He grinned, "It's a hard way to earn a living".

Bradford recovered from their previous week's loss at Castleford to thrash Sheffield 64-22 at Odsal. It was an incredible game in which 36 points were scored in

1996
SUPER
LEAGUE
SEASON
ROUND BY ROUND

ROUND 1

ROUND 2

ROUND 2

TOP: Super League kicks off in style as the PSG players celebrate a famous opening night 30-24 victory over Sheffield Eagles

LEFT: Tommy Martyn and Karle Hammond in jubilant mood after seeing off Wigan 41-26 at Knowsley Road

ABOVE: Andrew Schick high-steps another season for Castleford Tige in their thrillingly close 26-23 matc against third Title favourites Leeds

ROUND 3

LEFT: Oldham Bears' Joe Faimalo barges his way through the PSG defence in a 24-24 draw
CENTRE: Bradford Bulls' Sonny Nickle looks to off-load during the 31-24 victory over London Broncos
BOTTOM LEFT: Leeds' Jim Fallon grabs Oldham's Francis Maloney but can't stop his side going down 25-16
BOTTOM RIGHT: Karle Hammond halts Bradford's Gary Christie - Saints going on to win 26-20

ROUND 3

ROUND 4

ROUND 5

LEFT: Keiron Cunningham in another clos[e] shave for St Helens as they see off Halif[ax] Blue Sox 28-30

CENTRE: Jason Robinson scorches past PSG's Fabien Devecchi as Wigan stroll [to a] comfortable 76-8 winners

BOTTOM LEFT: Sheffield Eagles' Anthony Farrell on the rampage in a 20-12 victory against Castleford Tigers

BOTTOM RIGHT: London beat Leeds 20-2[?] with a little help from Russell Bawden

ROUND 6

ROUND

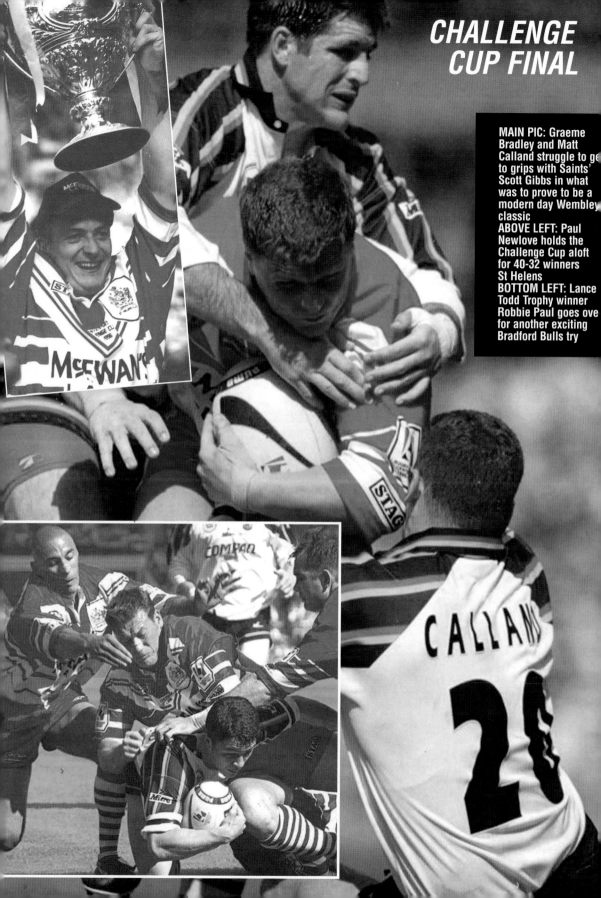

MAIN PIC: Graeme Bradley and Matt Calland struggle to get to grips with Saints' Scott Gibbs in what was to prove to be a modern day Wembley classic

ABOVE LEFT: Paul Newlove holds the Challenge Cup aloft for 40-32 winners St Helens

BOTTOM LEFT: Lance Todd Trophy winner Robbie Paul goes over for another exciting Bradford Bulls try

ROUND 7

LEFT: Darren Shaw hits the Saints defence in Lor
Broncos' thrilling 24-22 defeat at Knowsley Rd
BELOW: Anthony Gibbons romps away in Leeds'
14-40 defeat of Paris at the Charlety Stadium
BOTTOM LEFT: Derek McVey off-loads for St Hel
in their classic 24-25 victory at Warrington
BOTTOM RIGHT: Castleford old-stager Lee Crooks
can't stop the Tigers going down 20-21 v London

ROUND 7

ROUND 8

ROUND 8

LEFT: Bradford Bulls' James Lowes puts one over on his old Leeds team-mates in the 54-8 whitewash at Odsal
ABOVE: Workington's Jason Palmada halted in his tracks by Oldham's Darren Abram and Martin Crompton as Town come out on top 27-29 to record their only away win of the season
BOTTOM LEFT: Halifax' John Bentley can't halt Sheffield Eagles' Keith Senior in the 33-30 win at Thrum Hall
BOTTOM RIGHT: Leeds' Barrie McDermott comes in for some Wigan attention as his side go down 20-40 at Headingley

ROUND 10

ROUND 10

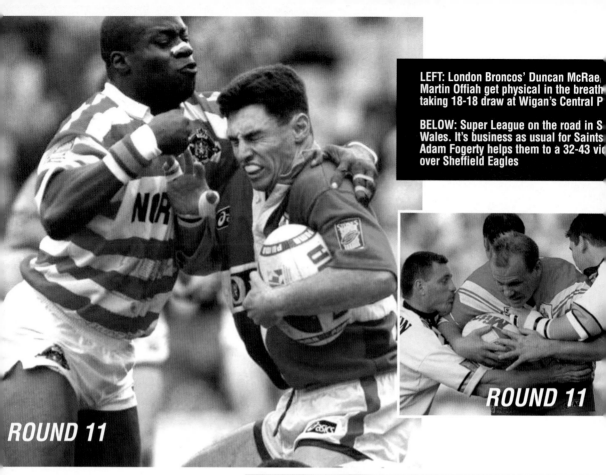

ROUND 11

ROUND 11

ROUND 1

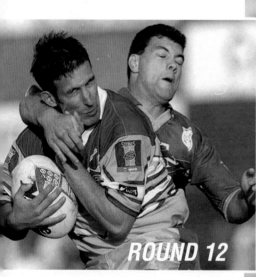

ROUND 12

TOP: Wigan's Gary Connolly in the thick of it as Saints are beaten 35-19 in the Central Park cauldron
ABOVE: Laurent Lucchese can't make ground as Paris go down valiantly 24-26 to Warrington
RIGHT: Stuart Spruce and the Bradford Bulls run out 6-22 winners at London Broncos

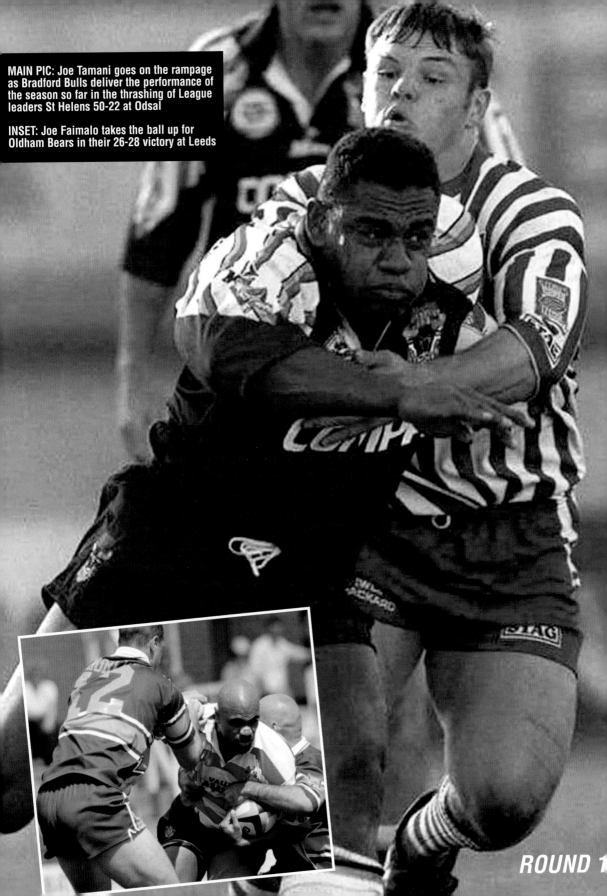

MAIN PIC: Joe Tamani goes on the rampage as Bradford Bulls deliver the performance of the season so far in the thrashing of League leaders St Helens 50-22 at Odsal

INSET: Joe Faimalo takes the ball up for Oldham Bears in their 26-28 victory at Leeds

ROUND 1

GHT: Saints one week, Wigan the next. There's little
n of brotherly love as Robbie and Henry Paul go head
head in 12 man Bradford Bulls' astounding 20-12 win.

OW: Cumbrian woe continued as Warrington full-back
Penny battles through the Workington defence. Wire
me out on top 4-49

ROUND 16

ROUND 17

ROUND 17

LEFT: Almost a shock as the improving Paris St Germain and
Dion Bird run the mighty Wigan close, 20-24

ABOVE: Castleford's big Aussie Andrew Schick runs into Sheffield
Eagles' Lynton Stott as the Tigers win 36-31

ROUND 18

ROUND 1

ROUND 19

ABOVE: James Lowes and the Bradford Bulls celebrate a resounding 18-56 win at Headingley

RIGHT: Broncos new boy Martin Offiah gets off to a winning start as London beat Warrington 20-13

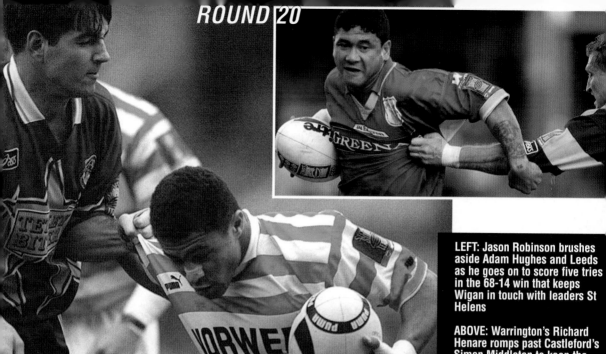

LEFT: Jason Robinson brushes aside Adam Hughes and Leeds as he goes on to score five tries in the 68-14 win that keeps Wigan in touch with leaders St Helens

ABOVE: Warrington's Richard Henare romps past Castleford's Simon Middleton to keep the top four pressure on London and help Wire to a 38-24 win

OUND 21

IGHT: St Helens' Steve Prescott gets the ball way as Saints beat Sheffield Eagles 68-2

BOVE: Halifax Blue Sox captain Karl arrison has a hand in shocking high-flying radford Bulls 26-27 at Odsal

ROUND 21

WE ARE THE CHAMPIONS!: The champagne corks fly at Knowsley Road as Bobbie Goulding and his talented team-mates lift the first summer Super League Trophy for St Helens after brushing aside Warrington 66-14.

ABOVE: Wigan's Jason Robinson attempts to give Bradford Bulls' Paul Cook the brush-off as the cherry and whites make home advantage tell in a 42-36 absolute thriller!

LEFT: London Broncos' Peter Gill comes under the close scrutiny of Chris Joynt and Adam Fogerty in their bruising 25-14 defeat at St Helens

PREMIERSHIP FINALS

SOMETHING TO CELEBRATE AT LAST!: Andy Farrell *(RIGHT)* holds aloft the Super League Premiership Trophy after Gary Connolly *(TOP)* and the rest of the Wigan side killed off St Helens' treble hopes with a 14-44 victory at Old Trafford.

ABOVE: Salford Reds' Steve Blakeley and Sam Panapa celebrate their 19-6 Divisional Final victory over Keighley Cougars in the curtain raiser to the main match.

the opening quarter, split evenly. Bulls coach Brian Smith prophesied that whichever side got its defence together first would go on and win with ease. Fortunately for him, it was the Bulls.

With their defensive worries sorted, Matt Calland grabbed the initiative to link with Joe Tamani, who sent Robbie Paul in for the first of his two tries, and the Bulls romped away out of sight.

London Broncos got back into gear, too, with a 34-6 success at Workington, despite having Gavin Allen sent off after just thirteen minutes. Sadly for Town, their demise was highlighted by a crowd of just 1,400.

Oldham Bears upset the form book by winning at Halifax. The Blue Sox' big win in London just a week earlier seemed a distant memory as the Bears produced one of their inimitable fighting performances to lift themselves two places with a 20-14 win.

The victory was based upon a tight defence and a top drawer two-try display from David Bradbury, who fully deserved the big raps from his coach. "David showed a glimpse of his potential today. I've been telling him all year how good he could be and that he should set his sights on gaining a tour spot," commented Goodway.

In Paris, Warrington very nearly came a cropper thanks to a much improved display by the French. John Kear, seconded to the strugglers by the RFL, appeared to have worked wonders when his new side led 24-20 inside the last 10 minutes. But a late effort from Paul Sculthorpe rescued his side, and left Kear ruing the fact that Paris had crossed the line nine times but only managed to ground the ball on five occasions.

"We got the points," summed up John Dorahy. "We stole the points," sighed one of his players in the background.

Leeds came up with their best effort yet to defeat Castleford 25-18. Barrie McDermott's try on the stroke of halftime, despite suffering a dislocated elbow in the previous tackle, sparked a second half revival from the Loiners. After being 12 points down in as many minutes, Leeds turned it around thanks to a great all round display from Dean Clark, who led his side with professionalism and a steadying influence that had been sadly lacking all season.

Nigel Wright returned to the Wigan side at the end of June for the first time in eleven months after his dreadful injury problems.

He appeared as a late substitute in the 21-0 win at Warrington, as Wigan handed out a lesson in clinical finishing. "When you step up against top class opposition you have to take every scoring opportunity," said a dejected John Dorahy. "We failed to do that and consequently ended up losers."

But Dorahy was also scathing of the referee. "I felt we just didn't get the bounce of the ball, and the only thing I have to say about Mr Presley is that I don't mind if I never see him again."

For Wigan, Va'aiga Tuigamala played heroically after flying to Auckland and back within three days for the aborted Oceania Cup. He'd already left Britain when the decision to cancel was made, and he had no alternative but to get straight on the plane and fly back. "If Inga plays like that after flying 24,000 miles round the world, I wish

June

he'd been hijacked," joked Alex Murphy, to which Graeme West replied: "Inga's that tired he wishes he'd been hijacked too!"

Apollo Perelini had accompanied Tuigamala on his jaunt, and the Saints prop also turned out to help his side recover from their first defeat of the season by beating Leeds 42-16. Perelini's exploits weren't quite as heroic as Tuigamala, as he came off the bench for the final thirty minutes, but he still played a major part by providing the impetus for a late surge that brought six tries in the final quarter.

The Bradford Bulls journied to London and produced a first class defensive effort to deny the Broncos' fluent attack and win the game 22-16. The highlight was a superb individual try by Robbie Paul, when he took the ball from Graeme Bradley some 60 yards out and bamboozled the Broncos defence to send fullback Greg Barwick the wrong way, and sprint over unopposed. "You might as well take the fullback out of the equation when Robbie Paul is in a one-on-one situation," said Broncos' manager Robbie Moore.

Paris travelled to Oldham buoyed by their recent improved showings, but couldn't prevent another defeat as the Bears strolled to a comfortable 24-6 success.

Halifax made it five successive away wins with a 24-20 effort at Castleford, leaving Steve Simms seriously pondering wearing the red and white away strip at Thrum Hall. "It must be that new kit," he joked. "Maybe the players should start sleeping in it!"

And Workington ended the month as they had started it, with another defeat, this time at Sheffield Eagles, for whom Richard Chapman stole the show on his debut with a two try display.

TABLES AT END OF JUNE

STONES SUPER LEAGUE

	P	W	D	L	For	Agst	Diff	PTS
St Helens	14	13	0	1	598	295	303	26
Wigan	14	12	1	1	572	192	380	25
Bradford Bulls	14	10	0	4	474	282	192	20
Warrington	14	9	0	5	353	344	9	18
London Broncos	14	7	1	6	376	321	55	15
Sheffield Eagles	14	7	0	7	417	412	5	14
Oldham Bears	14	6	1	7	305	402	-97	13
Halifax Blue Sox	14	5	1	8	347	350	-3	11
Castleford Tigers	14	5	0	9	349	370	-21	10
Leeds	14	4	0	10	324	422	-98	8
Paris St Germain	14	2	1	11	278	568	-290	5
Workington Town	14	1	1	12	203	638	-435	3

DIVISION ONE

	P	W	D	L	For	Agst	Diff	PTS
Salford Reds	12	11	0	1	451	197	254	22
Keighley Cougars	13	10	1	2	332	195	137	21
Huddersfield Giants	13	8	0	5	338	208	130	16
Featherstone Rovers	12	7	2	3	346	219	127	16
Hull	12	8	0	4	340	238	102	16
Widnes	12	7	0	5	271	231	40	14
Wakefield Trinity	13	5	1	7	282	293	-11	11
Dewsbury	12	4	1	7	171	355	-184	9
Whitehaven	13	3	0	10	180	352	-172	6
Batley Bulldogs	13	1	2	10	152	404	-252	4

DIVISION TWO

	P	W	D	L	For	Agst	Diff	PTS
Hull KR	14	13	0	1	646	210	436	26
Hunslet Hawks	14	12	0	2	465	225	240	24
Swinton Lions	14	11	0	3	496	218	278	22
Doncaster Dragons	14	9	0	5	369	338	31	18
Carlisle	14	8	0	6	420	282	138	16
South Wales	14	7	0	7	351	356	-5	14
York	14	7	0	7	297	401	-104	14
Leigh Centurions	14	6	0	8	388	308	80	12
Barrow Braves	14	3	0	11	215	404	-189	6
Bramley	14	3	0	11	236	476	-240	6
Chorley	14	3	0	11	197	572	-375	6
Prescot Panthers	14	2	0	12	205	495	-290	4

JULY
The running of the Bulls

July was the month of the Bull.

After their clinical defeat of the Broncos at the end of June, Bradford faced up to their toughest run in Super League, in the knowledge that they had the opportunity to decide the eventual destiny of the Super League title.

With leaders St Helens and second placed Wigan to visit Odsal on consecutive Friday nights, victory against only one of the two giants would virtually hand the title to the other.

Six points adrift of Saints at the top, the Bulls had only a remote chance of winning the league, but they had objectives of their own.

Graeme Bradley, who was becoming one of the most influential figures in the game as the summer wore on, explained to Super League Week: "A win against Saints will mean we'll definitely finish in the top four, and that in itself would be a tremendous achievement, given the vast amount of changes at the club in such a short amount of time."

And this against the backdrop of rumours about the impending departure of coach Brian Smith, who'd been strongly linked with Sydney club Parramatta.

St Helens were up first, and they had problems of their own. Bobbie Goulding picked up an ankle injury in the win against Leeds the previous Sunday, and was on crutches in the early part of the week. By Friday he was still struggling, and he failed a fitness test before the game.

His place was taken by John McAtee, the former Academy international. Saints, still lacking Chris Joynt, and the rest of the rugby league world were shocked by the way Bradford destroyed them that bright summer's night.

"Raging Bulls" might have become a cliche since the de Niro film, but on this occasion it could not have been more apt.

Bradford hit St Helens with six tries before half-time. When Jon Scales added another three minutes into the second half the table-toppers were staring down a scoreline of 38-0. And with Welsh centre Scott Gibbs, already destined for a return to rugby union, sent off for leading with his elbow, a possible rout was on the cards.

Ex-Saints centre Paul Loughlin produced another cracking display, hours after having an appeal upheld against a two match ban imposed for a late high tackle against the Broncos. He almost put Scales over in the first minute, and time and again he and Bradley combined down the left to punch holes in Gibbs' centre until, at 26-0 down, the Welshman's frustration got the better of him, and Stuart Cummings immediately reached for the red card.

July

But Saints showed the resilience of potential champions with a second half comeback, with the Bulls themselves reduced to twelve men when Karl Fairbank was marched for a high tackle. They scored four tries of their own, restricting Bradford to only one, to finish the game with a semblance of self respect, with the final scoreline at 50-22.

The result meant that Wigan had to win their home game against Castleford Tigers that same night to go to the top of the Super League.

With the Tigers' slump in form - they'd lost at Leeds and at home to Halifax since beating the Bulls three rounds previously - Wigan's task didn't appear to be too much of a problem.

As it turned out, in a season of close finishes, that game produced the most dramatic conclusion of them all.

League Express reporter Mike Latham nominated Wigan loose-forward Andy Farrell for the "Nerves of Steel" award after the England captain kicked a last second penalty from all of 40 metres out to give Wigan a one point victory. Sensational would be an understatement.

Controversy raged once again because of the circumstances of the penalty.

With the scores locked at 24-24 with only three minutes on the clock, Frano Botica gave the Tigers an astonishing one point lead with a drop-goal that the crowd thought would be the final scoring act of the game.

Fiji win the Pacific Festival of Rugby League in Auckland, beating a New Zealand XIII in the final 28-8....the League announces that Scotland will play Ireland in Glasgow in a month's time....Maurice Lindsay pleads with clubs to fast-track South Wales into Super League in 1997....Alex Murphy and Brian Smith engage in a war of words over the success of Super League

Cas then had to weather a ferocious Wigan attack which ended with Va'aiga Tuigamala losing possession in a five-man tackle over the line.

All the Tigers had to do was hang on to possession and watch the clock run down. But Tony Smith, after a tackle by Simon Haughton, took an eternity to get his feet, seemingly injured. Aussie referee Stephen Clark deemed that he was feigning in an attempt to slow the game down, sin-binned Smith, and left Farrell with the pressure kick of his career.

Graeme West was brutally honest after the game. "We were very lucky," he said.

Castleford officials thought so too, and let Clark know in no uncertain terms, prompting a complaint to referees' executive Greg McCallum.

It was a sickener for the Tigers, who had fully deserved to inflict Wigan's first defeat at Central Park since Wakefield Trinity's 13-20 victory there in February 1994.

"We came out with two points and showed courage," said West. "We take each week as it comes, but this next week is sure to be a tough one." He was right.

The next morning Brian Smith announced at a hastily arranged press conference that he would be leaving the Bulls at the end of the season to coach Parramatta.

There was also enough drama to go around at the bottom of the table, with the

Jeremy Donougher receives his marching orders from referee Russell Smith v Wigan. Despite this setback the 12 man Bradford Bulls went on to record a memorable win

reviving Paris Saint-Germain travelling to Derwent Park to take on Town, only two points below them at the foot of the table.

The omens for Town looked shaky, with long-time favourite Colin "Buck" Armstrong sold to second division Swinton, and Kiwi Jason Palmada put out on loan to neighbours Whitehaven. But they had brought over full-back Abram Fatnowna from Australia, once tipped to be the new Wendell Sailor at Brisbane Broncos, and played as if this really was their Grand Final - defeat would have left them in a hopeless situation.

Another import, one of Paris' belated signings, New Zealander Phil Shead, was sent off for striking with only ten minutes left on the clock, with Town 14-4 up thanks to a try from Lafaele Filipo and five goals from Wayne Kitchin.

But Patrick Entat's irrepressible leadership brought PSG back into the game. His bomb gave a try to Dion Bird and Fred Banquet's conversion left an unbearable last four minutes.

Town held on at 14-10 to join Paris on five points, but still in twelfth place, with a 137 worse points' difference.

Just above PSG, Leeds' fortunes refused to improve as they crashed at home to Oldham Bears.

Jason Temu scored a last gasp winner at the end of a move that covered the length of the field, as Oldham won their fourth game out of the last five.

"We've not spent much money but we work hard," said a delighted Andy Goodway after the 28-26 win.

July

"We've had so much adversity to overcome we never give in."

Leeds were rocked when Tony Kemp failed a fitness test before the kick off to compound their injury crisis, and nothing had been heard at Headingley of the whereabouts of props Neil Harmon and Harvey Howard, both out of contract and seeking moves. Harmon was all set to join Paris, until the RFL decided that a transfer fee would be payable and the French lost interest. Howard headed off to Australia where he was a big hit in the Optus Cup with Western Suburbs.

Halifax registered their second home win of the season - the first one coming at the start of June against Sheffield Eagles - beating fourth placed Warrington 25-16.

Great Britain winger John Bentley scored his eleventh try of the season but, astonishingly, his first at Thrum Hall. Kiwi Martin Moana grabbed two, while Paul Sculthorpe was in the sin bin early in the second half for refusing to hand over the ball on the last tackle. A John Schuster drop-goal five minutes from the end of the game - while team-mates Michael Jackson and Fereti Tuilagi were both in the bin for professional fouls - confirmed the two points for the Blue Sox.

London Broncos' 45-6 thrashing of Sheffield Eagles in the Saturday night game was ominous for the Wire, as the run for top-four places shaped up.

London kept the ball alive in a superb performance that had Tony Currie purring. "We released the harness from the players and let them express themselves," he said. "It was a good win. It will breed confidence."

Currie unveiled 17-year-old full-back Tony Martin, a star of the Broncos' successful Academy side, and the youngster established himself as a first grade regular for the rest of the season.

In the first division, Keighley Cougars received a fatal blow to their Championship hopes on the weekend that news of a takeover of the club by a local business consortium was announced. Huddersfield Giants hammered them 37-10 at Cougar Park. Both clubs had lodged applications to the RFL for "fast-track" membership of the Super League, along with Hull.

"I don't think a team like Bradford can back that up two weeks in a row against a team like Wigan - Wigan by 20 points."

Shaun McRae, smarting from the defeat at Odsal, was way off the mark as Bradford took on Wigan at the start of Round 16. Seventeen and a half thousand fans flocked to Odsal on that Friday night for a game which represented everything that Super League could deliver.

It was the biggest crowd at Odsal for a league match since 1950, and one which witnessed a pulsating eighty minutes of football.

After 25 minutes it looked as though McRae had read his cards correctly. Wigan were already 10-0 up, through tries to Danny Ellison and Henry Paul, and a Farrell conversion, when Aussie Jeremy Donougher was dismissed by Russell Smith for a high tackle on Simon Haughton. But far from crushing the Bulls, Donougher's departure energised them, with Bernard Dwyer and James Lowes putting in huge displays in the pack, and Robbie Paul coming into the game with lightning injections of pace. A try from Paul Medley on the half-hour, awarded by the video referee and goaled by Steve McNamara, made it 10-6 at the break. And within four minutes of the restart, Dwyer was equalising on the left. Five minutes later the Bulls were in the lead via Jon Scales, who added the clincher after a Farrell penalty, ten minutes from time. It ended 20-12 on a memorable night.

It had been a huge occasion, none more so than for Brian Smith, who was to sever his links with the Bulls at the end of the season.

"To do what we did with twelve men from ten points down and with all the hype that preceded the game, was pretty special," he said. "It is right up there with the best moments of my career."

The result had given St Helens a gilt-edged chance to take back the top spot.

And their Super League challenge was re-born, as Saints put on a brilliant performance at Knowsley Road against the Blue Sox.

Back were Bobbie Goulding and Chris Joynt, and it was the big second rower who scored the crucial try just before half-time, after a rough, tough forty minutes that saw Karle Hammond and Martin Moana sin-binned after a flare-up.

"They caught us on a good day," said McRae, after the 56-20 victory. "Whoever played us was in for a pretty horrendous time."

Ex-Castleford centre Richie Blackmore announces he wants to return to England from New Zealand.....Wigan chairman Jack Robinson calls for a longer season

The relegation battle took another astonishing twist as Paris Saint-Germain came back from the dead to beat London Broncos at the Charlety Stadium on Bastille Day.

"We proved to everybody tonight that we can stay in Super League," said Michel Mazare, after the great escape that was this 24-18 win.

London looked to be in the driving seat after Kevin Langer dummied his way over for an 18-12 lead with only nine minutes left. Four more minutes passed before PSG launched a desperate attack, keeping the ball alive in the Broncos' quarter. A speculative overhead pass from Vincent Wulf left space for Aussie winger George Wilson to step his way over.

Danny Smith, cut by the Broncos earlier in the summer, added the conversion to level the scores.

With seconds remaining Pierre Chamorin's drop-goal attempt was blocked but the Paris skipper recovered the ball, went left and found Wilson who squeezed in at the corner. Smith converted, and the near ten thousand crowd celebrated with a rendition of the Marseillaise.

They weren't singing in Workington though, as a week of optimism turned to despair with a 49-4 thrashing by Warrington at Derwent Park.

Paul Sculthorpe was brilliant for the Wire. Town, who lost star turn Abram Fatnowna to injury on his debut the week before, couldn't get a fair bounce. Their chances of survival, in the light of PSG's result, were now looking slim.

Mid-table, Sheffield Eagles kept the pressure on fifth placed London after a see-saw battle against Leeds at Bramall Lane. Eagles were coasting it at 16-0 at the break,

Halifax Blue Sox' Mike Umaga set a Super League record
as he became the first player to score five tries in a game

but four unanswered tries in an 18 minute spell, two from Marvin Golden, and one each from Gary Mercer and David Hulme, plus four Graham Holroyd conversions and a drop goal, gave Leeds an incredible nine point lead.

But back came the Eagles, as Keith Senior and Lynton Stott scored tries to make it 33-30.

Castleford bounced back from the disappointment at Central Park nine days earlier with a 30-20 win over the Bears at Watersheddings.

Oldham led 16-4 at the break, and looked set to complete their first double over the Tigers for 20 years. But, with Tony Smith buzzing, Cas' came back with a vengeance, scoring all their five tries in the second forty. Chris Smith's 70th minute try gave them the lead, and Junior Paramore scored the clincher just before the final hooter.

Mike Umaga set a Super League record when he became the first player to score five tries in a game, as Halifax Blue Sox demolished Workington Town by 74-14. Halifax had Aussie Johnny Brewer on debut, but his introduction was overshadowed by the scoring feat of the Western Samoan.

With six rounds to go in Super League 1996, the run-in appeared to favour Wigan rather than Saints.

Wigan had two tricky away games at Sheffield and Paris, three home fixtures which they could be expected to win, and one game they were tipped, by most pundits, to struggle in - away at London Broncos.

After taking on Oldham away, Saints had to face an horrific run of three consecutive away matches - at London, Castleford and Paris - before meeting Sheffield and Warrington at Knowsley Road in the last two games of the season.

Wigan were looking to bounce straight back from their shock at Bradford in that trip to Paris, which in theory shouldn't have posed too many problems for them.

But things just didn't go to plan, and they came within an inch of handing the Championship on a plate to St Helens at the Charlety.

Things were evidently not quite right on the field, and rumours started to grow that off the field there were problems too.

They seemed to be confirmed when Shaun Edwards, who was in Graeme West's original squad as a substitute, failed to appear in Paris. Reports indicated that Edwards was unsettled by rumours that the Wigan board, keen to get within the new salary cap for 1997, were looking to off-load the Great Britain scrum-half.

Edwards' absence didn't seem to matter at all for the first hour of the game in Paris. After repelling early pressure from the Parisians, Wigan sailed into an 18-2 lead with tries from Va'aiga Tuigamala, Jason Robinson and Kris Radlinski. But the never-say-die French almost stole the game, coming back to 18-16 with only three minutes remaining, before Andy Johnson followed up Henry Paul's kick to seal the win. Pierre Chamorin pegged another back and at 24-20, Wigan had had a lucky escape.

London Broncos announce the imminent signing of Martin Offiah....Wigan make a move to sign Tongan prop Lee Hansen from Widnes.....St Helens sign Auckland Warriors reserve grade prop Julian O'Neill.....Paris sign Justin Bryant, cut by the Broncos after a bust up in Paris with coach Tony Currie....South Wales fast-tracked into Super League by the Rugby League Council.....first division Champions elect Salford Reds sign Andy Platt from Auckland Warriors...

Saints meanwhile looked far more impressive in a 54-18 demolition of Oldham at Boundary Park. Shaun McRae summed up the match succinctly.

"It was dicey at times," he said. "18-14 at half-time and then 24-18.

"But to win the second half like that was a comprehensive victory."

The point-a-minute finale, orchestrated by Bobbie Goulding's distribution and Apollo Perelini and Paul Newlove's powerhouse running, set up Saints for those three away matches which would ultimately decide if they were to last the pace.

"The Championship will definitely go to the wire," predicted McRae, with chilling accuracy this time. "I don't see anyone beating Wigan, so we've got to win all our games."

After Round 17 it was apparent that the Bradford Bulls hadn't been completely drained by their heroics against Wigan and Saints.

Warrington's young Welsh star Iestyn Harris was the centre of controversy
as he failed to appear in Wire colours

They were forced to put in an almighty effort at Wilderspool in the Saturday night TV game to win by 30-20.

It was a game full of incident. Even before the kick-off controversy raged as Iestyn Harris failed to appear in Warrington colours, ostensibly because of a knee injury. It transpired that the Wales stand-off was in dispute with the club. Three days later he was put on the transfer list at £1.35 million.

The game had been billed as a grudge match between Brian Smith and Alex Murphy because of the public argument they had conducted over the merits and de-merits of Super League.

But the two shook hands before the kick-off of another hard-fought encounter.

Wire took a 10-4 lead into the break, but it could have been much bigger. Twice, marvellous work by future Great Britain full-back Stuart Spruce denied them over the line.

But Graeme Bradley inspired the Bulls to victory in the second half, scoring a try himself and making two more.

"He's a funny sort of player," said Smith, of the man he had brought with him from St George in Sydney.

"You see him in training and you think he is not going to last another week. But again he did it when it was critical."

The game boiled over on the hour, when Sonny Nickle, who had already had a tete-a-tete with Paul Sculthorpe, and Mark Forster were sin-binned for fighting while, on the other side of the field, Richard Henare was seeing red and punching Glen Tomlinson for not much reason. Henare subsequently copped a two match ban after the incident was put on report.

When Forster returned he probably wished he hadn't . When he collected a kick-through in his own in-goal, he was bundled into a TV cameraman by Jon Scales and Steve McNamara. Sky TV were not thrilled at the damage to the camera.

"Why McNamara and the other kid were not pulled up for a dangerous tackle was diabolical," blasted Wire coach John Dorahy. The incident was investigated by the RFL, but no action was taken.

London Broncos recovered their composure and moved back to within a point of fourth placed Warrington, with a 33-18 win over Leeds at The Valley.

Leeds gave debuts to new signing from Huddersfield, full-back Marcus St Hilaire but as a cost cutting measure - and to the utter disbelief of all Loiners fans - the team was forced to travel down to the match on the day of the game, on one of the hottest days of the year.

Not surprisingly they got off to a slow start, and found themselves 24-0 down at half-time.

In the second forty they scored three tries, but it was too little too late.

The absence of any Leeds' director at the game fuelled speculation that the club was about to be taken over by the new owners of Leeds United soccer club. But when asked for comment, an official revealed that the directors just all happened to be on holiday.

Castleford effectively killed off Sheffield Eagles' hopes of a top-four play-off place with a last-gasp effort in the oven-hot conditions at Wheldon Road.

Dean Lawford looked to have clinched a 31-30 win for the Eagles with a 75th minute drop-goal, and when Mark Aston sent a kick into the Cas' in-goal in the final seconds the result looked a foregone conclusion.

But Graham Steadman collected the ball and threw an outrageous long pass to substitute Simon Middleton, who broke down the left. The ball was fanned across field before David Chapman was sent in at the corner for one of the best tries of the season. Frano Botica kicked the touchline conversion for a 36-31 Tigers' win.

Round 18 opened on Friday night at Central Park, with the potential for Wigan to re-claim the top berth.

That night they took on Halifax, with Saints due to make the daunting trip to the Broncos the following day.

But Wigan's decision to off-load Martin Offiah's contract, seen as a sound business move by most people in the game, and the increasing rumours about the future of Shaun Edwards, overshadowed their televised game, with 'club in crisis' stories hogging the headlines.

Edwards denied that he had made himself unavailable through anything but injury.

"It really offended me if they were insinuating I was not injured," he blasted. "I always give 100% for Wigan. Every player declares himself unfit when injured. No player has played with more injuries than me.

"I'll put my record against any player on that."

Steve Simms had promised Wigan a tough game after last week's hammering of Workington, and that is what they got. Still, Wigan managed to eke out a 32-8 lead, with Gary Connolly in superb form before limping off and signalling a mighty fightback by the Blue Sox, with three tries in the last half hour. But Wigan held on for a 34-26 win to put the pressure on St Helens.

And Saints themselves got the mother of all pressure games at The Valley.

Shaun McRae heaved a huge sigh of relief as his side twice came back from the dead, in what many would pick as the best game of the Super League 1996 season.

"It's easy for me to say it was a great game because I am the winning coach," said McRae.

"I'm gutted." was Tony Currie's reaction after a 32-28 reverse.

"But it was the way in which they got through which gutted me."

The video ref was one of the best innovations in Super League and on this occasion he was to decide the outcome of this game and the ultimate destiny of Super League.

The video ref's decision was vital in Apollo Perelini's life saving try for St Helens at London Broncos

Saints had come back from a six point deficit, after leading 12-2 early in the first half, through tries to sub Vila Matautia and Scott Gibbs, playing his last game for Saints before being sold to Swansea union club. But a 70 metre try set up by Peter Gill, and scored by Steve Rosolen in the 72nd minute, looked to have decided the game.

But Saints snatched it in incredible fashion. With some awesome defence they kept the Broncos in their own quarter, and Tony Rea's clearance kick only reached half-way. Then London skipper Terry Matterson was put on report for

London Broncos captain Terry Matterson was put on report for a high tackle on Saints' Steve Prescott

a high tackle on Steve Prescott. But with two minutes on the clock, Bobbie Goulding opted to tap the ball instead of taking the draw with a penalty goal.

Determined work by Karle Hammond put Apollo Perelini over the line. The Samoan was on his back, but managed to ground the ball to the satisfaction of the video ref.

The Broncos argued that there'd been an improper play the ball in the build up to the try, and Matterson was sin-binned after letting Stuart Cummings know his feelings, but Goulding's conversion made it 32-28 and Saints were back on top. of the table.

Headingley experienced a second coming as coach Dean Bell pulled on the number 38 shirt to lead his charges to a vital 34-12 win over Paris Saint-Germain.

'Playing is not something I want to do," admitted Bell, "but it was out of necessity. I enjoyed the physical contact, but the best thing was to get the win."

Indeed it was.

Defeat would have seen PSG leapfrog the Loiners.

Bell himself scored a late try to the delight of the six and a half thousand supporters who remained faithful to the club, which was claiming poverty as the reason for denying Bell the top flight players that he needed.

The game itself was not without incident, Paris' Justin Bryant being sent off for a high tackle on the half hour, after only six minutes on the field.

The video clearly showed that referee Colin Morris had made a bad error - he'd made a similar mistake the previous week in the division two promotion decider between Hunslet and Swinton.

Bryant did obstruct Mick Shaw as he chased his own kick through, but there was no contact with the head at all. Morris was relieved of his next appointment.

July

The Bulls' phenomenon continued with almost ten thousand people watching their Sunday night game with Oldham.

After the thriller against Wigan this was a more one sided affair, with the Bulls rattling up 30 points in the first half against injury-ravaged Bears. Aussie Glen Tomlinson was rewarded for a top display at Warrington with a start, and was chosen as the League Express Gamestar. But the man he would have to dislodge, Robbie Paul, emphasised the size of his quest to become a regular choice by scoring a hat-trick of tries in a 56-0 win.

Sheffield kept the battle for the final top-four place alive by beating Warrington at Bramall Lane. Wire lost both props, Mark Hilton and Gary Chambers, through injury in the first ten minutes of the game. Mark Aston was in superlative form in an eventual 28-22 win for the Eagles.

Workington Town were fast running out of time and games to escape relegation. They introduced Ian Watson at scrum-half - on loan from Salford Reds - but the Tigers had too much power and ran out 46-20 winners, with Richard Russell back to his best on return from injury.

TABLES AT END OF JULY

STONES SUPER LEAGUE

	P	W	D	L	For	Agst	Diff	PTS
St Helens	18	16	0	2	764	411	353	32
Wigan	18	15	1	2	668	283	385	31
Bradford Bulls	18	14	0	4	630	336	294	28
Warrington	18	10	0	8	462	431	31	20
London Broncos	18	9	1	8	500	401	99	19
Sheffield Eagles	18	9	0	9	518	546	-28	18
Castleford Tigers	18	8	0	10	486	467	19	16
Halifax Blue Sox	18	7	1	10	492	474	18	15
Oldham Bears	18	7	1	10	371	568	-197	15
Leeds	18	5	0	13	431	529	-98	10
Paris St Germain	18	3	1	14	344	658	-314	7
Workington Town	18	2	1	15	255	817	-562	5

DIVISION ONE

	P	W	D	L	For	Agst	Diff	PTS
Salford Reds	16	15	0	1	596	253	343	30
Featherstone Rovers	17	11	2	4	509	301	208	24
Keighley Cougars	16	11	2	3	404	272	132	24
Hull	16	11	0	5	427	307	120	22
Huddersfield Giants	17	10	0	7	461	270	191	20
Widnes	16	8	0	8	333	332	1	16
Wakefield Trinity	16	7	1	8	365	363	2	15
Dewsbury	16	5	1	10	221	458	-237	11
Whitehaven	17	4	1	12	260	448	-188	9
Rochdale Hornets	17	2	1	14	284	508	-224	5
Batley Bulldogs	16	1	2	13	170	518	-348	4

DIVISION TWO

	P	W	D	L	For	Agst	Diff	PTS
Hull KR	18	17	0	1	876	246	630	34
Swinton Lions	18	15	0	3	627	255	372	30
Hunslet Hawks	18	15	0	3	604	267	337	30
Carlisle	18	12	0	6	566	353	213	24
South Wales	18	10	0	8	465	434	31	20
Doncaster Dragons	18	10	0	8	413	455	-42	20
Leigh Centurions	18	8	0	10	495	392	103	16
York	18	7	0	11	354	521	-167	14
Barrow Braves	18	4	0	14	290	552	-262	8
Bramley	18	4	0	14	283	662	-379	8
Chorley	18	4	0	14	271	653	-382	8
Prescot Panthers	18	2	0	16	239	693	-454	4

AUGUST
Race for the finishing line

August provided the tensest of climaxes to Super League 1996.

The month opened in the certainty that the title was now definitely a two horse race between the "old firm", Wigan and St Helens.

After 18 rounds, with four more to go, Saints, courtesy of Terry Matterson's last minute touchline goal at Central Park back in June, sat one point clear at the top with Wigan still breathing down their necks.

In short, St Helens could not afford even to drop a point, with Wigan having the better points difference by 70. Any slip from the Knowsley Road men would be exploited in the most complete fashion by the defending Champions.

It was in that context that St Helens backed up for their second stern test in a week, this time at Wheldon Road, in the Friday night game.

Castleford Tigers had experienced a mixed season, and could not shake off their "unpredictable" tag. But at the start of August they were arguably having their best spell of the whole season, with the memory of the heartbreak of Central Park a month earlier being erased by three consecutive victories at Oldham and Workington, and at home to Sheffield.

Saints had, of course, produced a mighty effort six days earlier at The Valley, and no-one could know, not even Shaun McRae, how much that might have taken out of them.

For the first half-hour it appeared that the leaders had made a full recovery, and were back into the swing of things, when they shot into a 10-2 lead through tries by Paul Newlove and Anthony Sullivan. But a Jason Flowers try - the full-back managed to reach his own kick through under the sticks first, despite being felled by Derek McVey en-route - and two goals to Frano Botica levelled the scores at the break.

Saints' fans began to get slightly edgy, but breathed easier when Sullivan pounced on a Goulding kick to the corner for his second try - his 100th for the club - and then sub Tommy Martyn got a fourth try on 64 minutes. One Goulding conversion gave them a ten point lead, and St Helens looked home and dry.

But Cas, perhaps sensing that the TV viewers required yet more drama, produced another heartstopper, as Tony Smith burrowed under from dummy-half on 66 minutes, and Frano Botica converted to set up a pulsating last fifteen minutes.

All seemed well for Saints with the match moving into injury time, until, with literally seconds left on the clock, Cas' full-back Flowers was streaking clear for what seemed like a certain try under the posts.

Amazingly, full-back Steve Prescott and winger Joey Hayes pegged back Flowers,

79

bringing him down two metres short of the line for the tackle of the season, which kept St Helens' title dream alive with a 20-16 win.

"Desperate situations call for desperate men," said a breathless McRae after the game.

"I could see a whole season's work go before us in just a flash.

"We had to pull something out and we did."

The following night, Wigan produced what Graeme West called his side's best performance of the season - a 54-12 win against Sheffield Eagle at Bramall Lane.

And the brilliant Henry Paul commented: "We're finding our character back, and we want to win and win well.

"There's a great spirit among the players, and we'll kick on strong for the rest of the season."

Paul scored twice as Wigan inflicted Sheffield's first defeat in the city on the Eagles for the second season running.

And Shaun Edwards proved his heart still belonged to the Riversiders, when he

St Helens' Steve Prescott who, together with team-mate Joey Hayes, pulled off the tackle of the season on Castleford's Jason Flowers

appeared as substitute in the 66th minute, scoring a try ten minutes later to the delight of the Wigan faithful who had made the trip across the Pennines.

There was controversy at The Valley, where the Broncos took up pole position in the battle for the fourth spot with a 20-13 victory.

Martin Offiah's debut for London was overshadowed by the eventual circumstances of his new club's win.

An angry Alex Murphy was seen to have words with referee Russell Smith at the final whistle, after London's clinching try in the 76th minute. TV replays seemed to show that Peter Gill had used a shepherd before providing the scoring pass to Darryl Pitt.

"We thought that Gill was interfering with play," said John Dorahy. "We will go away and look at the video, but it is the second week running that we had a zero penalty count in the second half."

"They should take a look at the tape of our game at St Helens earlier in the season if they think they were hard done by," responded Tony Currie.

Offiah made Duncan McRae's opening try in the 27th minute. Earlier he had bombed a try when spilling McRae's kick to the corner.

Nevertheless Offiah's appearance after weeks of uncertainty, gave The Broncos a PR boost in the capital.

Not that Currie was overly impressed with the disruption.

"The lads are a little bit down as they are the type of side that needs a meticulous preparation," he said.

"And all this on-off business with Martin's transfer hasn't helped."

It was now, even arithmetically, impossible for either London or Warrington to catch Bradford in third place, after the Bulls recorded their biggest ever winning score at Headingley since 1945.

Ironically it was a try by ex-Loiner Paul Medley, converted by an even more recent Leeds player, Paul Cook, that passed the milestone.

A young Leeds side had pegged back a 16-0 deficit to 16-14 late in the first half, before Paul Loughlin set up the Bulls' points onslaught with a try just before the hooter.

Matthew Elliott, Brian Smith's assistant, is named as the new head coach at Bradford Bulls.....Warrington sign Auckland Warriors prop Dallas Mead......Featherstone Rovers transfer list stars Martin Pearson and Steve Molloy.....Super League-bound Salford Reds move in to sign former Great Britain prop Andy Platt from Auckland Warriors and Penrith Panther John Cartwright....

Paris Saint-Germain had stayed in England all week to help their preparations for the game against Halifax. But it didn't do them much good, as the Blue Sox continued their impressive end of season form with a 56-10 rout.

It was only 22-10 at the break, but two-try Martin Moana - the Kiwi stand-off now established as a loose forward - inspired Halifax to an impeccable second half showing, that saw the Blue Sox leap over Castleford into seventh spot, with sixth placed Sheffield Eagles to visit the following week.

Oldham Bears' Martin Crompton inspired his side to victory at Derwent Park ending any hopes Workington Town had of Super League survival

"Town out of time" read the League Express headline for the Workington-Oldham match report.

The Martin Crompton-inspired Bears scuppered any lingering hopes of Super League rugby in Cumbria in 1997 with a 30-14 win at Derwent Park.

After a half-hour of Wigan's Friday night game with beleaguered Leeds in the first game of Round 20, it looked as though the title would be decided in the unlikeliest of circumstances.

Only five days before Leeds were going down to a humbling defeat to neighbours Bradford at Headingley, while Wigan were back to their imperious best at Sheffield.

After seven minutes the match was going predictably to form, when Jason Robinson shrugged out of a tackle to open up a 4-0 lead.

But the next 20 minutes were all Leeds, as Kiwi Dean Clark and teenage second-rower Adrian Morley inspired the Loiners to their best spell of the season.

The crowd was stunned, as former Wiganer Mike Forshaw scored two tries and Graham Holroyd kicked three goals to give Leeds a 14-4 lead.

It might have been bigger but for the video ref, who ruled out efforts by Clark and Morley during that golden period.

In the ten minutes before the break the game turned around completely. First, David Hulme was sin-binned for holding down and Robinson scored his second try. Then some elementary errors gave Wigan the position for three more tries from Va'aiga Tuigamala, Craig Murdock and Gary Connolly. Wigan were ten points up. In the second half Wigan scored 44 more points, with Robinson ending with five tries to equal Mike Umaga's record for Super League.

Shaun Edwards came on after 50 minutes to score two tries prompting chants from the terraces of "Edwards for Chairman".

Under eight thousand people turned out to watch a superb 80 minutes of football. "I don't know why the people didn't turn up," commented Graeme West after the 68-14 success. "We can't do much more than that."

Wigan were back on top but, not for the first time, only for 24 hours, as St Helens won their third gruelling away match in a row, this week at the Charlety Stadium.

John Joyner signs a new 12 month coaching contract with Castleford Tigers after approaches from Aussie club Perth Western Reds.....Rob Smyth suffers damage to his cruciate ligament against Leeds, ruling him out of the Great Britain tour to the southern hemisphere....the Australian Rugby League block contracted players Jason Robinson, Gary Connolly and Lee Jackson from playing for Great Britain.

Warrington and Wigan had both struggled in Paris, and the Broncos had fallen to a last minute defeat there. But Saints, after the thrillers of the previous two rounds, were well up to the task, and ran out 32-12 winners.

John Kear, for one, was convinced he had seen the title winners that night.

"We asked Saints a load of questions in very tricky situations," he said. "We thought they would make mistakes.

"They not only had the answers to those questions, but even some we never got the chance to pose. They looked like a champion side to me."

Paris had been hit that day by rainstorms, and the greasy conditions not only kept the Parisians away - this was PSG's lowest crowd of the Super League season, just over 4,000 - but led to a glut of handling errors.

Shaun McRae switched Karle Hammond back to loose-forward, drafted in Andy Haigh, and moved Alan Hunte into the centre, with Paul Newlove on the bench to rest a foot injury, and Scott Gibbs departed.

"I've always thought that Hammond, Goulding and Martyn as the middle three would be my best option," said McRae, "but because of injuries I've never had much chance to use it.

"I certainly liked the look of it tonight."

Hammond had a top game, and Anthony Sullivan collected two tries for the second week running, as Saints left themselves a two match run-in at Knowsley Road against Sheffield and Warrington.

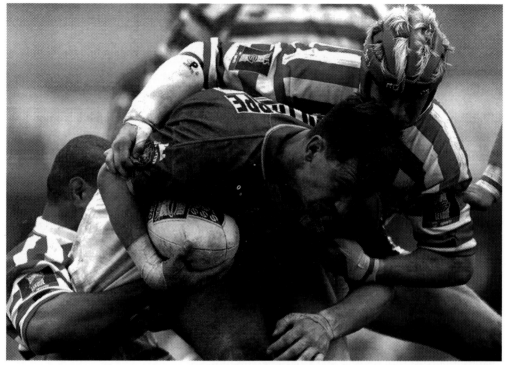

Warrington's young Great Britain tourist Paul Sculthorpe was in great form
and earned the praise of his coach John Dorahy

The contest for the last Premiership play-off spot ran and ran.

Warrington, in fifth, were first up against the Tigers at Wilderspool.

18 year old Paul Sculthorpe, on the eve of the selection of the Great Britain touring party, was in great form. scoring a first half try and making two others as the Wire raced into a 20-4 half-time lead.

Which had John Dorahy raving about his young star.

"He's very similar to the great Ray Price, with the effort and intensity he puts into his game," said Joe Cool.

"As far as ability and skill go, he's up there with the best. At this stage in his development I rate him better than Denis Betts or Phil Clarke. When he's at his optimum age he'll be some player.

"Already he's almost up to Dick Huddart standard, and that is high praise."

Cas, who had prop Dean Sampson sent off for a back-hander on Wire's youngster Warren Stevens, never threw in the towel, but had to settle for second place in this match, Warrington emerging 38-24 victors.

They moved into fourth, but it didn't last long, with London Broncos eking out two points at Watersheddings. Martin Offiah scored his first try for his new club when he supported Peter Gill, after a Kevin Langer break. Paul Davidson then barged over to make it only 6-4 at the break and then, only three minutes after the restart, Martin Crompton dived over under the posts, Francis Maloney converted, and the Bears had the lead.

Form prop Tony Mestrov snatched the lead back for the Broncos, before Adie Belle scooped up a loose ball to put Oldham 14-12 in front.

But tries in the last 15 minutes from David Krause and Offiah sank the Bears, and moved the Broncos back into fourth spot.

In Sheffield, the Eagles maintained their 100% Super League record at the Don Valley - in what turned out to be their last game at the athletics stadium.

In the process Halifax

Martin Offiah scored his first try for London Broncos against Oldham Bears at Watersheddings

missed the chance, for then at least, to leapfrog the Eagles into sixth spot. Sheffield ran out 42-28 winners, with Ryan Sheridan, Eagles' classy half-back, who had been sidelined for the biggest part of the season, along with Aussie back-rower Paul Carr, spearheading a commanding second half performance.

The Super League curtain was brought down at Derwent Park with what was Workington's best display of the season.

At half-time they had the high-flying Bulls worried, 8-6 to the good, through a Mike Bethwaite try and two Ian Watson goals, against a Stuart Spruce effort. But with Paul Penrice in the sin-bin, minutes after Jeremy Donougher had given Bradford the lead, the Bulls stretched out to 24-8. In other games Town would have folded. But not this time, as they fought back to finish the match 14-28 in arrears.

In the first division, Salford Reds removed any mathematical possibility of being overtaken at the top with a 21-4 win over nearest rivals Keighley Cougars.

Then it was Wigan's turn to have another twenty four hours at the top.

London Broncos had, three weeks earlier, almost decided the title, when they

Lively young scrum-half Craig Murdock was keeping seasoned veteran
Shaun Edwards out of the Wigan starting line-up

pushed St Helens so close at The Valley. Now, on the Saturday night of Round 21, it was the turn of Wigan to enter "The Valley of Death" as the Broncos home ground was quickly becoming known.

Over ten thousand folk turned out to see Britain's most famous League team, the Broncos' biggest crowd of the season, and hundreds of thousands more TV viewers saw Wigan at their very best - for the last 25 minutes of the game at least.

Until then the London pack was superb, bottling up the Wigan attack with some awesome defence.

Once again Graeme West continued with his policy of starting with Cumbrian Craig Murdock at scrum-half, with club skipper Shaun Edwards on the bench, where he remained for those first 55 nerve-wracking minutes.

When Edwards was introduced, Wigan were on the rack at 9-6 down.

With his first touch of the game, Edwards was scooting 40 metres after a Mick Cassidy break, for the try under the posts that gave Wigan the lead - one they were never going to give up.

Tries followed from Henry Paul, Jason Robinson, Andy Johnson and Va'aiga Tuigamala to eventually take Wigan home by 34-13.

The importance of Edwards' intervention was noted by Graeme West: "Things were getting a bit stagnant on the pitch," he said. "Shaun was chafing at the bit to get on. He's got a lot of control around the middle. Craig Murdock gets the ball to the backs quickly, but he doesn't yet have the control of the forwards as Edwards has."

Edwards himself recognised the importance of his score, but predicted that St Helens would not falter in their last two games: "My try was crucial, and then we scored again straight away," he said. "That changed the course of the game.

"We are still in the hunt, but we need favours from other teams.

"I don't think St Helens will slip up."

Tony Currie was once again in inimitable form: "The Wigan Boys Brigade could have come down here in the second half and fallen over the try-line with the amount of ball we gave them." With Warrington likely to beat Oldham at Watersheddings the following day, Currie could see that play-off place slipping away.

St Helens, after coming through a trial-by-fire in their last three games away from home, returned to Knowsley Road to set themselves up for a high-scoring finale.

Plans to form a company to promote and market Super League were revealed.....Jacques Fouroux, the moving force behind Paris Saint-Germain announces he will resign as chairman of the club....chief executive Robbie Moore quits London Broncos and is replaced by retiring player Tony Rea....

The Champions-elect had already beaten their penultimate opponents, Sheffield Eagles, "away from home" in Cardiff two months earlier, and they made light of the Eagles this time around.

Anthony Sullivan and Karle Hammond each scored hat-tricks, and fellow Great Britain tourist- to-be Steve Prescott got four tries as Saints romped to a 68-2 win.

"Goals were set and goals were achieved," purred McRae, after watching his side at their very best.

Now only local rivals Warrington, in the very last game of the whole Super League season, lay between them and their first league title since 1975.

Warrington were moving back into fourth as a sparkling hat-trick from New Zealander Richard Henare - picked up from second division Carlisle in the Centenary season - showed there was life after Iestyn.

Another Kiwi, Kelly Shelford, who had been on the transfer list himself for most of the season, filled in admirably for Harris, who was by now not even allowed to train with the club who held his contract, as Wire eventually shook off the Bears 42-24.

At "Fortress Odsal" in a rip-roaring local derby Halifax Blue Sox brought the Bulls down to earth, by inflicting the first home defeat of the season on Bradford, ironically in the very last game.

Over thirteen thousand flocked to see Brian Smith's last home game in charge, but the Blue Sox were in no mood to give him a perfect send off, as John Schuster dropped a last minute goal to give them a shock 27-26 victory.

"Any loss is disappointing," said Smith, "this one is no worse." But it was not a perfect way to bid farewell to the Bradford faithful, to whom he had delivered so much.

David Chapman and Castleford Tigers were just too strong
for a valiant Paris St Germain side at Wheldon Road

At the bottom end of the table, Leeds coach Dean Bell reflected on a thumping 68-28 win over Workington Town: "One win doesn't pay the Leeds public back for what they suffered this year, but maybe that was the first instalment."

And Paris proved that they would compete till the very end as John Kear took his side to his hometown club and gave the Tigers - with John Joyner blooding several youngsters from their talented Academy side - a mighty shock, Cas eventually being relieved to hear the final hooter that left the score at 22-18 in their favour.

And so to the ultimate weekend of Super League 1996.

There had been so many thrilling matches in the previous 21 rounds that it had crept up on us all so quickly.

In the Championship race, Wigan were first up on Saturday in what was to be a mere formality - a home fixture against relegated Workington Town.

According to Ross O'Reilly he had set his side - with an average age of 20 - the modest goal of "not giving up and trying to the end."

There was a hat-trick for Henry Paul as Wigan blew Workington aside in record-breaking style

By half-time they were 42-0 down and forty minutes later, 78-4, with a Mark Johnson try seven minutes from the end proving that they hadn't given up.

They were just outgunned, with Henry Paul and young prop Steve Barrow collecting hat-tricks from a total of fourteen tries.

Wigan were back on top with a 133 better points difference than Saints - who could afford nothing less than a win to take the title when they met Warrington at Knowsley Road two days later.

On that same Saturday night Bradford Bulls were stuttering to a 27-14 win at Paris. PSG finished their first Super League season with a crowd of over 6,000, and said goodbye to John Kear, the man from RFL headquarters sent to revive the team's fortunes in mid-season. Not many would deny that he achieved that.

At Thrum Hall, in what may turn out to be Halifax's last ever first grade game at the famous stadium, the Blue Sox finished their season with a flourish against Leeds, running out 64-24

89

winners. It meant Steve Simms' men, who went seven rounds without a victory at the start of the season, finished in sixth spot in Super League.

"I thought in many of the opening six or seven games we played better than in some of our wins," said a weary Simms. "The players can rest now. They are both physically and mentally exhausted, and they can prepare to explode into action in Super League 1997."

Dean Bell gave credit to his youngsters and said: "I need to be on the plane in the next three or four days. We need to talk to people out there. The club is four or five players short of what is necessary."

Halifax went sixth because Oldham Bears beat Sheffield at Watersheddings in a thrilling final act at the infamous stadium. Scott Ranson scored a hat-trick as the Bears recovered from a 21-6 half-time deficit to win 34-25, and cement eighth position.

London kept their play-off hopes alive, and gave Warrington every incentive to turn over St Helens the following day, by hammering a despondent looking Castleford Tigers, who finished a disappointing ninth in the table, by 56-0. Broncos' form three-quarter Greg Barwick scored four tries as London romped to a 56-0 win.

Tony Currie knew that the Broncos' fate depended on events 200 miles away on Merseyside 24 hours later.

"It is hard for me to think of anything today, because I know our season may be over at 4pm tomorrow."

And so to Knowsley Road on Bank Holiday Monday afternoon for literally the final game - the 132nd match in Super League.

There was plenty at stake for both clubs, but everyone accepted that Wire would need a flying start to knock Saints off their unstoppable stride.

It couldn't have turned out worse for them, as Tommy Martyn opened Saints' account in the second minute, when he collected Joey Hayes speculative crossfield kick for the first try.

St Helen ran in thirteen more as Warrington wilted under the pressure, to the delight of almost all the 18,000 fans come to witness the climax to the season.

There was plenty of emotion on display as Saints completed the double for the first time in thirty years with this 66-14 rout.

Bobbie Goulding, whose stirring leadership had driven Saints on through the tough campaign, summed it all up.

"Warrington came here looking for a top four spot," he said after the game, "but it was never in any doubt that we'd win.

"It was just nerves that we had to overcome. We were glad to score the first try - that settled us a lot.

"Shaun's prepared us well all year," concluded Goulding. "It's been a great all round performance by the coaching staff and the players too.

"The lads have been a credit to themselves, to their families and to the club.

"I can't speak highly enough of them."

The St Helens players celebrate a resounding victory against Warrington and, more importantly, the historic first ever summer Super League title.

McRae himself had guided his team through many a rough crossing and could afford a moment's satisfaction.

"What we have been able to do over the last few weeks is regroup, focus and compete," he said.

"When you've got those things at your club, you're always going to have a chance.

"When I first got here, everybody talked about how the St Helens backs could match anybody, but the forwards maybe lacked a little bit in the middle and a little bit on the left side of the chest.

"I think we've shown a lot of sides that that's not the case."

They certainly had.

SEPTEMBER
Destination: Old Trafford

And so, after six months of intense competition, the final placings that had been so keenly contested were settled.

A week after the thrilling finale to Super League '96, thoughts turned towards the Premiership play-offs and a lucrative final appearance at Old Trafford.

The placings meant that champions St Helens would entertain London Broncos, and Wigan would host Bradford Bulls. In the lower divisions, Salford, the division one Champions, would play Hull Kingston Rovers, who had topped division two, while Keighley Cougars would play Hull.

For Wigan, it was a final chance to salvage some silverware and stop their arch-rivals from picking up the treble. But their Central Park clash with the Bulls was never going to be easy. Bradford were determined to reach Old Trafford and gain some reward for an outstanding campaign, whilst at the same time sending Parramatta-bound coach Brian Smith back home with a tangible thankyou. It all added up to an enthralling contest.

In the end, Smith's departure was overshadowed by Shaun Edwards, who scored four tries in a brilliant individual performance to steer Wigan to the final. It was a breathtaking encounter, with fifteen tries, great individual skills, and gutsy team spirit that had fans on the edge of their seats in a rollercoaster of a game.

Edwards summed it up perfectly: "That was one of the best games I have ever played in," he said immediately afterwards.

Bradford had gone into the game without in-form fullback Stuart Spruce, and lost Sonny Nickle with a broken arm after just seven minutes. They struck first, however, when Graeme Bradley went over for the first of what would become a hat-trick of tries.

Not for the first time, the game produced an intruiging battle between the Paul brothers, Henry gaining the early advantage on his younger brother by sending Edwards over. But Robbie showed his own elusiveness when cutting right through the home defence, and ignoring a slap on the mouth from Edwards to score a brilliant try. The incident sparked a brief flurry of punches, and a couple of sin-binnings, but eventually both sides settled down to give the watching TV audience a treat.

The game swung one way and then the other, until a three try burst in nine minutes from Wigan put them 32-16 ahead and seemingly out of sight. But incredibly, the Bulls' hit back to stun Central Park and tie the game at 32-32. At that point, the game could have gone either way, but Edwards' fourth try restored his sides' lead. Andy Farrell added a goal, but still the Bulls weren't finished, and Bradley's third brought them back to within two points.

Wigan's Andy Farrell was desperate for his side to win the Premiership Final
and stop Saints making off with a famous treble

It was finally settled when Edwards made a late break and sent winger Danny
Ellison scorching over in the last minute for the decisive score. The final hooter
sounded, and it was the only thing that settled a remarkable match.

The Bulls' season was over, but their fans went back across the Pennines

93

reasonably happy reflecting on six months of remarkable progress on and off the field that offered real hope of major success in Super League '97.

For Wigan - and Edwards in particular, who had now scored ten tries in the last five games since regaining his place - it meant another trip to Old Trafford, and minds were already being focussed on the last chance of lifting a trophy.

The following day, at Knowsley Road, St Helens overcame a mighty mauling from a tough London Broncos side to set up what pundits were calling "The Decider" against Wigan.

But Saints were made to work hard for their victory. London were still upset at suffering two heartbreaking defeats at the hands of the Champions, and the Broncos were fired up for revenge. They stuck to their game plan like glue. They hit hard, ran strong and straight, and frustrated the normally free-flowing Saints.

Saints coach Shaun McRae stormed afterwards: "The Broncos camp have always been very outspoken, and have always complained about controversial defeats. But three-nil to us is comprehensive enough.

"We expected roughhouse tactics, but we are not a side who likes to take a backward step. We like to keep within the rules, and if we're not allowed to play an open game we'll mix it with anybody. It was obvious they were out to upset us."

The Broncos plan almost worked. Saints struggled to find their rhythm, and were knocked out of their stride with some huge hits.

Bradford's Robbie Paul agrees a £75,000 three-month deal with Harlequins, and at the same time agrees to a new four-year contract with the Bulls....St Helens enquire about Auckland Warriors centre Richie Blackmore....South Africa win race to host next Student World Cup in 1998....Warrington list 18 players worth a total of £465,000. Biggest shock is Lee Penny, on offer at £120,000

Approaching the break, Saints were just 12-8 ahead and looking vulnerable. But winger Anthony Sullivan struck in the 39th minute to give his side a little breathing space. It was to prove a crucial score, as the second half continued pretty much the same as the first forty. Each side managed just one further try each,as the penalties kept flowing from the whistle of Stuart Cummings.

Sullivan sealed the game with his second, mid-way through the half, when Steve Prescott defused a bomb behind his line. Bobbie Goulding took a quick tap on the twenty to re-start, and sent Sullivan tearing away on a 70 metre sprint to the line.

London managed a late effort through Graham Strutton, but Saints ended victors by 25-14. The town was buzzing in anticipation of completing the treble against their fiercest rivals from just a few miles down the road.

The divisional semi-finals went as expected. Keighley Cougars defeated Hull 41-28, but only after the game had been held up for twenty minutes when a crash barrier gave way and fans spilled onto the pitch.

Salford Reds dispatched a gutsy Hull KR side 36-16 to set up a showdown between division one's top two.

Shaun Edwards led his
Wigan side magnificently

Wigan ruthlessly shot down St Helens bid for a clean sweep with a vintage performance at Old Trafford that saw them retain the Premiership Trophy in style.

Their 44-14 win was one of the best displays by any team throughout the whole year. Led magnificently by Shaun Edwards and Andy Farrell - who collected the man-of-the-match award to add to the Man of Steel accolade he had picked up earlier in the week - Wigan put on an exhibition of fast free-flowing football and solid effective defence that never allowed Saints a look-in.

Winger Danny Ellison scored a hat-trick to confirm his emergence as a potent attacking force, just as Kris Radlinski had done twelve months earlier. Gary Connolly threatened danger every time he touched the ball, and the Saints defence was dragged cruelly from side to side by the directional running of Henry Paul, Va'aiga Tuigamala and Jason Robinson.

Poor Saints had a nightmare. They couldn't control the ball, and seemed devoid of a kicking game. True, they had the upset of lacking Chris Joynt and Vila Matautia through injury, and the scoreline suggested at half time they were still in the hunt at 18-8 down.

But Wigan were always in control, as Saints' coach Shaun McRae admitted.

"We were up against a very committed side, and the London game probably worked against us," he said. "We were glad to hear the final hooter, but we should

95

remember all the good times we have had this year.

"We competed well for the first forty, but we have a very young side, and the pressure they've been subjected to over the last six weeks finally took its toll."

Wigan's Shaun Edwards found it hard to contain his delight.

"It was a very special final for me," he smiled. "People keep saying how good the opposition was, but today we beat them convincingly. We nullified their kicking game and our tactics were spot on."

Andy Farrell agreed.

"We were desperate to win, and there was no way we were going to let Saints get all three trophies," he said.

Warrington deny coach John Dorahy is to quit and join Illawarra....Leeds confirm they are the subject of a takeover bid, and could leave Headingley....South Wales place in Super League in doubt because of financial worries....Bradford boss Chris Caisley is appointed chairman of newly formed Rugby League (Europe) Ltd....Michael Potter, the Western Reds and former St George fullback joins Bradford as assistant coach....Sheffield fail in audacious bid for Warrington's Iestyn Harris

"We've been in top form for the last six or seven games, and we are really looking forward to next season. But Saints deserve credit for what they've done this year. They've been up there all season, with everyone trying to knock them off. But they held out well and deserve what they've got."

The game attracted over 35,000 to Old Trafford, and was preceded by the divisional final, won 19-6 by Salford Reds, for whom Sam Panapa played his last game before hanging up his boots for good, against the Keighley Cougars.

THE STONES GOLD AWARDS

Man of Steel...Andy Farrell
Player of Year ....Robbie Paul
Young Player of Year ....Keiron Cunningham
Coach of Year ....Shaun McRae
Division One Player...Nathan McAvoy
Division Two ....Stanley Gene
Referee of Year...Stuart Cummings

2
THE INTERNATIONAL SCENE

GREAT BRITAIN TOUR OF OCEANIA

WHEN it became clear that Great Britain's proposed 1996 Tour of Australia and New Zealand would not happen because of the switch to summer and the effects of the Super League-ARL war, the RFL had a straight choice.

Either they called the whole thing off or went against Maurice Lindsay's vow made after the financially crippling 1990 Tour and visited the Super League-aligned New Zealand as a stand alone venture.

Lindsay had forecast that trips to take on solely the Kiwis would never happen again, owing to the fact that as Tour Manager, and before he became the RFL's Chief Executive, he had returned home with a loss approaching £750,000.

But six years later, circumstances were different.

At a press conference to announce the revised schedule, he pointed to the increased awareness of League in New Zealand thanks to the Auckland Warriors, and the televising of games from Britain and Australia via satellite.

He was sure the crowds would be far greater than in 1990. Furthermore, as chairman of the Super League World Board, he had a commitment to pushing forward a showpiece first-ever tour under the Super League banner.

To cancel now would be handing the initiative back to the ARL.

Urged on by support from Super League, the RFL agreed to an autumn tour down under, adding Papua New Guinea and Fiji to the schedule.

It led to a very messy few months for everyone connected.

Over 3,000 supporters had booked to watch the Lions in Australia in June. The itinerary was changed, modified, adjusted and then changed again.

By the time they departed for New Zealand in September, the bookings were down to less than 300.

The 1996 Lions were headed up by manager Phil Lowe, with Phil Larder as Head Coach assisted by Gary Hetherington and Welsh national coach Clive Griffiths.

The four selected 32 first choice names plus a back-up squad of 13 potential tourists.

There were plenty of surprises. Shock call-ups for Tulsen Tollett, Keith Senior, Bernard Dwyer and Brian McDermott. And no place for Martin Offiah.

There was a recall for hooker Lee Jackson, dropped by Newcastle Knights, but selected ahead of strong candidates James Lowes, Johnny Lawless and Paul Rowley.

Larder also picked Gary Connolly and Jason Robinson, despite them being contracted to the ARL who had refused them permission to play in the World Nines.

Explaining his reasoning, Larder said: "My job is to pick a team to win test matches, not to suit Australia."

In the end, Larder had to bow to pressure and the ARL trio were replaced.

On Offiah, he said: "He has the ability but not the enthusiasm for a six-week tour."

It was a very young squad, with an average age of 23 and led by skipper Andy Farrell who was just 21 himself.

Seventeen of the squad had yet to make their Great Britain debut, and Adrian Morley, Paul Sculthorpe and Keiron Cunningham were still eligible for the supporting Academy Tour, but would all go on to play in the Test series.

It was also the biggest ever squad for one of the shortest tours, featuring just ten games but with the real possibility of a couple of extra games in Australia tagged on the end, depending on which way the Super League court case went.

Manager Lowe, with 1990 in his mind and already fearing more huge losses, said: "An Australian section will be financially advantageous. It would be very easy to put an extra week on the end, but it depends on what happens in Sydney."

THE 1996 LIONS

Andy Farrell,
Captain..Wigan
Denis Betts,
Vice-Captain ....Auckland Warriors

Dave Bradbury......................Oldham Bears
Paul Broadbent................Sheffield Eagles
Mick Cassidy....................................Wigan
Jason Critchley...............Keighley Cougars
Keiron Cunningham ....St Helens
Bernard Dwyer ....Bradford Bulls
Bobbie Goulding ....St Helens
Karle Hammond..........................St Helens
Neil Harmon ....Leeds
Iestyn Harris............................Warrington
Joey Hayes...................................St Helens
Alan Hunte ....St Helens
Chris Joynt ....St Helens
James Lowes ....Bradford Bulls
Barrie-Jon Mather ....Western Reds
Brian McDermott.................Bradford Bulls
Steve Molloy.........................Featherstone

Adrian Morley...................................Leeds
Terry O'Connor ....Wigan
Rowland Phillips ....Workington
Daryl Powell...................Keighley Cougars
Steve Prescott.............................St Helens
Kris Radlinski ....Wigan
Jon Roper ....Warrington
Paul Sculthorpe.......................Warrington
Keith Senior ....Sheffield Eagles
Tony Smith ....Castleford
Stuart Spruce ....Bradford Bulls
Anthony Sullivan..........................St Helens
Tulsen Tollet....................................London

Original selections who withdrew were;
John Bentley *(personal reasons)*
Gary Connolly, Jason Robinson,
Lee Jackson *(ARL contracted)*
Shaun Edwards *(knee operation)*
Steve McNamara *(hand injury)*
Paul Newlove *(hamstring injury)*

A shadow squad was also announced from which Alan Hunte, Jonathan Roper, Jason Critchley, James Lowes and Daryl Powell were called up before the Lions departed.

The remainder of the shadow squad was: Paul Atcheson *(Oldham)*, Nathan McAvoy *(Salford)*, Steve Blakeley *(Salford)*, Ryan Sheridan *(Sheffield)*, Craig Murdock *(Wigan)*, Barrie McDermott *(Leeds)*, Simon Haughton *(Wigan)* and Steve McCurrie *(Widnes)*.

The travel weary Great Britain players wait at Port Moresby Airport for the final leg of the journey to Lae, Papua New Guinea. A journey which took a mammoth 47 hours.

Papua New Guinea

The journey from Manchester to Lae in Papua New Guinea was never going to be easy. But when the squad assembled at the airport and bid fond farewells to their loved ones, no-one was prepared for the marathon that lay ahead.

The first leg was straight forward enough. Manchester to Singapore, with a twelve hour stop before the onward journey.

The Lions used that stop to freshen up at a nearby hotel and have a quick training session. The heat and humidity of Singapore was ideal to get the players partly acclimatised for what would greet them in Papua New Guinea.

But for Bernard Dwyer, it was a nightmare. He finished the session with badly blistered feet and was advised to rest for a week. Before he had even arrived in PNG, he was out of contention for the opening two games.

"I have suffered all summer with them, but nothing as bad as this," Dwyer reflected. "It has been terrible having to watch the rest of the lads - you don't really feel part of things."

Worse lay ahead. On arrival at Port Moresby, the Lions were made to wait over five hours in the stifling heat. No air-conditioned luxury lounge that professional sportsmen would normally expect.

Eventually, they made their connection to Lae, and arrived 47 hours after leaving Manchester.

And there was a blessing in disguise.

The original plan had been to dump the luggage at the hotel and immediately board a bus for the PNG National Cup Final, where the Lions would be guests of honour.

Their late arrival meant that plan had to be aborted. No bad thing when news filtered through that a riot had broken out amongst the locals, and four people had been shot!

For the entire duration of their stay, the Lions were placed under armed guard at their hotel, hidden away behind tall fences topped with barbed wire.

When they did venture out, it was for the flight to Mount Hagen for the opening game.

And Phil Larder was mightily pleased when his first Tour selection came up with an outstanding performance against a highly competitive PNG Presidents XIII side.

"I travelled out here with an open mind about our likely team for the first test in New Zealand," said Larder .

"Tony Smith, Rowland Phillips and captain Daryl Powell did enough to fight their way onto the bench on Saturday, while props McDermott and Molloy, and loose forward Karle Hammond also staked a strong claim."

Larder had special praise for teenagers Keith Senior and Adrian Morley, who made their Great Britain debuts in totally alien circumstances.

But the most eye-catching performance came from one of the tour's most surprising selections. Oldham second rower Dave Bradbury won the first players' player award.

He scored a well taken try, but it was his big-hitting defence which marked him out as a genuine Test contender. And the 24 year old revealed that the credit for that belonged to Tour vice-captain Denis Betts, ironically one of the men he was aiming to replace.

Bradbury sat next to Betts on the morning flight, from Lae to Hagen, and said: "Denis told me to concentrate on my defence and the rest would look after itself. He is a good friend of Andy Goodway. I think Denis learned a lot off Andy, and Andy has probably asked him to keep an eye on me."

But it wasn't such a great start for Neil Harmon, who was concussed making his first tackle of the game. He needed lengthy treatment, including extra oxygen, before being helped off. Fortunately Harmon's injury was not as serious as it first looked.

The Lions started with two tries in the first five minutes, but were then contained by the Papuans, and became frustrated when James Lowes had two tries disallowed.

The interval score was just 12-4, but Great Britain pulled away in the second half when Lowes' third effort was allowed. Karle Hammond added another and there were two in as many minutes from Tony Smith.

The Test side took the field four days later in incredible heat and humidity for Great Britain's first international proper under the Super League banner.

Late call-up Daryl Powell, GB captain for the midweek game v PNG President's XIII, gets to know some local tribesmen

And it was a Test in every meaning of the word. The lead changed hands five times, with the Lions trailing 16-12 at the interval, and the ultimate difference was an impeccable kicking display by Bobbie Goulding, and an awful one by Elias Paiyo.

The Lions were seemingly in control at 32-20, with Goulding having landed six goals from six attempts and scored a try. But two tries by the Kumuls in the closing minutes, after Goulding had seemingly made the match safe with one of his crosskick specials to Kris Radlinski, led to a frantic finale.

The Lions were mightily relieved to hear the final whistle and the locals were left reflecting on what might have been.

Lam had a quiet first half, but still managed to get on the scoresheet with a try after he had set one up for Hull KR's Stanley Gene. Marcus Bai had a strong game in the centre, but the star for the Kumuls was dreadlocked fullback Robert Sio.

His every touch of the ball was greeted with an excited gasp of anticipation from the home crowd and he went on to score a sensational individual try late on in the game.

PNG skipper Adrian Lam, however, acknowledged Goulding's contribution. "He kicked very well. If we had his feet on our side we would have won," he said.

Goulding was one of just three British players, along with Stuart Spruce and Joey Hayes, to play the full eighty minutes. The Lions exploiting the unlimited interchange rule to make a grand total of 26 substitutions.

They also pushed the rules on water carriers to the limit and, early in the second half, Phil Larder was told to stay off the pitch by referee Stephen Clark.

"I did a lot of talking out there to keep the lads going," said Goulding. "I was reasonably happy with my distribution."

THE GAMES IN PAPUA NEW GUINEA

PAPUA NEW GUINEA PRESIDENTS XIII 8
GREAT BRITAIN 34
at Mount Hagan, Wednesday 25th September

PNG PRESIDENT'S XIII
1 Oliver John
2 David Tiki
3 Ivan Mosotea
4 Paul Paha
5 Chris Itam
6 Fati Buka
7 Anton Mal
8 David Sari
9 Luke Daniel
10 Eremas Batkin
11 Billy Akin
12 Andrew Norman
13 Elias Kamakic
Subs
14 Agi Tete
15 Oscar Zutu
16 Andrew Kaiyaman
17 Peter Sune

Tries: Itam (9), Tiki

GREAT BRITAIN
1 Steve Prescott (St Helens)
2 Jonathan Roper (Warrington)
3 Barrie-Jon Mather (Western Reds)
4 Keith Senior (Sheffield Eagles)
5 Jason Critchley (Keighley Cougars)
6 Daryl Powell (Keighley Cougars)
7 Tony Smith (Castleford)
8 Steve Molloy (Featherstone Rovers)
9 James Lowes (Bradford Bulls)
10 Brian McDermott (Bradford Bulls)
11 David Bradbury (Oldham Bears)
12 Mick Cassidy (Wigan)
13 Karle Hammond (St Helens)
Subs
14 Tulsen Tollett (London Broncos)
15 Neil Harmon
16 Adrian Morley (Leeds)
17 Rowland Phillips (Workington Town)

Tries: Senior (2), Bradbury (5), Hammond (50), Lowes (60),
Smith (75, 77)
Goals: Prescott 5

League Express Men of the Match
PNG: Elias Kamakic
Great Britain: David Bradbury

Penalty count: 12-4
Half-time: 4-10
Referee: Tony Kim (Port Moresby)
Attendance: 2,000

PAPUA NEW GUINEA 30
GREAT BRITAIN 32
at Lae, Saturday 28th September

PAPUA NEW GUINEA
1 Robert Sio
2 James Kops
3 Marcus Bai
4 Robert Tela
5 David Gomia
6 Stanley Gene
7 Adrian Lam
8 Ben Bire
9 Elias Paiyo
10 Raymond Karl
11 Noide Yer
12 David Westley
13 Bruce Mamando
Subs
8 Simon Kundi
14 Reuben Ruing
17 Max Tire
18 Obert Batia

Tries: Gene (7), Garnia (23), Lam (40), Bire (62, 74), Sio (78)
Goals: Payo 3

GREAT BRITAIN
1 Stuart Spruce
2 Joey Hayes
3 Kris Radlinski
4 Alan Hunte
5 Anthony Sullivan
6 Iestyn Harris
7 Bobbie Goulding
8 Paul Broadbent
9 Keiron Cunningham
10 Terry O'Connor
11 Denis Betts
12 Chris Joynt
13 Andy Farrell
Subs
14 Tony Smith
15 Rowland Phillips
16 Daryl Powell
17 Paul Sculthorpe

Tries: Cunningham (3), Goulding (27), Radlinski (43, 71),
Sullivan (56)
Goals: Goulding 6

League Express Men of the Match
PNG: Raymond Karl
Great Britain: Bobbie Goulding

Penalty Count: 5-4
Half-time: 16-12
Referee: Stephen Clark (Australia)
Attendance: 10,000 (Est)

Fiji

The Lions arrived in Fiji still struggling against the heat and humidity but thankful of facilities a little more westernised.

Fiji is a country which simply can't get enough of Rugby League at the moment, and the tour followed the World Nines in Suva six months earlier.

This time the games would be on the opposite side of the island, centred around Nadi where support was known to be not quite as enthusiastic as the eastern side but still considerable.

The first game was against a Fijian Presidents XIII at Lautoka, about an hour north of Nadi.

Against a back-drop of mountains draped with tropical rain forest, the British, led for the first time by Bradford's James Lowes, gave the new nation

Wigan's Terry O'Connor gave a powerhouse performance against a Fijian President's XIII after losing his test place

a lesson in unit defence and tough individual tackling that set the platform for a 42-16 win.

Up front, Wigan's Terry O'Connor was smarting from losing his place in the test line-up after disappointing in PNG. He gave a towering performance in the first quarter, making impressive yardage and hitting hard in defence, and it was no surprise he got the call as players' man of the match.

His starting partner, Neil Harmon, was playing his first full game since his infamous on-off transfer from Leeds to Paris - that's four months without a run - so after an industrious eighty minutes Larder was keen to give the man with no club the wraps after the game.

"I thought Neil Harmon was the pick of the forwards tonight," he said. "Particularly when you consider that he hasn't played a full game of competitive football for so long.

"But all the forwards played well as did the half-backs."

Late call up Karle Hammond took the biggest accolades however, back in his old position of stand-off.

The 22 year old collected a try hat-trick to lead the tour try-scoring charts, and had a hand in two others.

His second score was the most crucial when the Brits appeared to have lost their momentum after the half-time break.

A big bonus for the Lions was the form shown by Adrian Morley.

Morley, still only 19, had impressed no end in the midweek games, and insiders were predicting that if his form continued, he'd be pushing for a place in the test team before the end of the tour.

Larder had already stated his selection policy was to pick purely on form, something he felt was vital to the success of the tour so far.

"I believe that's why we have got such tremendous team spirit," he said. "Everybody feels they are part and parcel of the squad. They are not just here for the ride and they will all get a chance, if they perform, of getting a test shirt."

The days leading up to the Lions first-ever Test in Fiji were filled with mounting speculation about the decision of the appeal judges in Sydney.

After months of waiting, the verdict would be handed down on the Friday, 24 hours before the Test.

It meant a nervous time for many of the players, and talk after training almost inevitably centred around what a Super League victory or loss would mean to them.

A win, they thought, would mean in the short term an extension to the tour and a clash with the Kangaroos. Not everyone relished that prospect, but word was that it would happen.

When news came through of Super League's comprehensive win, it shocked everyone. Being Super League aligned everyone on tour hoped, even expected, they would win. But to overturn every single judgement was beyond their wildest dreams.

The British media on tour rang London for the BBC broadcast, and heard an ecstatic Maurice Lindsay say the celebrations would include a match between Australia and Great Britain.

The journalists relayed the news to the Lions, who weren't too chuffed about the prospect of an extra two weeks on tour.

They were even more disappointed that Lindsay never bothered to ring them to pass on the news. For all Lindsay knew, the people that mattered, the players, may not have even heard of Super League's victory yet he was telling the rest of the world that they would play the Aussies.

But the most pressing matter for the players was the following day's Test. Fiji were an unknown quantity on their own soil. Twelve months earlier they had played

Great Britain Tour

England at Central Park and surprised everyone with a gutsy second half performance in conditions far removed from anything they had ever experienced before.

And the narrow two point Test victory in Papua New Guinea was still fresh in the Lions' minds.

The Fijians did all they could to disrupt the Lions, arriving thirty minutes late, having assured them that morning that the game would kick off at 3.00pm, and keeping them stood out in the searing heat for over an hour.

Once the game started, there was never any doubt about the result. Britain stormed to a 30-0 interval lead and went on to record a record 72-4 win.

Bobbie Goulding collected his first-ever hat-trick and broke John Holmes record for points-in-a-test with a 32 point haul.

"Records are there to broken," beamed Goulding.

"But it was a tremendous all-round team performance out there today."

"We played that game on fear," added Larder.

"Certainly me and Faz (skipper Andy Farrell) didn't want to be part of the first British team to be beaten in Fiji.

"I thought it was a top class performance, a very courageous performance."

But it was one of the most physical encounters seen in recent years and a test for the young Brits in any sense of the word, despite the overwhelming scoreline.

"It was tough game out there, some really big hits from both teams," said Larder. "There was no room for anybody who wanted to take a backward step."

The game erupted in the 17th minute when, with Britain already leading 10-0, Denis Betts and former Fiji captain Livai Nalagilagi squared up to each other.

The Fijian threw the first punch and a free-for-all started in earnest.

The brawl involved all 26 players on the park and took at least two minutes for Kiwi referee Jim Stokes to break up.

When he managed to restore some kind of order, he could do nothing but give the two initial combatants ten minutes each in the sin-bin, and then award a penalty, somewhat arbitrarily, to Fiji.

But the fire was not quite dampened as stand-off Inoke Ratudina prepared to kick for touch.

Sheffield Eagles' prop Mal Yasa, incited by something said to him, charged a full thirty metres out of the line to continue a battle with Goulding. Goulding managed to get out of the big bloke's way and to give him a sly jab before Yasa's teammates managed to make him think again.

But Stokes had little option other than to show Yasa the red card.

Britain answered back with tries by Andy Farrell and Powell's second. And when Goulding registered the first of his three, the game was as good as won.

Goulding completed his hat-trick after the break, Stuart Spruce and Alan Hunte weighed in with two each while Mick Cassidy and Keith Senior, on his debut, also got on the scoresheet.

The spirits amongst the whole squad at a special reception that night could not have been higher.

THE GAMES IN FIJI

FIJI PRESIDENTS XIII	....	16
GREAT BRITAIN	....	42

FIJI	....	4
GREAT BRITAIN	....	72

FIJIAN PRESIDENTS XIII
1 Eparama Navale
2 Paula Baravilala
3 Jamesa Davi
4 Waisake Kattuerata
5 Jonathan Vatubua
6 Ilaita Tokalaudau
7 Mosese Maraivalu
8 Napoliani Lomaloma
9 Alipate Noilea
10 Levi Bilivalu
11 Isimeli Soqe
12 Tabua Raiwaqauuka
13 Tevita Topu
Subs
14 Ovalase Toduadua for Ovalase (25)
15 Jonie Koroi for Kattuerata (38)
16 Wacanieli Botenakadau for Maraivalu (28)
17 Jiuta Suita for Raiwaqauuka (20)
Kattuerata for Bilivalu (36)

Tries: Koroi (48), Baravilala (74), Navale (75)
Goals: Tokalaudau 2

GREAT BRITAIN
1 Steve Prescott
2 Joey Hayes
3 Barrie-Jon Mather
4 Keith Senior
5 Jason Critchley
6 Karle Hammond
7 Tulsen Tollett
8 Neil Harmon
9 James Lowes
10 Terry O'Connor
11 Dave Bradbury
12 Mick Cassidy
13 Chris Joynt
Subs
14 Anthony Sullivan for Prescott (48BB)
Prescott for Sullivan (53BB)
15 Steve Molloy for O'Connor (50)
16 Adrian Morley for Cassidy (20)
17 Bernard Dwyer for Bradbury (30)
Cassidy for Joynt (35BB)
Joynt for Cassidy (40BB)
Bradbury for Joynt (75)

Tries: Hammond (14, 63, 73), Hayes (8), Tollett (29),
Senior (34), Cassidy (37), Critchley (69)
Goals: Prescott 5

Sin-bin: Tollett (68) - dissent

League Express Men of the Match
Fiji XIII: Eparama Navale
Great Britain: Terry O'Connor

Penalty Count: 9-6

Half-time: 0-26
Referee: T Nunu (Fiji)
Attendance: 2,700 est

FIJI
1 Waisale Sovatabua (Sheffield Eagles)
2 Paula Baravilula (Nabua)
4 Manoa Thompson (Penrith)
3 Joe Tamani (Bradford Bulls)
5 Stan Tulevu Canterbury Bankstown)
6 Inoke Ratudina (Nadera)
7 Kalavati Naisore (Lautoka)
8 Pio Kumbawe (Canberra)
9 Meli Kaidroka (Nadera)
10 Mal Yasa (Sheffield Eagles)
11 Ian Sagaitu (Canberra)
12 Joe Dakuitoga (Sheffield Eagles)
13 Livai Nalagilagi (Penrith)
Subs
14 Vula Dakuitoga (Canberra) for Kumbawe (48)
15 Waisake Vatabua (Naisori) for Nalagilagi (43)
16 Sam Marayawa (Canberra) for Dakuitoga (43)
17 Ulaisi Wainidroa (Canberra) for Kaidroka (48)

Try: Marayawa (64)

Sin-bin: Nalagilagi (17) - fighting
Dismissal: Yasa (19) - fighting

GREAT BRITAIN
1 Stuart Spruce (Bradford Bulls)
2 Alan Hunte (St Helens)
3 Kris Radlinski (Wigan)
4 Daryl Powell (Keighley Cougars)
5 Anthony Sullivan (St Helens)
6 Iestyn Harris (Warrington)
7 Bobbie Goulding (St Helens)
8 Paul Broadbent (Sheffield Eagles)
9 Keiron Cunningham (St Helens)
10 Brian McDermott (Bradford Bulls)
11 Denis Betts (Auckland Warriors)
12 Paul Sculthorpe (Warrington)
13 Andy Farrell (Wigan)
Subs
14 Tony Smith (Castleford Tigers) for Harris (62)
15 Steve Molloy (Featherstone Rovers) for Broadbent (29)
16 Keith Senior (Sheffield Eagles) for Spruce (35)
17 Mick Cassidy (Wigan) for Sculthorpe (62)
Spruce for Sullivan (40)
Broadbent for McDermott (48)

Tries: Sullivan (9), Powell (14, 25), Farrell (21),
Goulding (36, 57, 72), Hunte (42, 51), Spruce (48, 61),
Cassidy (67), Senior (75)
Goals: Goulding 10

Sin-bin: Betts (17) - fighting

League Express Men of the Match
Fiji: Kalavati Naisore
Great Britain: Bobbie Goulding

Penalty Count: 7-9

Half-time: 0-30
Referee: Jim Stokes (New Zealand)
Attendance: 5,000 est

107

New Zealand

AND so on to what everybody knew would be the business end of the tour - the three match series in New Zealand.

The Lions flew out of Fiji on a high, but four weeks later they left the shores of the Land of the Long White Cloud on a very definite low.

It had all started fairly promisingly with the arrival of the Lions creating a surge of media interest.

Both the major terrestrial TV stations featured League prominently on their lunchtime and evening bulletins, showing footage of the Test match in Nadi, concentrating on the brawl rather than the tries, and featuring Denis Betts as the player that everybody knew.

The Kiwis meanwhile were in the middle of a two match series with Papua New Guinea, which did little to create public interest or

The young British Lions side would look to experienced tour vice-captain Denis Betts for inspiration

improve the credibility of the New Zealand Rugby League (NZRL) which had come out of the Super League/ARL feud rather badly.

ARL boss Ken Arthurson had fingered Carden for what he saw as the "biggest act of treachery" for siding with News Corporation, and for the reported knockdown price of $2 million (£1 million) a year.

It was a prominent reason given for the man in the street staying away from the PNG Tests.

Though the PNG games received "live" coverage (in fact they were delayed by an hour), the crowds were woeful, with the second match attracting only 2,000 people in Palmerston North, near the south of the North Island.

The results did little to encourage the belief in a wider international future for League - 62-8 and 64-0 - as the Kumuls appeared to have little heart for the fight away from home.

Their inspirational skipper, ARL contracted Adrian Lam, though allowed to front up against Great Britain three weeks earlier, was refused permission to play in the second Test (he'd been unavailable the week before because he was leading a Port Moresby representative team against an ARL Kangaroos team).

The ARL's bar prompted PNG coach Bob, brother of Brisbane boss Wayne, Bennett, to pronounce Lam's club coach Phil Gould, who had communicated the decision, "a pig of a man".

The record win for New Zealand in Test match rugby managed to obscure what was glaringly obvious to most people inside and on the edges of the Lions' camp - the Kiwis had put together a formidable national side on the back of the Auckland Warriors and the recent involvement of players in the Aussie competition.

Coach Frank Endacott would later claim that if Britain had left behind Jason Robinson, Paul Newlove, Gary Connolly and Martin Offiah, then he had as many big guns unavailable.

True, the mercurial Paul brothers had stayed to pick up bumper cheques back in English rugby union, and former Castleford star Tawera Nikau, now with Cronulla, was unavailable for personal reasons, but Endacott hadn't showed a great liking for any of them in the past and his current selection was running hot.

For the opening game in New Zealand, against a Lion Red Cup XIII, Larder decided to give his Test thirteen a run out.

The Lion Red Cup (LRC) is New Zealand's national competition, a revolutionary concept when it was introduced three seasons ago in a country whose League was traditionally organised on regional lines.

But the LRC, although providing a good level of rugby, has been denuded of its best talents by the Warriors and by the English game. The Lions, fielding the same starting thirteen that overwhelmed Fiji in record-breaking style, five days before, were expected to cope comfortably with what the locals had to offer.

The opening salvos indicated that they would, but six minutes from the end they could quite easily have lost the match when former Wakefield Trinity stand-off David Bailey struck a sweet drop-kick toward the posts that looked all the way a one-pointer.

But it hit the right upright before bouncing into the arms of replacement prop Steve Molloy.

And then it was Britain's turn as some marvellous inter-play between Andy Farrell, Denis Betts and Adrian Morley took them back up field and Daryl Powell provided the pass to put Anthony Sullivan in at the left corner for what would have been the winning try.

But, to the utter disbelief of the British boys, local referee Grant Wallace, with the undivided support of 5,000 Aucklanders, called a scrum for a forward pass.

Before then, the Lions were shocked to be 14-4 down approaching the break. It needed something special to bring them back into a game they had looked like coasting in the first quarter.

Stuart Spruce produced that something special.

The Bulls' full-back moved into dummy-half on his own ten metre line, sidestepped the first line and out-raced the cover for a spectacular individual score. Harris's conversion made it 14-10 at the break.

But when Gus Malietoa-Brown put his side further ahead, the Lions were back to square one until Keiron Cunningham and Daryl Powell tries pulled it back level and set up that frantic final ten minutes.

Lion Red Cup coach Graeme Norton, who masterminded New Zealand's World Nines victory in Fiji back in February, pointed out after the game that this was New Zealand, and not the Pacific Islands.

"They've come here through Fiji but in New Zealand the level of football is much higher," he said.

"This will be a good indication of how hard it is going to be and the size of the challenge they will face from the Kiwis.

"We commanded them territorially."

Larder, however reserved any flattery for his opponents, putting the blame for the disappointing performance fairly and squarely on his own players' shoulders.

"We played very badly," he said. "We didn't play the way we had trained.

"We didn't go forward too much and we were far to ambitious with the ball.

"Our ball control against Fiji had been 81 per cent but it dipped to 42 per cent.

"And we made 18 or 19 errors which you cannot do at this level of football."

Larder spent the weekend reviewing the video time and time again. After strolling through Papua New Guinea and Fiji, suddenly the pressure was on. His midweek side were due to play a strong New Zealand XIII - effectively a Kiwi 'B' side - in Wellington, yet his Test team hadn't been able to beat a bunch of semi-pros.

Test places were certainly at stake as the Lions travelled south, but they produced a very patchy performance against a powerful Kiwi outfit.

The New Zealand second string - with bags of Auckland Warriors experience - won a fine victory, and Kiwis with English League backgrounds all played major roles.

Former Wakefield scrum half Aaron Whittaker had an off night with his goal kicking but his kicks from general play were head and shoulder above anything the tourists could produce.

And Hitro Okesene, a popular guest at Carlisle, produced a thunderous display up front. Former Featherstone, Sheffield and Oldham winger Iva Ropati opened the scoring and looked strong and fast with the ball and Shane Endacott, son of national coach Frank and never a huge success in his time at Hull, scored two killer tries.

The game was also the beginning of what would become a catalogue of cock-ups surrounding the organisation of the Tour.

It was switched from the original venue of Athletic Park in downtown Wellington, New Zealand's capital city, when it was realised no-one had arranged a drinks' license. Considering the game was sponsored by Lion Red, this was more than a minor hiccup.

The game was therefore switched, at very late notice, to Fraser Park at Lower Hutt, a forty-five minute drive out of town. It was too late to change newspaper advertisements, but the real choker was that Fraser Park didn't have a drinks license either!

It was far from an ideal venue. The stands were separated from the playing area by a softball pitch, complete with back-net, so it was hardly surprising that most of the crowd made their way to the touchline to witness the match at closer hand.

Add to this the presence of a PA/DJ whose sole purpose seemed to be to rouse the Kiwi selection to victory and we had a fairly unique international event.

The action on the pitch was fierce and the result could have gone either way .

"It was a game between two very evenly matched sides," said coach Phil Larder.

"But we should have had a substantial lead by half-time. We blew two obvious chances and effectively two handling errors cost us 18 points."

"One or to players let us down.

"But for the guys in test team there was no gloom and doom."

Gary Hetherington, Larder's lieutenant on the touchline was even more sanguine: "We just never got a roll on and it was just one of those games where almost everybody was a little bit flat," he said.

Chris Joynt did enough to prove his fitness for a place on the Test bench and Keith Senior was confident in everything he did.

But the star performance came from Wigan prop Terry O'Connor, who was a giant in the tough exchanges up the middle to earn a starting place in the Test series opener just four days later.

The team for the First Test showed a couple of changes to the one that had rattled up a record score against Fiji.

Larder had been concerned at the showing against the Lion Red Cup side, and juggled things around searching for that winning formula.

Terry O'Connor replaced Brian McDermott at prop, Chris Joynt was on the bench for Steve Molloy, and 19 year-old Leeds forward Adrian Morley was in line for a debut, taking Mick Cassidy's bench spot.

Britain weathered an almighty bashing in the first quarter and went ahead through Alan Hunte, who outjumped the Kiwi cover to collect Bobbie Goulding's cross-field kick.

Denis Betts added a second just before the break, and Goulding's goals put the Lions 12-2 ahead and seemingly in total control of the game.

But two crucial incidents were to turn the game on its head.

The first came after 54 minutes. Goulding tried another kick towards Hunte's wing, but this time Kiwi winger Richard Barnett got there first. He stepped round the first line of defence, straightened up and sprinted towards the Lions line.

Stuart Spruce, solid as a rock at the back until then, was wrong-footed, but in a desperate attempt to slow Barnett down the Bradford Bull attempted a tackle, managing to collect a gaping gash on the side of his head.

His withdrawal meant the introduction of Sheffield Eagle Keith Senior, who dropped into the centre, with Kris Radlinski moving to full-back.

Then came the second, decisive incident, with just eight minutes remaining.

Senior had settled reasonably well on his debut, and Spruce's departure and the subsequent re-organisation was being overcome.

But fellow debutant, Adrian Morley, was sin-binned for holding onto Sean Hoppe too long in a tackle. Something that had gone on all through the game from both sides, but only now had referee Bill Harrigan decided to act.

Down to twelve men and with a rookie in the centre, the Kiwis knew exactly how to expose the Lions.

Canterbury's John Timu did the real damage down the left as the Kiwis exploited their one man advantage to the full, stretching the British line, with skipper Matthew Ridge popping up everywhere to keep the ball alive and Gene Ngamu firing out the final telling long balls.

Within a minute of Morley's departure, Timu had crashed over. Ridge converted the try, and the pair repeated the trick two minutes later for a 16-12 lead. Ridge rubbed salt in the wound with a last gasp drop goal, and a 12-4 Lions lead had evaporated within eight minutes to a heartbreaking Test defeat.

It would be hard to argue with anybody who claims Morley's sin-binning won New Zealand the Test.

And Lions' coach Phil Larder was among that group.

"I said to Adrian that there is no doubt in my mind, and I don't think there can have been a doubt in anybody's mind, that if it hadn't been for the sin-binning we would have won the match," he said.

"But that is no reflection on Adrian because we had been working on slowing down the play the ball all week. The criticism is firmly on the shoulders of the referee."

Denis Betts agreed.

"I feel for Mozzer," he said sympathetically. "It was nothing bad against him, he was just unfortunate to be in that situation. Our defence had been solid all game and we didn't think they would score a try no matter how many times they had the ball as long as we had 13 men. But defending with twelve men so late in the game was tough."

Morley added: "It was the worst moment of my life. I just did what I thought was right. After the game I couldn't look anyone in the face, but the lads were great."

On the Saturday morning after Ericsson there was disappointment, but no mood of

A BLOW BY BLOW ACCOUNT OF THE FIRST TEST

Time	Event	Score
9 mins	O'Connor penalised for not getting back ten metres - RIDGE penalty	2-0
22 mins	Goulding crossfield kick plucked out of the air by Hunte	2-4
23 mins	GOULDING conversion from touch	2-6
31 mins	Joynt flicks out wonder ball and Radlinski sends in BETTS	2-10
48 mins	Broadbent held down by Young, GOULDING penalty	2-12
59 mins	RIDGE penalty for Radlinski holding down	4-12
72 mins	Morley sin-binning	
73 mins	Ngamu hits TIMU with long ball	8-12
74 mins	RIDGE converts	10-12
76 mins	TIMU repeats the trick	14-12
77 mins	Ridge converts from touchline	16-12
79 mins	RIDGE drop-goal from 40 metres	17-12

impending disaster as preparations began for the second Test in Palmerston North - an hour's flight to the south - the following Friday. The Lions had given their all. But for a bit more rub of the green, they would have been leading the series 1-0.

Instead, the New Zealand Rugby League had got a perfect result in terms of promoting the Test series and Rugby League to the sports-mad country.

But coach Phil Larder was still seething about the Morley sin-binning that had cost his side the game. "For us to lose somebody through a sin-binning is very harsh," he said. "But for either team to lose a player with nine minutes to go for an offence that has been committed right through the game, to me, is absolutely nonsense."

"Saying that we can go down to Palmerston for the Second Test with confidence is irrelevant - we have already been out there and won a match, but then thrown it away."

All in all there were no huge problems looming for the Lions.

There was, as there always is, disappointment for some players. Two wingers, Keighley Cougars Jason Critchley and Joey Hayes of St Helens - who had won a cap against Papua

New Guinea - had both limped off at Lower Hutt and were diagnosed as having knee cartilage problems that would possibly require surgery. In short, their tours were over and they were booked on flights back home the following Thursday.

On the Monday morning, Larder drafted in Academy captain Nathan McAvoy as substitute for the Tuesday night midweek game against the New Zealand Maori in Whangarei, about two hours drive north of Auckland. The nineteen year old Salford Red scored two tries in the Young Lions' 35-14 defeat by the Junior Kiwis in the Academy Test the previous Friday

Larder was reluctant to name any of his starting test team with the crucial second Test only three days away. The Test side travelled south on the Monday for Palmerston North, while the midweek team stayed in Auckland to prepare for the Maori game.

Leeds teenager Adrian Morley asked Larder for a start to help him get over his nightmare Test debut and the coach obliged.

"I want to play a full 80 minutes on Tuesday because I haven't started a game yet - every game I have played I've come on as a sub," explained Morley.

Two other substitutes from the Test, Tony Smith and Keith Senior, also got starts.

When Larder named his starting line-up there was a hint of an eventual injury crisis in the camp. McAvoy was listed on the right wing, with former Wigan centre Barrie-Jon Mather, now with Aussie club Perth Western Reds, on the bench.

A hamstring injury to Daryl Powell was proving slow to clear up and Mather would replace him in Friday's Test if he didn't come through. Mather's only appearance that night in Whangarei was as a sand carrier, demonstrating that the worry was a real one.

The Lions could have done with a win but they bungled and bumbled their way to a 40-28 defeat in front of a rapturous crowd.

This wasn't a bad Maori side - under coach Cameron Bell it had already beaten Tonga, Western Samoa and Papua New Guinea in 1996 - and it was led by the enigmatic former Castleford loose-forward Tawera Nikau, who but for a personal disagreement with former clubmate Richie Blackmore, would have surely been the Test lock.

There was also a cameo appearance from former London favourite Neville Ramsay, who came on from the bench to run the British defence around the park with his constant probing and clever distribution.

There were also a number of Auckland Warriors in the side, emphasising a theme that was going to re-occur - the Warriors club had and was lifting the standard of New Zealand Rugby League. The question was, had Super League done the same for the English game?

But while wider questions had still to be answered, this game was decided, once again, by British mistakes. The Lions had scored the first try which had given them a 6-2 lead, with Steve Prescott converting in reply to a penalty from Maori scrum-half Paul Howell, when the first blooper came.

The usually-dependable Bernard Dwyer, who had scored the try, ran out a kick from his own line. But Maori stand-off, Jamie Stevens, ripped the ball from his grasp to score the simple try, which, with Howell's second goal, gave the home side an 8-6 lead. It was a lead they never lost and after 25 minutes the Lions were staring down an embarrassing hammering at 20-6.

But Smith and Oldham Bear Dave Bradbury got them back into contention, only two points in arrears at the break until another huge gaff handed the initiative back to the

113

Maori. This time it ws the youngster McAvoy who collected a deep kick. It took a big a two man hit for him to spill the ball with no cover around him. Ramsay collected and ambled over.

That put the Maori eight points in front again and Great Britain never got closer. Marlon Gardiner's fine effort in the left corner - significantly after Dwyer and Neil Harmon had both dropped the ball - stretched the Maori out to 30-18 and the game was gone.

Steve Prescott and James Lowes scored tries from kicks into the in-goal, interspersed by winger Jason Walker slipping Jon Roper's tackle on the right, but David "Doc" Murray, released by the Warriors and who had excelled in this game and for the President's XIII a week earlier, had the final say at the death when he won the race to his own kick through.

The Lions, laid pretty low by another disappointing display set off straight back on the three-hour journey along the narrow, winding route through the forests and over the mountains, that is State Highway One.

On the trip north their bus had been involved in a minor accident with another coach but the return leg was uneventful. The peaceful trip was a stark contrast to the drama that was to unfold over the next 24 hours.

The following morning, coach Larder, who had flown up to Whangarei the day before, flew back to Palmerston North to-rejoin the Test team, expecting to meet up with the midweek squad, who were due to travel down by bus, the same day.

The game against the Maori proved to be the parting shot for the mid-week side - the "ham-and-eggers" as they had begun to call themselves.

Somebody at Red Hall had suddenly realised that, without a midweek game in the final week of the tour at Christchurch, some of the squad would be left with little to do but have themselves a holiday at the expense of the RFL.

The players were given the news they were to fly home early the following morning after manager Phil Lowe cobbled together a list of "surplus to requirement" players.

It was a bombshell, not just for the players concerned, but for the rest of the party, and Larder who besides having to now work with a bare minimum 21 man squad for the last two Tests - two of the most crucial games in British Test history - didn't get the chance to thank the players for their efforts on the tour.

"It was tough and it was tough for me personally," he admitted. "It was very tough for Andy Farrell and one or two of the players who have made close friendships."

It was tough for the rejected Lions too. Ironically, with no more games to play in and only the remotest chances of making the Test side, there were several who were ready to return home.

But the suddenness of the decision and the lack of consultation left them all, to a man, absolutely fuming.

Twelve players, including Joey Hayes and Jason Critchley, were booked on flights, either home, or to Sydney, where they had already planned holidays, on the Thursday.

The "dirty dozen" made the most of their last hours with a big night out in Auckland that continued into the early hours.

The situation, with all the Lions' management hundreds of miles away in Palmerston North, was a ready made opportunity for the media to have a laugh at League's expense.

National TV station, TV3, certainly took the chance to make the players and the sport look very silly as they herded the players, looking distinctly the worse for wear, into

114

Rowland Phillips' hotel room the morning after. As the lead story on the main sports news bulletin, it wasn't a pretty sight. And when midweek captain James Lowes was prompted to say a few words to the camera about the obvious paradox between the big bucks era of Super League and what had been portrayed as a penny-pinching move, the damage to the game's credibility was complete.

On the same morning, Keith Senior was given a reprieve and flown down to "Palmy". Bradford Bulls' prop Brian McDermott, who wasn't in the best of spirits after losing his place in the Test team, was also asked to stay.

But having already revised his own arrangements and those of his girlfriend, who had originally had flights booked to meet him in Australia in twelve days time, McDermott's exasperation resulted in him declining the offer.

As a postscript, the eleven players headed off for Auckland International Airport, having to pay their own taxi fares and the 20 dollars (£10) departure tax.

Down in Palmerston, the mood was one of confusion.

If the decision had been made before the start of the tour, there would have been no problem but the handling of the situation felt like a kick in the collective guts.

Larder and his management team were now faced with a huge ask.

Larder never once blamed the events for what was to pass, but the disruption was obvious to everybody around the party. And logistically, difficulties that were to arise were entirely predictable.

If the 21 men who remained had all been one hundred per cent fit, there would have been few worries.

However, when Larder and his remaining squad members who had fronted against the Maoris arrived in Palmerston North, resources were starting to look a little thin.

First there was Powell's hamstring, causing the re-think on Senior.

St Helens pair Bobbie Goulding and Alan Hunte, whose training was disrupted by knocks taken in the the First test, weren't looking good.

Stuart Spruce had also suffered mild concussion at Ericsson.

And then there was Tony Smith, the only cover for Goulding at scrum half.

Smith, who had won his place on the Test bench in the very first game of the tour at Mount Hagen, had been bitten by an insect in Fiji. He had scratched at the irritation since that time until the wound had become badly infected. When he arrived from Whangarei it needed urgent hospital attention, so much so that medical staff at Palmerston North hospital insisted that the Castleford half-back should be kept in overnight.

Smith remained there for three nights, although he sneaked out for his meals to the team's hotel. But everybody knew that his chance of making either of the remaining Tests were slim.

And that was the build up for a Test match that Britain just had to win to stay in the contest.

Palmerston North is a flat inland city, famous for its university, but with a population of only 40,000. Projections of a 16,000 full house were thought a little optimistic.

But 12,000 souls did turn out to witness another belter of a Test match and the Kiwis clinch their first series against Great Britain since 1984.

Again the match could easily have gone either way in a game that Britain had in their grasp at half-time, but let slip under tremendous pressure from the Kiwis.

Great Britain Tour

For Kiwi coach Frank Endacott it was a personal triumph after a disappointing international season last year.

His only change to the previous week was to relegate former Castleford centre Richie Blackmore to the bench and bring in Ruben Wiki of Canberra, mainly for his big-hitting defence. Wiki paid him back two-fold with two tries either side of half time.

"It's another foot forward on the international scene," said the genial Endacott after the game. "We were third on the international rankings prior to this series, but it's fair to say that we should be called number two at this stage.

"We had to come from behind again, but we showed character and patience to come back and we all know that the game lasts for eighty minutes, not seventy.

"We put a lot more pressure on Bobbie Goulding this week and their kicking game was nowhere near as good. So it showed we had done a bit of homework there."

The Lions could count themselves fortunate to head into the break with a 13-8 lead. Matthew Ridge kicked the first points of the game with a penalty for offside to enter the record books as New Zealand's highest points scorer in Test history. He'd come into the game level with the 40 year record of Des White, on 132 points from 21 games.

But the Lions took the lead when a brilliant Farrell-Betts combination opened up the Kiwis on the right and Alan Hunte raced inside Ridge for the try. Goulding converted and then dropped a goal for a 7-2 lead.

Wiki got his first, but after Iestyn Harris stole the ball in a one-on-one tackle on giant prop Grant Young, Stuart Spruce created the space for Betts to crash over on the right.

Goulding converted from the touchline on the stroke of half-time.

But a Goulding penalty was all that the Lions could produce in the second half as Wiki ran in his second, courtesy of a superb pass from Stephen Kearney, and then stand-off Gene Ngamu produced the sucker punch when he duped Daryl Powell straight from a scrum.

A BLOW BY BLOW ACCOUNT OF THE SECOND TEST		
10th min	Sean Hoppe drops Jones' kick in in-goal	
18th min	MATTHEW RIDGE kicks penalty for offside in front of posts	2-0
26th min	ALAN HUNTE cuts inside Ridge for first try	2-4
27th min	BOBBIE GOULDING conversion	2-6
31st min	GOULDING drop-goal	2-7
33rd min	RUBEN WIKI crashes over from John Timu break	6-7
34th min	RIDGE converts	8-7
38th min	DENIS BETTS takes three men over on right	8-11
39th min	GOULDING converts	8-13
51st min	Stephen Kearney sends WIKI 40 metres to the line	12-13
61st min	GOULDING penalty for interference at play the ball	12-15
65th min	GENE NGAMU scores direct from scrum	16-15
66th min	RIDGE conversion	18-15
72nd min	Betts prevents Syd Eru from grounding the ball	

There were plenty of heroics from Britain, not least Spruce's and Bett's try-saving tackles on Stacey Jones and Syd Eru. But the disappointment in the British camp couldn't be hidden.

"It's hurt us, really hurt us, but we'll recover and bounce back," coach Larder promised.

"It will be another tough game next week, make no mistake about that."

And though it would have been a soft option to blame the bizzare events of midweek, neither Larder or captain Andy Farrell took it.

"I don't think it affected us," Larder insisted.

"It was tough and it was tough for me personally. It was very tough for Andy Farrell and one or two of the players who have made close friendships.

"But it happened on Tuesday. We are professional people. We talked about it, we've soaked it in and we recovered from it. There's no way you can use that as an excuse.

"I thought we played very well. If that had affected us we would have been looking at players who perhaps didn't give a hundred per cent commitment.

"But I can't fault any of my players. They really put their bodies on the line.

"I am very proud of every one of them."

Farrell agreed: "When you go out there you are playing for yourself and for your team," he said. "You can't let anything distract you, as much as we were disgusted with what's gone on."

But no-one could deny, despite both Tests being as close as close could be, the pressure was well and truly on Great Britain.

Kiwi coach Frank Endacott, for one, wasn't going to let the Lions forget it. "I wouldn't have said it two weeks ago," he said, "but I think 3-0 is a possibility now. We're not going to relax at all."

And so to Christchurch.

After the cosmopolitan character of Auckland, the capital of the Canterbury region seemed much more sedate and relaxed. And the Lions had a full week to recover and prepare for the face-saving Test at famous cricket ground Lancaster Park.

But things didn't quite work out.

As the team prepared to leave for Christchurch from Palmerston North, team doctor Anwar Zanar decided that Tony Smith's tour was over and he should return to England.

The 21 man squad was now 20, surely enough with one game remaining.

It was, until a quick glance at the walking wounded from the second Test was made.

Larder's scrum-half cover was back in England and as chance would have it Bobbie Goulding was one of a string of players with a worrying knock. Which led to the tour management pondering the recall of London Broncos' Tulsen Tollett, sent home a week before as surplus to requirements.

It was a story that ran all week. Tulsen even made the front page of "The Press", the daily newspaper of the South Island. The management hung on, and hung on, waiting on Goulding's ankle to improve.

But it didn't, and on the Wednesday night Tollett, who was fortunately holidaying at his parents home in Sydney, got the call from Phil Lowe.

"It was hard to believe," said Tollett, "but at least I can say proper goodbyes to everybody!"

But Goulding wasn't the only worry.

Skipper Andy Farrell tore his quads (the muscles at the front of the leg) and broke down in training.

Kris Radlinski damaged a shoulder, Stuart Spruce had a bad in-growing toe nail and was unable to get his boot on let alone train, Daryl Powell had a trapped nerve in his neck and Anthony Sullivan a hamstring injury.

Alan Hunte had a hamstring problem too and an arm complaint too thrown in for good measure.

A 20-man squad, didn't look too promising and even the addition of Tollett the day before the Test, couldn't increase confidence.

Other, non-playing matters, also pre-occupied the New Zealand media.

When the Lions arrived in Christchurh on the Sunday, there was a bus waiting for them, but no liaison officer from the NZRL. Monday was Labour day, a public holiday in New Zealand, and it was a full 24 hours before anybody contacted the Lions management.

"We feel as though we are an embarrassment to the New Zealand Rugby League," said Larder. "We've got blazers and ties and flannels and we've not bloody worn them yet because we have not been invited yet to anything that warrants getting our make-up on.

"We're just a bit pissed off."

The day the papers ran the story, as did the national TV stations - it was the first story on the lunchtime News bulletin - the Lions were bombarded with offers of hospitality, none of them from the NZRL.

There were also problems about getting enough money to pay the players because of the holiday, and that was the story that hit the headlines among others on the poor organisation on the New Zealand leg of the tour.

Tour Manager Phil Lowe was at the end of his tether and even publically urged the RFL Council to seriously rethink the future of international Rugby League.

Lowe also revealed how he had had to save money wherever possible on the Tour.

He said he had to continually barter with hotel management to get accomodation and food costs down to a minimum. He also speculated that the Tour was expected to lose around £500,000 though NZRL chairman Graham Carden held a press conference on the day of the Test to offer his own estimates of losses.

"It's been a bad ten days for us," admitted Larder.

Tulsen Tollett had a wasted journey.

He didn't make the team for the Third test.

Phil Larder couldn't name his side until minutes before the kick-off but Bobbie Goulding, with the help of two pain-killing injections, took the field. As did Andy Farrell, who took an uncomfortable looking fitness test in front of the stand at Lancaster Park an hour before the game.

The two centres Daryl Powell and Kris Radlinski also carried injuries into the game, as did Stuart Spruce and Alan Hunte. Anthony Sullivan had been withdrawn the previous day and Barrie-Jon Mather replaced him.

Larder's other change was tactical with Karle Hammond taking Iestyn Harris's place at stand-off with the Welsh international starting on the bench.

Against the odds, Britain got off to a dream start. It had taken twenty minutes to break down the Kiwis in the previous two encounters but this night it took only four.

Frank Endacott had been forced to draft in union convert Marc Ellis onto the wing as replacement for Richard Barnett who twisted a knee seven days before.

Now Ellis is the darling of the Kiwi fans and a huge cheer goes up whenever he gets the ball. But the Lions targeted him in the early minutes and the tactic paid immediate dividends.

First Paul Sculthorpe ran at him, just held short. But from dummy-half, Denis Betts kept up his record of scoring in all the New Zealand Tests, by forcing his way through Ellis's tackle.

But an against the odds win was a dream that lasted only four minutes as John Timu, who had destroyed the Lions in Auckland, bust the tackle of Radlinski and Hunte and

118

rounded Spruce for an equalising score. Then, after Keiron Cunningham had damaged his shoulder allowing Bernard Dwyer to make his test debut, Betts' Warriors clubmate Stephen Kearney slipped a ball out of a tackle for Wiki to go in on the left. And in the five minutes before the break, New Zealand sealed it with two killer tries.

First Goulding, dummying to kick, shot a long pass to Hunte on the left. Gene Ngamu read it, intercepted and raced 50 metres down the left.

Three minutes later, with half-time approaching, Goulding put in a great a chip, but his palm-back to Hammond was dropped. Timu picked up, saw the wide open spaces and tore downfield.

Paul Broadbent, who had three big Tests, managed to halt Timu, but Ngamu was on hand to find Sean Hoppe with a long pass for the try of the series.

Harris had come into the fray on the half-hour and in the second half he showed his abilities playing at centre and then full-back when Spruce retired with an ankle injury.

After he had almost gone fifty metres for a wonder try, only to be brought down inches short by Ridge, he hit substitute Adrian Morley with a bullet pass and the

A BLOW BY BLOW ACCOUNT OF THE THIRD TEST

4th min	DENIS BETTS keeps up his record of scoring in every Test going over from dummy-half	0-4
5th min	BOBBIE GOULDING converts from touch	0-6
8th min	JOHN TIMU busts Radlinski and Hunte down the left centre	4-6
9th min	MATTHEW RIDGE convert	6-6
28th min	RUBEN WIKI crahes onto Kearney' ball out of the tackle on the right	10-6
36th min	Bobbie Goulding's long pass on half way is intercepted by GENE NGAMU	14-6
37th min	RIDGE converts from wide out	16-6
40th min	Timu collects a dropped ball in his own 20, races 50 metres before finding Ngamu, who puts in SEAN HOPPE in the right corner	20-6
43rd min	Iestyn Harris hits sub Adrian Morley with a crash ball and the Leeds teenager scores his first Test try under the posts	20-10
44th min	Goulding converts	20-12
52nd min	HOPPE brushes off Harris and Spruce straight from a scrum	24-12
53rd min	RIDGE conversion	26-12
67th min	RIDGE powers under posts and converts	32-12
69th min	Daryl Powell sent off for dissent	

Leeds' teenager crashed over under the posts. 20-12 down, the Lions had their best spell but they couldn't get over again as Hoppe got his second and Ridge forced his way over for a final score of 32-12. It was New Zealand's biggest win over Great Britain and the first 3-0 series whitewash since 1984.

Kris Radlinski, who had played despite a painful shoulder injury, summed up the feeling amongst the Lions.

"You can't ask any more from the lads - they would die for each other," he said.

"I'm sure we'll be getting a bit of stick at home but I hope the people realise we gave it our best. It was just a matter of surviving towards the end."

On the day after the test there was more hospitality laid on for the Lions - a bus trip into the southern Alps for fun and frolics in the snow.

When the bus was due to leave, only four players were fit enough to take up the offer.

Coach Phil Larder made the trip, as did half-a-dozen from the British media. The whispers amongst the journos on the bus ride into the mountains centred around Larder and the vacant Sheffield Eagles coaching position.

Sure enough, on the return to Christchurch Larder confirmed he had agreed to coach the Eagles following Gary Hetherington's shock switch to Leeds.

With that, the media had a fresh story to file and the Tour was over.

Great Britain Tour

THE GAMES IN NEW ZEALAND

LION RED XIII 22
GREAT BRITAIN.....................................22
at Carlaw Park, Auckland,
Thursday 10th October

LION RED CUP XIII
1 Tama Hohaia (Waikato)
2 Marlon Gardiner (Bay of Plenty)
16 Cheaf Lee Fakavamoenga
(Counties Manukau)
4 Gus Malietoa-Brown
 (Counties Manukau)
5 Richard Stewart (North Harbour)
6 David Bailey (Waitakere)
7 Ben Lythe (Waitakere)
8 Donald Stewart (North Harbour)
9 Tukere Barlow (Waikato)
15 Vai Afoa (North Harbour)
11 Anthony Edwards (Waitakere)
12 Gareth Adams (Waitakere)
13 Jonathan Hughes (Waitakere)
Subs
14 Corrie Jamieson (North Harbour)
for Gardiner (68)
10 Leamy Tato (North Harbour)
 for Afoa (10)
3 Boycie Nelson (Waitakere)
for Fakavamoenga (65)
17 Vilai Kelemete (Hutt Valley)
for D Stewart (60)

Tries: Barlow (28), Hughes (35), Malietoa-
Brown (42)
Goals: Lythe 5

GREAT BRITAIN
1 Stuart Spruce (Bradford Bulls)
2 Alan Hunte (St Helens)
3 Kris Radlinski (Wigan)
4 Daryl Powell (Keighley Cougars)
5 Anthony Sullivan (St Helens)
6 Iestyn Harris (Warrington)
7 Bobbie Goulding (St Helens)
8 Paul Broadbent (Sheffield Eagles)
10 Brian McDermott (Bradford Bulls)
11 Denis Betts (Auckland Warriors)
12 Paul Sculthorpe (Warrington)
13 Andy Farrell (Wigan)
Subs
14 Tulsen Tollett (London Broncos)
for Goulding (68)
15 Steve Molloy (Featherstone Rovers)
for McDermott (29)
16 Adrian Morley (Leeds) for Betts (29)
17 Mick Cassidy (Wigan) not used
McDermott for Broadbent (56)
Betts for Sculthorpe (58)

Tries: Sullivan (21), Spruce (36),
Cunningham (48), Powell (62)
Goals: Harris 3

League Express Men of the Match
Lion Red XIII: Ben Lythe
Great Britain: Stuart Spruce

Penalty Count: 7-8

Half-time: 14-10
Referee: Grant Wallace (Auckland)
Attendance: 5,000 est

120

NEW ZEALAND XIII 30
GREAT BRITAIN.....................................22
at Lower Hutt, Wellington,
Tuesday 15th October

NEW ZEALAND XIII
1 David Murray (Auckland Warriors)
2 Iva Ropati (Auckland Warriors)
3 Anthony Swann (Auckland Warriors)
4 Whetu Taewa
(North Queensland Cowboys)
5 Richard Stewart (North Harbour)
6 Shane Endacott (Auckland Warriors)
7 Aaron Whittaker (Auckland Warriors)
8 Brad Malam (Auckland Warriors)
9 Denvour Johnson (Taranaki Rockets)
10 Hitro Okesene (Auckland Warriors)
11 Tony Tatupu (Auckland Warriors)
12 Bryan Henare (Auckland Warriors)
13 Logan Swann (Auckland Warriors)
Subs
14 Meti Noovao (Auckland Warriors)
for Johnson (60)
15 Mark Faumiuna (Penrith Panthers)
for Okesene (25)
16 Jerry Seu Seu (Counties Manakau)
for Swann (25)
17 Darren Avery (Canterbury Cardinals)
for Tatupu (25)
Okesene for Faumiuna (52)
Tatupu for Henare (70)

Tries: Ropati (8), Okesene (21), Taewa
(26), A Swann (43), Endacott (67,74)
Goals: Whittaker, Murray 2

GREAT BRITAIN
1 Steve Prescott (St Helens)
2 Joey Hayes (St Helens)
3 Barrie-Jon Mather (Perth Western Reds)
4 Keith Senior (Sheffield Eagles)
5 Jason Critchley (Keighley Cougars)
6 Tulsen Tollett (London Broncos)
7 Tony Smith (Castleford Tigers)
8 Neil Harmon (Leeds)
9 James Lowes (Bradford Bulls)
10 Terry O'Connor (Wigan)
11 Chris Joynt (St Helens)
12 Dave Bradbury (Oldham Bears)
13 Karle Hammond (St Helens)
Subs
14 Jon Roper (Warrington) for Hayes (37)
15 Rowland Phillips (Workington Town)
for Harmon (22)
16 Bernard Dwyer (Bradford Bulls) for
Critchley (40)
17 Mick Cassidy (Wigan) for Bradbury (31)
Harmon for O'Connor (57)
Bradbury for Lowes (72)

Tries: Hayes (17), Mather (32), Smith
(49), Hammond (72)
Goal: Prescott 3

League Express Men of the Match
NZ XIII: David Murray
Great Britain: Karle Hammond

Penalty Count: 4-6

Half-time: 14-10
Referee: Denis Hale (New Zealand)
Attendance: 3,000 est

FIRST TEST
NEW ZEALAND.....................................17
GREAT BRITAIN.....................................12
at Ericsson Stadium, Auckland,
Friday 18th October

NEW ZEALAND
1 Matthew Ridge (Auckland Warriors)
2 Sean Hoppe (Auckland Warriors)
3 Richard Blackmore (Auckland Warriors)
4 John Timu (Auckland Warriors)
5 Richard Barnett (Cronulla Sharks)
6 Gene Ngamu (Auckland Warriors)
7 Stacey Jones (Auckland Warriors)
8 Grant Young (Auckland Warriors)
9 Syd Eru (Auckland Warriors)
10 Quentin Pongia (Canberra Raiders)
11 Tony Iro (Hunter Mariners)
12 Stephen Kearney (Auckland Warriors)
13 Tyran Smith
(North Queensland Cowboys)
Subs
14 Marc Ellis (Auckland Warriors)
for Blackmore (69)
15 Joe Vagana (Auckland Warriors)
for Young (30)
16 Ruben Wiki (Canberra Raiders)
for Smith (34)
17 Logan Swann (Auckland Warriors)
for Iro (57)
Young for Pongia (31BB)
Pongia for Young (61BB)
Young for Vagana (64)
Iro for Swann (71)

Tries: Timu (73, 76)
Goals: Ridge 4
Drop-goal: Ridge

GREAT BRITAIN
1 Stuart Spruce (Bradford Bulls)
2 Alan Hunte (St Helens)
3 Kris Radlinski (Wigan)
4 Daryl Powell (Keighley Cougars)
5 Anthony Sullivan (St Helens)
6 Iestyn Harris (Warrington)
7 Bobbie Goulding (St Helens)
8 Paul Broadbent (Sheffield Eagles)
9 Keiron Cunningham (St Helens)
10 Terry O'Connor (Wigan)
11 Denis Betts (Auckland Warriors)
12 Paul Sculthorpe (Warrington)
13 Andy Farrell (Wigan)
Subs
14 Tony Smith (Castleford) not used
15 Chris Joynt (St Helens) for O'Connor (28)
16 Keith Senior (Sheffield Eagles)
for Spruce (56)
17 Adrian Morley (Leeds) for Sculthorpe (64)
O'Connor for Broadbent (53)
Broadbent for Joynt (74)

Tries: Hunte (22), Betts (32)
Goals: Goulding 2

Sin-bin: Morley (72) - holding down

League Express Men of the Match
New Zealand: John Timu
Great Britain: Denis Betts

Penalty Count: 4-6

Half-time: 10-2
Referee: Bill Harrigan (Sydney)
Attendance: 12,000 est

THE GAMES IN NEW ZEALAND

NEW ZEALAND MAORI 40
GREAT BRITAIN....................................28
at Whangarei, Tuesday 22nd October

MAORI XIII
1 David Murray (Auckland Warriors)
2 Jason Walker (Bay of Plenty Stags)
3 Ricky Henry (Christchurch Shiners)
4 Whetu Taewa (N Queensland Cowboys)
5 Marlon Gardiner (Taranaki Rockets)
6 Jamie Stevens (Hawkes Bay Unicorns)
7 Paul Howell (Wellington Dukes)
8 Gavin Hill (Auckland Warriors)
9 Tukere Barlow (Waikato Congars)
10 Paul Rawhihi (Auckland Warriors)
11 Matthew Sturm
(Counties Manukau Heroes)
12 David Pearce (Canberra Raiders)
13 Tawera Nikau (Cronulla Sharks)
Subs
14 Neville Ramsay (Counties Manukau
Heroes) for Sturm (30)
15 John Farrar (Taranaki Rockets)
for Pearce (75)
16 Sonny Whakarau (Keighley Cougars)
for Barlow (60)
17 George Milner (Waikatere Raiders)
for Hill (3BB) and (12BB)
Hill for Milner (5BB)
Hill for Milner (40)

Tries: Stevens (10), Nikau (20), Murray
(24, 80), Ramsay (48), Gardiner (60),
Walker (70)
Goals: Howell 6

Sin-bin: Rawhihi (63) - elbow

GREAT BRITAIN
1 Steve Prescott (St Helens)
2 Nathan McAvoy (Salford Reds)
3 Keith Senior (Sheffield Eagles)
4 Tulsen Tollett (London Broncos)
5 Jon Roper (Warrington)
6 Karle Hammond (St Helens)
7 Tony Smith (Castleford Tigers)
8 Steve Molloy (Featherstone Rovers)
9 James Lowes (Bradford Bulls)
10 Brian McDermott (Bradford Bulls)
11 Adrian Morley (Leeds)
12 Mick Cassidy (Wigan)
13 Bernard Dwyer (Bradford Bulls)
Subs
14 Dave Bradbury (Oldham Bears)
for Cassidy (20)
15 Rowland Phillips (Workington Town)
for Harmon (29BB)
16 Barrie-Jon Mather
(Perth Western Reds) not used
17 Neil Harmon (Leeds) for Molloy (11BB)
Harmon for McDermott (54)
McDermott for Phillips (70)
Molloy for Phillips (70)

Tries: Dwyer (9), Smith (32), Bradbury
(36), Prescott (65), Lowes (73)
Goal: Prescott 4

League Express Men of the Match
Maori XIII: Tawera Nikau
Great Britain: Karle Hammond

Penalty Count: 7-12
Half-time: 20-18
Referee: Gary Allcock (Auckland)
Attendance: 6,000 est

SECOND TEST

NEW ZEALAND..................................18
GREAT BRITAIN................................15
at Palmerston North Showgrounds,
Friday 25th October

NEW ZEALAND
1 Matthew Ridge (Auckland Warriors)
2 Sean Hoppe (Auckland Warriors)
16 Ruben Wiki (Canberra Raiders)
4 John Timu (Auckland Warriors)
5 Richard Barnett (Cronulla Sharks)
6 Gene Ngamu (Auckland Warriors)
7 Stacey Jones (Auckland Warriors)
8 Grant Young (Auckland Warriors)
9 Syd Eru (Auckland Warriors)
10 Quentin Pongia (Canberra Raiders)
11 Tony Iro (Hunter Mariners)
12 Stephen Kearney (Auckland Warriors)
13 Tyran Smith
(North Queensland Cowboys)
Subs
14 Marc Ellis (Auckland Warriors)
for Barnett (63)
15 Joe Vagana (Auckland Warriors)
for Young (47)
3 Richard Blackmore (Auckland Warriors)
for Wiki (62)
17 Logan Swann (Auckland Warriors)
for Iro (47)
Iro for Smith (70)

Tries: Wiki (33, 51), Ngamu (65)
Goals: Ridge 3

GREAT BRITAIN
1 Stuart Spruce (Bradford Bulls)
2 Alan Hunte (St Helens)
3 Kris Radlinski (Wigan)
4 Daryl Powell (Keighley Cougars)
5 Anthony Sullivan (St Helens)
6 Iestyn Harris (Warrington)
7 Bobbie Goulding (St Helens)
8 Paul Broadbent (Sheffield Eagles)
9 Keiron Cunningham (St Helens)
10 Terry O'Connor (Wigan)
11 Denis Betts (Auckland Warriors)
12 Paul Sculthorpe (Warrington)
13 Andy Farrell (Wigan)
Subs
14 Barrie-Jon Mather (Perth Western
Reds) for Sullivan (56)
15 Steve Molloy (Featherstone Rovers)
for O'Connor (34)
16 Karle Hammond (St Helens)
for Joynt (69)
17 Chris Joynt (St Helens)
for Sculthorpe (26)
O'Connor for Broadbent (56)
Broadbent for Molloy (71)

Tries: Hunte (26), Betts (38)
Goals: Goulding 3
Drop-goal: Goulding

League Express Men of the Match
New Zealand: Stephen Kearney
Great Britain: Denis Betts

Penalty Count: 7-8

Half-time: 8-13
Referee: Graham Annesley (Sydney)
Attendance: 12,000 est

THIRD TEST

NEW ZEALAND..................................32
GREAT BRITAIN................................12
at Christchurch,
Friday 1st November

NEW ZEALAND
1 Matthew Ridge (Auckland Warriors)
2 Sean Hoppe (Auckland Warriors)
3 Ruben Wiki (Canberra Raiders)
4 John Timu (Auckland Warriors)
5 Marc Ellis (Auckland Warriors)
6 Gene Ngamu (Auckland Warriors)
7 Stacey Jones (Auckland Warriors)
8 Grant Young (Auckland Warriors)
9 Syd Eru (Auckland Warriors)
10 Quentin Pongia (Canberra Raiders)
11 Tony Iro (Hunter Mariners)
12 Stephen Kearney (Auckland Warriors)
13 Tyran Smith (Queensland Cowboys)
Subs
14 Anthony Swann (Auckland Warriors)
for Smith (63)
15 Joe Vagana (Auckland Warriors)
for Young (8BB)
16 Richard Blackmore
(Auckland Warriors) for Ellis (42)
17 Logan Swann (Auckland Warriors)
for Kearney (29)
Young for Vagana (22BB)
Kearney for Iro (48BB)
Vagana for Young (61)
Iro for L Swann (68)

Tries: Timu (8), Wiki (28), Ngamu (36),
Hoppe (40,52), Ridge (67)
Goals: Ridge 4

GREAT BRITAIN
1 Stuart Spruce (Bradford Bulls)
2 Alan Hunte (St Helens)
3 Kris Radlinski (Wigan)
4 Daryl Powell (Keighley Cougars)
5 Barrie-Jon Mather (Perth Western Reds)
6 Karle Hammond (St Helens)
7 Bobbie Goulding (St Helens)
8 Paul Broadbent (Sheffield Eagles)
9 Keiron Cunningham (St Helens)
10 Terry O'Connor (Wigan)
11 Denis Betts (Auckland Warriors)
12 Paul Sculthorpe (Warrington)
13 Andy Farrell (Wigan)
Subs
14 Iestyn Harris (Warrington) for Powell (30)
15 Chris Joynt (St Helens) for O'Connor (28)
16 Adrian Morley (Leeds) for Sculthorpe (40)
17 Bernard Dwyer (Bradford Bulls) for
Cunningham (22)
O'Connor for Broadbent (51)
Powell for Spruce (58)

Sin-bin: Powell (69) - dissent
Dismissal: Powell (69) - dissent

Tries: Betts (4), Morley (43)
Goals: Goulding 2

League Express Men of the Match
New Zealand: Gene Ngamu
Great Britain: Andy Farrell

Penalty Count: 5-7

Half-time: 20-6
Referee: Steve Clark (Sydney)
Attendance: 9,000 est

121

Great Britain Tour

THE ACADEMY TOUR

FIRST TEST
JUNIOR KIWIS **35**
GREAT BRITAIN ACADEMY **14**
at Ericsson Stadium, Auckland,
Friday 18th October

JUNIOR KIWIS
1 Joe Galuvao (Auckland)
2 Leslie Vainakolo (Auckland)
3 David Kidwell (Canterbury)
4 Tai Savea (Auckland)
5 Charlie Kennedy (Auckland)
6 Scott Nixon (Canterbury)
7 Hare Te Rangi (Bay of Plenty)
8 Robert Henare (Illawarra)
9 Shane Beyers (Canterbury)
10 Frank Watene (Auckland)
11 Matthew Rua (Manly)
12 Darren Hewitt (Bay of Plenty)
13 Shaun Norton (Canterbury)
Subs
14 Monty Beetham (Auckland)
for Norton (65)
15 Kyle Leuluai (Auckland)
for Hewitt (26)
16 Gareth Cook (West Coast)
for Watene (70)
17 Phillip Leuluai (Auckland)
for Watene (22BB)
Watene for P Leuluai (30BB)
Hewitt for Henare (60)

Tries: Rua (10), Henare (28, 41),
Beyers (48), Kennedy (52),
Te Rangi (65)
Goals: Savea 5
Drop-goal: Te Rangi

GREAT BRITAIN ACADEMY
1 Daryl Cardiss (Wigan)
2 Marvin Golden (Leeds)
3 Paul Johnson (Wigan)
4 Nathan McAvoy (Salford Reds)
5 Danny Arnold (St Helens)
6 Craig Dean (Halifax Blue Sox)
7 Gavin Brown (Leeds)
8 Neil Baynes (Wigan)
9 Ian Talbot (Wigan)
10 Nick Fozzard (Leeds)
11 Jamie Field (Leeds)
12 Paul Highton (Halifax Blue Sox)
13 Ian Knott (Warrington)
Subs
14 Ian Watson (Salford Reds)
for Brown (43)
15 Terry Newton (Leeds)
for Baynes (32)
16 Gary Broadbent (Widnes)
for Dean (60)
17 Lee Milner (Huddersfield Giants)
for Highton (39)
Baynes for Newton (65)
Dean for Cardiss (70)

Tries: McAvoy (2, 35), Cardiss (70)
Goal: Knott
League Express Men of the Match
Kiwis: Robert Henare
Great Britain: Daryl Cardiss

Penalty Count: 5-7
Half-time: 11-8
Referee: D Pakieto (New Zealand)

SECOND TEST
JUNIOR KIWIS **27**
GREAT BRITAIN ACADEMY **24**
at The Showgrounds, Palmerston
North, Friday 25th October

JUNIOR KIWIS
1 Joe Galuvao (Auckland)
2 Leslie Vainakolo (Auckland)
3 David Kidwell (Canterbury)

4 Tai Savea (Auckland)
5 Charlie Kennedy (Auckland)
6 Scott Nixon (Canterbury)
7 Hare Te Rangi (Bay of Plenty)
8 Robert Henare (Illawarra)
9 Shane Beyers (Canterbury)
10 Frank Watene (Auckland)
11 Phillip Leuluai (Auckland)
12 Darren Hewitt (Bay of Plenty)
13 Shaun Norton (Canterbury)
Subs
14 Monty Beetham (Auckland)
for Hewitt (55)
15 Kyle Leuluai (Auckland)
for P Leuluai (30)
16 Gareth Cook (West Coast)
for Norton (55)
17 John Toelupe (Wellington)
for Henare (20)
Henare for Toelupe (40)

Tries: Henare (9, 58), Vainakolo
(16), Galuvao (41), Te Rangi (68)
Goals: Savea 3
Drop-goal: Te Rangi

GREAT BRITAIN ACADEMY
6 Gary Broadbent (Widnes)
2 Marvin Golden (Leeds)
3 Paul Johnson (Wigan)
4 Nathan McAvoy (Salford Reds)
5 Danny Arnold (St Helens)
1 Daryl Cardiss (Wigan)
7 Craig Dean (Halifax Blue Sox)
8 Neil Baynes (Wigan)
9 Ian Talbot (Wigan)
10 Jamie Field (Leeds)
11 Paul Anderson (St Helens)
12 Lee Milner (Huddersfield Giants)
13 Ian Knott (Warrington)
Subs
14 Ian Watson (Salford Reds)
for Cardiss (56)
15 Kevin O'Loughlin (St Helens)
for Golden (26)
16 Jon Clarke (Wigan)
for Talbot (69)

LIONS SQUAD TOUR STATS

17 Terry Newton (Leeds)
for Baynes (68)

Tries: Cardiss (29), Johnson (35),
Anderson (38, 78), McAvoy (55)
Goals: Knott 2

League Express Men of the Match
Kiwis: Robert Henare
Great Britain: Paul Anderson

Penalty Count: 9-5
Half-time: 10-16
Referee: Rodney Horn (New
Zealand)

THIRD TEST
JUNIOR KIWIS **37**
GREAT BRITAIN ACADEMY **36**
at Lancaster Park, Christchurch,
Friday 1st November

JUNIOR KIWIS
1 Joe Galuvao (Auckland)
2 Lesley Vainikolo (Auckland)
3 David Kidwell (Canterbury)
4 Tai Savea (Auckland)
5 Charlie Kennedy (Auckland)
6 Scott Nixon (Canterbury)
7 Hare Te Rangi (Bay of Plenty)
8 Robert Henare (Illawarra)
9 Shane Beyers (Canterbury)
10 Frank Watene (Auckland)
11 Phillip Leuluai (Auckland)
12 Darren Hewitt (Bay of Plenty)
13 Shaun Norton (Canterbury)
Subs
14 Monty Beetham (Auckland)
for Vainikolo (66)
15 Kyle Leuluai (Auckland)
for P Leuluai (51)
16 Gareth Cook (West Coast)
for Hewitt (66)
17 John Toelupe (Wellington)
for Watene (28)
P Leuluai for Henare (60BB)
Henare for Toelupe (66)

Tries: Te Rangi (4,60), Kennedy
(10), Vainikolo (29,51), Toelupe
(34), Hewitt (44)
Goals: Savea 4
Drop-goal: Nixon

GREAT BRITAIN ACADEMY
1 Gary Broadbent (Widnes)
2 Marvin Golden (Leeds)
3 Paul Johnson (Wigan)
4 Nathan McAvoy (Salford Reds)
5 Danny Arnold (St Helens)
6 Daryl Cardiss (Wigan)
7 Craig Dean (Halifax Blue Sox)
8 Jamie Field (Leeds)
9 Jon Clarke (Wigan)
10 Neil Baynes (Wigan)
11 Terry Newton (Leeds)
12 Ian Knott (Warrington)
13 Paul Anderson (St Helens)
Subs
14 Ian Watson (Salford Reds) for
Dean (25)
15 Wayne Flynn (Wakefield Trinity)
for Knott (52)
16 Damian Munro (Halifax Blue
Sox) for Arnold (48)
17 Kevin O'Loughlin (St Helens)
for Newton (35)
Newton for Baynes (56BB)
Baynes for Newton (59)

Tries: Knott (150, Broadbent (28),
Clarke (39), Anderson (66), Watson
(70), McAvoy (78)
Goals: Knott 3, Watson 3
League Express Men of the Match
Kiwis: Lesley Vainikolo
Great Britain: Neil Baynes

Penalty Count: 11-5
Half-time: 20-18
Referee: Gary Baxter (Wellington)

OTHER TOUR GAMES;

AUCKLAND u19's **16**
GREAT BRITAIN ACADEMY **48**
Auckland: Tries: Daganaysi, Butt,
Knight.
Goals: Welsh, Beverly
GB Academy: Tries: Arnold 2, Dean
2, Cardiss, Knott, Fozzard, Highton,
St Hilaire
Goals: Knott 6

CENTRAL DISTRICTS XIII **38**
GREAT BRITAIN ACADEMY **30**
Cent. Dist: Tries: Lalatoa, Clarke,
Toelupe 2, Talau, Gibson, Roberts
Goals: Ruwhiu 5
GB Academy: Tries: Munro, Flynn,
Broadbent, Watson, Newton,
Anderson
Goals: Watson 3

MAORI COLTS **10**
GREAT BRITAIN ACADEMY **36**
Maori: Tries: Stowers
Goals: Morgan 3
GB Academy: Tries: O'Loughlin,
Gilmour, Brown, Kitching 2, Clarke,
St Hilaire
Goals: Watson 3, Anderson

CANTERBURY u19's **14**
GREAT BRITAIN ACADEMY **44**
Canterbury: Tries: Lawrence (18),
Kopelani (73), McCausland (80)
Goal: Tia Tia
GB Academy: Tries: Munro 3, Salter
2, Hilaire, Brown, Golden. Goals:
Knott 6

	Tests	Tour games	Total App	Tries	Goals	Drop-goals	Points
Bobbie Goulding	5	1	6	4	23	1	63
Steve Prescott		4	4	1	17		38
Karle Hammond	2	4	6	5			20
Tony Smith	3	3	6	4			16
Alan Hunte	5	1	6	4			16
Keith Senior	2	4	6	3			12
Daryl Powell	5	2	7	3			12
Stuart Spruce	5	1	6	3			12
Anthony Sullivan	4	2	6	3			12
Denis Betts	5	1	6	3			12
James Lowes		4	4	2			8
Dave Bradbury		4	4	2			8
Mick Cassidy	1	5	6	2			8
Joey Hayes	1	2	3	2			8
Kris Radlinski	5	1	6	2			8
Keiron Cunningham	5	1	6	2			8
Iestyn Harris	5	1	6		3		6
Barrie-Jon Mather	2	4	6	1			4
Jason Critchley	3	1	4	1			4
Tulsen Tollet	5		5	1	4		4
Adrian Morley	2	4	6	1			4
Andy Farrell	5	1	6	1			4
Bernard Dwyer	1	3	4	1			4
Jon Roper		3	3				0
Steve Molloy	2	4	6				0
Brian McDermott	1	3	4				0
Neil Harmon		4	4				0
Rowland Phillips	1	3	4				0
Paul Broadbent	5	1	6				0
Terry O'Connor	4	2	6				0
Chris Joynt	4	2	6				0
Paul Sculthorpe	5	1	6				0
Nathan McAvoy		1	1				0

THE WORLD NINES, FIJI

Graham Clay

The staging of the inaugural World Nines in the Pacific paradise of Fiji was meant to herald the beginning of global Super League. The row with the ARL, and the islands' worst rainfall in years conspired to reduce the event to rather less than this grand image.

The tournament was originally intended to succeed the highly popular World Sevens, which had previously been held in Sydney.

But the Super League-ARL row resulted in the old competition continuing as normal, complete with a 'Great Britain Select' side that fielded those who had already departed to the ARL.

For Fiji, Great Britain had split into the guise of England and Wales. Included in their squads were Gary Connolly and Martin Hall respectively, neither nation expecting any problems, even though the pair had signed ARL contracts.

Unfortunately, the ARL didn't quite see it that way, and ordered the pair to withdraw. The lateness in taking such action - the players were told just before midnight on the eve of the competition - infuriated Super League officials.

Bob Abbott, an ARL executive, was accused of deliberately trying to sabotage the prestigious launch of Super League.

He had placed enormous pressure on the two Wigan players, threatening legal action and the prospect of massive financial complications if they didn't comply.

With no time to consider the best course of action, Connolly and Hall reluctantly had to step down and assume the role of water carriers.

Undeterred, and their resolve strengthened, Super League bosses went ahead.

Sixteen teams arrived in Suva, including Scotland, Ireland, Italy, USA, Japan and Morocco. Added to the South Sea island nations such as Tonga, Western Samoa and Cook Islands, plus the dominant forces of Australia and New Zealand, the organisers were confident of a competition befitting of the title 'World' Nines.

The opening day had 24 games scheduled from 10.00am through till late night. Australia kicked the whole thing off, with a 30-0 stroll against Western Samoa, played under gathering storm clouds.

England were next, and eventually saw off a determined effort from Tonga to run out 18-4 winners. Andy Farrell opened the scoring, his Wigan team-mate Kris Radlinski added a second, and Castleford's Tony Smith wrapped the game up.

A 34-0 thrashing of Morocco followed just after lunch, with a hat-trick for Martin Pearson and a brace for Keighley's Phil Cantillon.

World Nines

Two wins from two and everything seemed to be going to plan.

Enter Italy and the rain.

England, expecting a walkover on their way to meeting the big boys in the next round, were given an almighty shock. Italy produced a stunning display, fast and fluent on attack, strong and tight in defence.

Wigan's Rob Smyth eventually saved his side's blushes with a late 40 yard sprint for the game's only try.

The win meant England topped Group B ahead of Tonga, and were drawn to play Australia, Western Samoa and Tonga in the following day's second round.

The atrocious weather killed off that idea, a completely submerged pitch leaving the organisers with no alternative but to cancel the second day's play. Instead, it was decided to re-structure the third day and go straight into the semi-final stage. England would play Papua New Guinea, who had topped Group D and inflicted a 14-12 defeat on Wales in the process.

That defeat condemned the Welsh to the Trophy competition for the runners-up in each group. Clive Griffiths' side were always going to have an uphill battle in a very tough group, and took credit for hard-earned wins against Cook Islands (10-8) and Fiji (8-6). They were drawn to face Tonga in the semi-final.

With all the re-draws complete, players, officials and media retreated to the event headquarters at the Tradewinds Hotel.

Then the bombshell hit.

Already humbled by being forced to cancel a day's play, news began to filter through that the ARL had won the court case against Super League.

Hoards of people gathered around the lone television screen in the hotel bar to hear Justice Burchett hand down his verdict.

The Australian players, with Mal Meninga and Laurie Daley to the fore, looked at each other in bewilderment. Maurice Lindsay was in his room talking with lawyers and preparing a media statement in his capacity as World Super League Chairman.

Eventually, the players were taken to a local community centre for an urgent meeting, and to hear a message from Super League chief executive, John Ribot.

Suddenly, the Nines had been almost forgotten.

Gary Connolly, forced to sit out the Nines after threats from the ARL, watches from the sidelines.

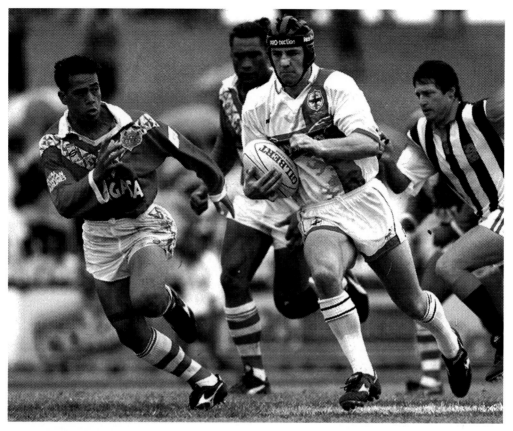

Warrington's Paul Sculthorpe
splits the Tongan defence

An hour later, Lindsay emerged to give his reaction. He informed the press that the players were unified in their support of Super League, and had faxed a statement, signed by every player, to News Limited re-asserting their loyalty. He claimed it was merely a setback, and an appeal would be launched.

With that, the weary players retired and the rest spent the night drowning their sorrows.

As day three dawned, the heavens were still pouring. Mechanical pumps and an army of workers were brought in to make the pitch playable, but by mid-morning worried officials were facing the prospect of cancelling the rest of the tournament.

Coupled with the events in Sydney, it was a scenario no-one wished to contemplate.

But the rain eventually stopped at around lunchtime, the hot sunshine quickly dried the mud-bath of a pitch, and everyone once again busied themselves with a determined effort to make a success of what was left.

Unbeaten England took to the field against Papua New Guinea for their semi-final

World Nines

DAY ONE RESULTS

Australia	30	Western Samoa	0	Western Samoa	8	Scotland	4
England	18	Tonga	4	Tonga	30	Italy	4
New Zealand	22	France	0	Ireland	16	France	12
PNG	4	Fiji	0	Fiji	10	Cook Islands	4
Scotland	12	USA	6	Australia	26	Scotland	6
Italy	18	Morocco	0	England	4	Italy	0
Ireland	20	Japan	4	New Zealand	20	Ireland	0
Wales	10	Cook Islands	8	PNG	16	Cook Island	10
Australia	30	USA	16	Western Samoa	14	USA	6
England	34	Morocco	0	Tonga	32	Morocco	0
New Zealand	42	Japan	0	France	16	Japan	0
PNG	14	Wales	12	Fiji	6	Wales	10

POOL TABLES

	P	W	D	L	F	A	PTS		P	W	D	L	F	A	PTS
England	3	3	0	0	56	4	6	Australia	3	3	0	0	86	22	6
Tonga	3	2	0	1	66	22	4	Western Samoa	3	2	0	1	22	40	4
Italy	3	1	0	2	22	34	2	Scotland	3	1	0	2	22	40	2
Morocco	3	0	0	3	0	84	0	USA	3	0	0	3	28	56	0

	P	W	D	L	F	A	PTS		P	W	D	L	F	A	PTS
PNG	3	3	0	0	34	22	6	New Zealand	3	3	0	0	84	0	6
Wales	3	2	0	1	32	26	4	Ireland	3	2	0	1	36	36	4
Fiji	3	1	0	1	16	18	2	France	3	1	0	2	32	38	2
Cook Islands	3	0	0	3	22	36	0	Japan	3	0	0	3	4	78	0

DAY THREE
(DAY TWO CANCELLED DUE TO WATERLOGGED PITCH)

BOWL COMPETITION
Cook Islands 14   Japan..........................6
USA...............................18   Morocco 4
3RD PLACE PLAY-OFF
Morocco 18   Japan..........................6
FINAL
USA..................................0   Cook Islands 22

PLATE COMPETITION
France 26   Italy 4
Scotland 4   Fiji 14
3RD PLACE PLAY-OFF
Scotland 34   Italy 0
FINAL
Fiji 18   France 8

TROPHY COMPETITION
SEMI FINALS
Western Samoa 32   Ireland 18
Tonga 6   Wales.......................16
3RD PLACE PLAY-OFF
Tonga 36   Ireland 8
FINAL
Wales 12   Western Samoa 8
(a.e.t - score 8-8 at full time)
Wales: T- Perrett, Atcheson, Watson
W Samoa: T- Laumatia   HT: 0-4

WORLD NINES CUP SEMI FINALS

England 14   Papua New Guinea 15
Eng: T- Wood 2, Flynn; G- Ford
PNG: T- Sio, Paiyo, Mamando; G- Paiyo; DG- Sio
HT: 6-10

Australia 8   New Zealand 10
Aust: T- Hetherington, Mullins
NZ: T- Kirwan, Vagana; G- Ngamu
HT: 4-6

THIRD PLACE PLAY OFF

England 10   Australia 14
(a e t - score 10-10 at full time)
Eng: T- Sculthorpe, Wood; G- Ford
Aust: T- Sailor, Beckett 2; G- Green
HT: 10-4

SUPER LEAGUE WORLD NINES CUP FINAL

New Zealand.................26   Papua New Guinea 10
NZ: T- Hoppe 2, Barnett, Ngamu, Kirwan; G- Ngamu 3
PNG: T- Kops, Gene; G- Paiyo

Man of the Tournament - Sean Hoppe (New Zealand)

in confident mood, but suffered an early setback when Tony Smith limped off with an ankle injury just minutes into the game. Shortly after, they fell behind to a try by Robert Sio in PNG's first real attack.

Elias Paiyo, the pint-sized hooker, put PNG further ahead with a 40 yard midfield break, outpacing the chasing Mick Cassidy. He scored in spectacular style, somersaulting before slamming the ball down to the delight of the 10,000 crowd.

Mike Ford and Adrian Flynn finally got England going when they combined to send Martin Wood tearing down the left wing. He stepped inside the cover and planted the ball under the posts.

Flynn pulled his side level just after the break, when Andy Farrell squeezed out a lobbed pass to unleash him on a 30 yard dash to the corner. But PNG refused to buckle, and they launched several exciting raids on the English line. Kris Radlinski made a crucial interception ten yards out when a

New Zealand skipper Sean Hoppe lifts the World Nines Trophy

try seemed certain and PNG, frustrated at not being able to break this stubborn defence, had to settle for a drop goal to put them 11-10 ahead.

It was to prove invaluable, as both sides added just one further try each. Wood got his second after more good work by Flynn, and with seconds remaining it appeared England had just done enough. But, in injury time, PNG threw the ball around and broke the scrambling defence to score with the very last pass of the game to earn an unlikely place in the World Nines Final.

Old enemies Australia and New Zealand now had to battle it out for the right to meet the Kumuls. Like England, the Aussies had won all their group games, including a 26-6 win against Scotland. New Zealand, too, were unbeaten, but their wins were against lesser opposition, with only Ireland offering any resistance before going down 20-0.

World Nines

Australia were the red-hot competition favourites, and went ahead early on when Ricky Stuart put new-boy Jason Hetherington over following a dazzling kick and chase by Andrew Ettingshausen. The Kiwis soon hit back through Nigel Vagana, who looked threatening with every touch. Gene Ngamu converted, and the Kiwis turned around 6-4 ahead.

Henry Paul went close after the re-start, but it was John Kirwan who extended the lead, when Laurie Daley shot out of the defensive line early to make an interception attempt. He missed, and Kirwan had the space to stroll in.

Brett Mullins brought it back to 10-8, but the Kiwis hung on for a great win, consigning Australia to a third-place play-off against England.

That was a thrilling game, and typical of a full 13-a-side clash between the two. At full time the scores were locked at 10-10, after England had led 10-4 at the interval. Paul Sculthorpe and Martin Wood had crossed for tries, with Mike Ford adding a conversion.

But, in sudden death extra time, Robbie Beckett got his second and vital try to earn third place for Australia.

Meanwhile, Wales were enjoying success in the consolation tournament. They dispatched Tonga in the semi-final, Jason Critchley grabbing two sensational tries in a 16-6 win. In the other semi, Western Samoa proved too strong for Ireland, and ran out convincing 32-18 winners.

The final was one of the games of the tournament. Wales fell behind to a Willie Poching try, but Iestyn Harris prompted and probed with thrilling 30 yard bursts that delighted the crowd.

Allan Bateman made a tremendous cover tackle as a Samoan winger sprinted 60 yards downfield, and that seemed to kick-start his team-mates. They turned around 4-0 in arrears, but levelled when, from the re-start, they forced a drop out and Gareth Stephens put Mark Perrett over.

Paul Atcheson added a second after some breath-taking free flowing football, and Salford's Ian Watson grabbed the winner after great approach play from Bateman and Atcheson.

All that remained now was the main final. As expected, New Zealand proved far too strong for PNG. Sean Hoppe, later to be declared man of the series, scored two tries and lifted the World Nines Trophy before a packed stadium. The smiles returned to the faces of Super League officials.

GREAT BRITAIN'S youngest ever tour captain, Andy Farrell, leads the Lions out for the First Test Match v New Zealand at the Ericsson Stadium, Auckland on October 18th

THE 1996 INTERNATIONAL YEAR

England's Paul Sculthorpe comes under pressure from the PNG defence during the 1996 Super League World Nines in Fiji

RIGHT: Wales' Iestyn Harris is brought down to earth by Western Samoa
ABOVE: Storm clouds ahead? Martin Hall ponders his predicament in the Welsh dug-out

TOP: Wales celebrate winning the "Trophy" CENTRE LEFT: England's Adrian Flynn in action against Tonga CENTRE RIGHT: Tony Smith scores an English try LEFT: New Zealand's Henry Paul on the loose for the Super League World Nines winners in the final against Papua New Guinea

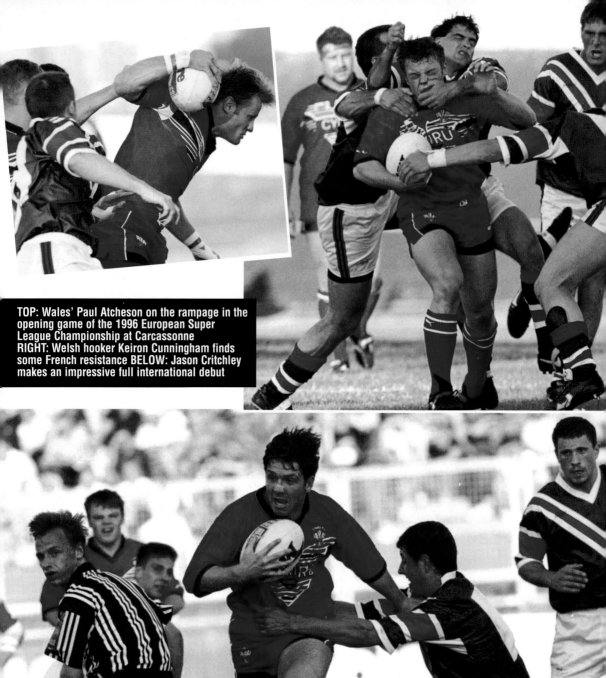

TOP: Wales' Paul Atcheson on the rampage in the opening game of the 1996 European Super League Championship at Carcassonne
RIGHT: Welsh hooker Keiron Cunningham finds some French resistance **BELOW:** Jason Critchley makes an impressive full international debut

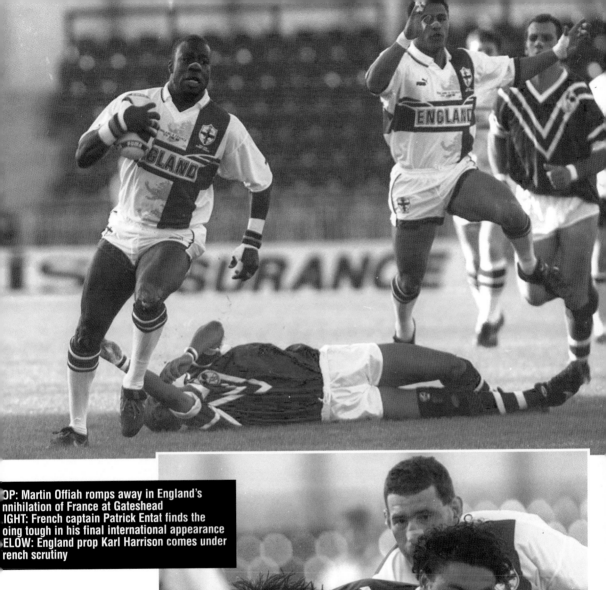

OP: Martin Offiah romps away in England's
nnihilation of France at Gateshead
IGHT: French captain Patrick Entat finds the
going tough in his final international appearance
ELOW: England prop Karl Harrison comes under
French scrutiny

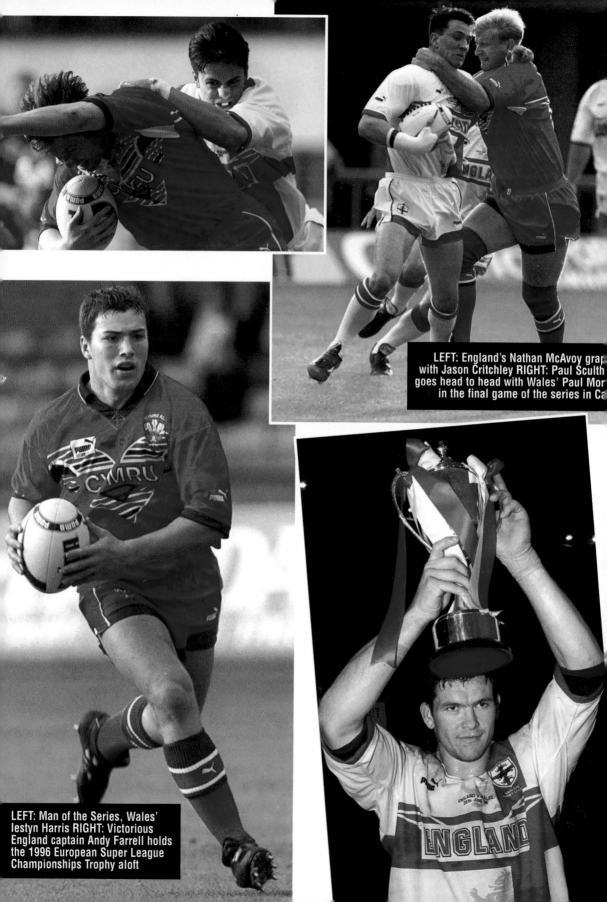

LEFT: England's Nathan McAvoy grap
with Jason Critchley RIGHT: Paul Sculth
goes head to head with Wales' Paul Mor
in the final game of the series in Ca

LEFT: Man of the Series, Wales'
Iestyn Harris RIGHT: Victorious
England captain Andy Farrell holds
the 1996 European Super League
Championships Trophy aloft

TOP: Scotland beat Ireland 26-6 in Glasgow on August 6th. An inquisitive flag-waving Scottish public enter into the spirit of the occasion
LEFT: Scotland's Martin Ketteridge on the charge
BELOW: The Irish and Scottish players applaud the fans who had witnessed the historic event.

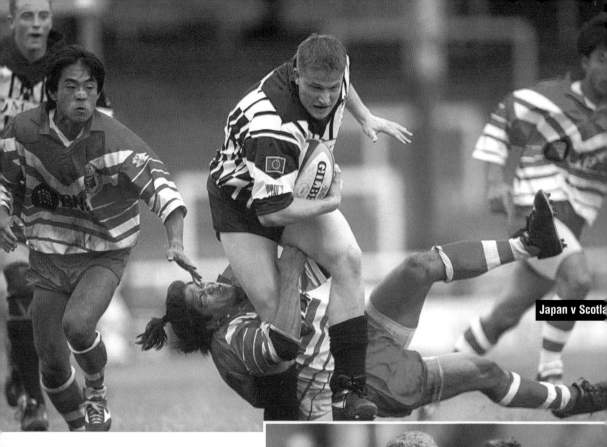

Japan v Scotland

The Halifax Student World Cup was held in August and was
the largest ever. Including teams from England, Ireland,
Scotland, Wales, Australia, New Zealand, Western Samoa,
France, South Africa, Japan, Russia/Moldova, and the USA
the tournament was an undoubted success which augurs
well for the future of international Rugby League.
On the following three pages we look back at some of
more memorable scenes on offer.

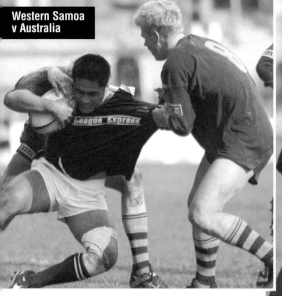

Western Samoa
v Australia

South Africa
v Russia/Moldova

England v France

: The opening parade in Warrington
VE: Japan v Scotland

ABOVE: Western Samoa v Ireland
LEFT: France v Scotland

Japan v Scotland

Western Samoa
v Australia

ABOVE: Bowl winners South Afr
celebrate their succe
BELOW: Reigning champions Australia
the Student World Cup yet aga

ABOVE: Manly celebrate winning the 1996 Optus Cup Grand Final, 20-8 v St George Dragons, at Sydney Football Stadium in September
LEFT: Daniel Gartner breaks clear for the Sea Eagles
BELOW: Former Leeds centre Craig Innes *(middle)* celebrates with team-mates Jim Serdaris and Daniel Gartner

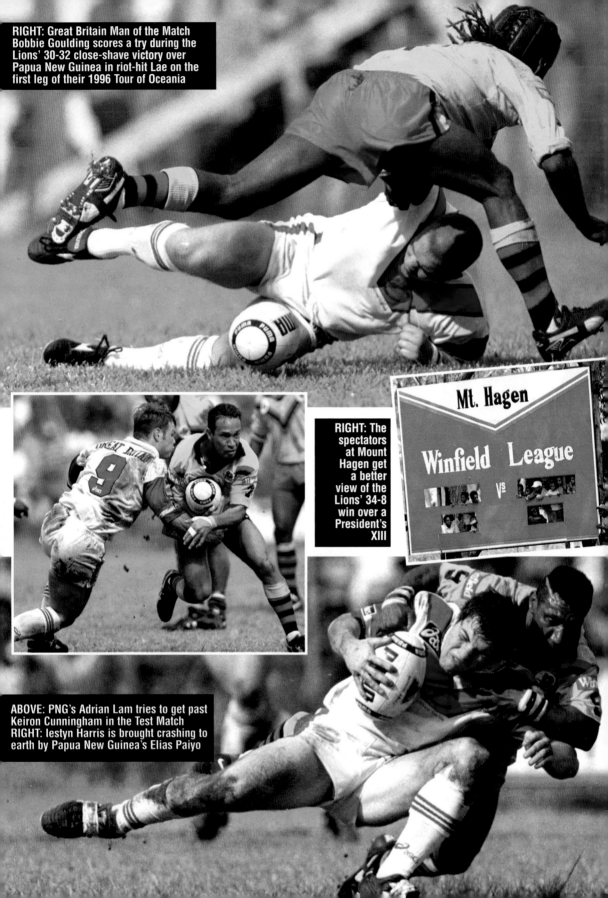

RIGHT: Great Britain Man of the Match Bobbie Goulding scores a try during the Lions' 30-32 close-shave victory over Papua New Guinea in riot-hit Lae on the first leg of their 1996 Tour of Oceania

RIGHT: The spectators at Mount Hagen get a better view of the Lions' 34-8 win over a President's XIII

Mt. Hagen

Winfield League

VS

ABOVE: PNG's Adrian Lam tries to get past Keiron Cunningham in the Test Match
RIGHT: Iestyn Harris is brought crashing to earth by Papua New Guinea's Elias Paiyo

LEFT: Auckland Warrior Denis Betts takes a pounding in the all-out brawl which took place during the Lions test match with Fiij. Britain went on to hammer the Fijians 72-4
TOP: A traditional Fiji warrior leads the pre-match haka
ABOVE: GB Doctor Zamar provides Daryl Powell with much needed oxygen at half-time as Paul Broadbent waits his turn

HT: Bradford Bulls' Brian McDermott es the ball up on his test debut
LOW: The smiling face of Fiji - a local enjoys the test match action

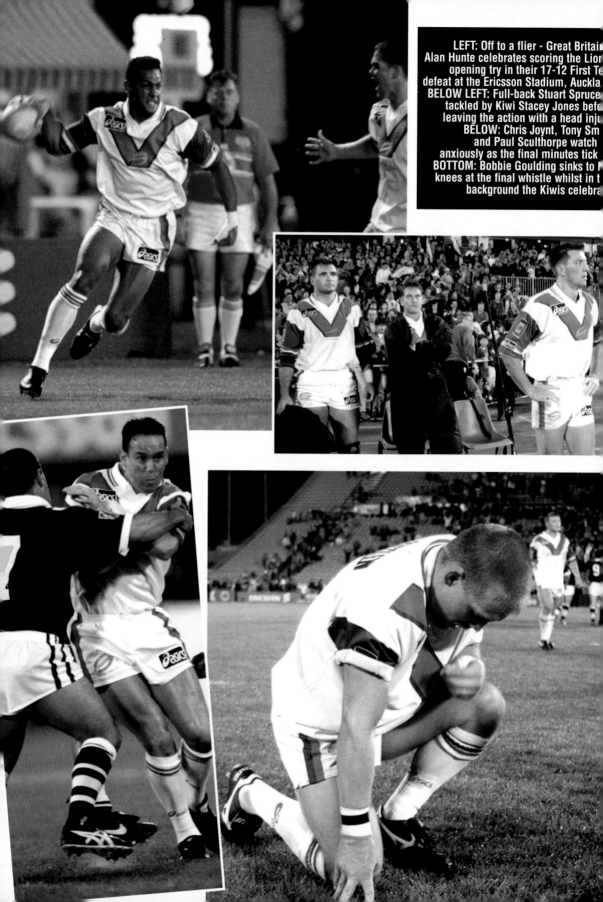

LEFT: Off to a flier - Great Britain's Alan Hunte celebrates scoring the Lions' opening try in their 17-12 First Test defeat at the Ericsson Stadium, Auckland

BELOW LEFT: Full-back Stuart Spruce is tackled by Kiwi Stacey Jones before leaving the action with a head injury

BELOW: Chris Joynt, Tony Smith and Paul Sculthorpe watch anxiously as the final minutes tick by

BOTTOM: Bobbie Goulding sinks to his knees at the final whistle whilst in the background the Kiwis celebrate

LEFT: Great Britain's youngest ever Tour Captain Andy Farrell tries in vain to lead his side to victory in the Second Test at Palmerston North. New Zealand went on to win the game 18-15 thereby clinching the series with a game still to go
BELOW : Inspirational Kiwi skipper Matthew Ridge attempts to find a way around Lions' centre and new Keighley Cougars player-coach Daryl Powell

BELOW: Maori dancers get into the spirit of things before the Lions' midweek match at Whangerei
RIGHT: Great Britain's Welsh winger Anthony Sullivan spills the ball under pressure from the Kiwi defence early in the Second Test

ABOVE: Sheffield Eagles' Paul Broadbent comes under close Kiwi attention during the third and final test at Lancaster Park, Christchurch on November 1st
RIGHT: New Zealand powerhouse Steve Kearney finds his way blocked by Saints duo Karle Hammond and Chris Joynt
BELOW: The victorious Kiwis celebrate a highly convincing record 32-12 win and a three test whitewash over the sad Lions

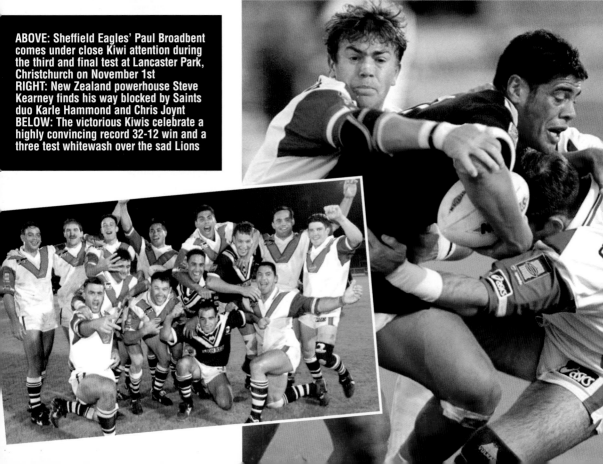

THE EUROPEAN CHAMPIONSHIPS

Tim Butcher

Buoyed by the huge success of the Centenary World Cup in the autumn of 1995, the International Board hurtled headlong into the ambitiously titled European Championships, scheduled to take place on three successive Wednesdays in the middle of June to avoid disruption to the Super League programme.

Ambitious and, in hindsight, a mistake.

The competition took the soccer Euorpean Championships head on in the battle for media and public interest.

Not surprisingly, League lost out. In fact it wasn't a contest at all.

Soccer's Euro '96 was the biggest sporting event held in this country since the World Cup of 1966. The media hype was over the top - not only newspapers, TV and radio were carried away by it all, but companies, eager to associate themselves with the soccer extravagana, joined the rush to have their products endorsed by the tournament. It was hard to drive or walk anywhere during those few weeks in the summer without seeing or hearing some mention of Euro '96.

Much of the fare was very ordinary. But the success of the England soccer team in getting to the semi-finals had the nation in a near state of hysteria as Rugby League's own version came to its own modest little climax in Cardiff on June 26th.

Alas, that was the night that the soccer team was reaching its own apotheosis at Wembley.

There was palpable relief, therefore, when the Wales-England game at Ninian Park attracted a crowd in excess of 5,000 people. But there was no getting away from the fact that the scheduling of the game was a huge blunder.

It left the whole tournament under a big question mark.

There were other big problems for the administrators.

The rumbling, acrimonious row between the Australian Rugby League and the Super League threatened to affect the preparations of England coach Phil Larder and his Welsh counterpart Clive Griffiths.

Wigan trio Gary Connolly, Jason Robinson and Martin Hall had all signed contracts with the ARL the previous spring, and had been kept out of the Fiji Nines in February, as the increasingly isolated ARL insisted on their non-participation.

Surpringly, this time the ARL voiced no objection, and the three were all cleared to play their parts in the Championships.

These storm clouds were nothing when compared to the problems faced by the

145

The European Championships

French national side. Having surprised a lot of observers by picking up five (ultimately invaluable) points in the opening rounds of Super League, Paris Saint-Germain were, by June, well and truly on the slide.

Not that they were lacking in ability and spirit. It was merely because they were fast becoming exhausted by the bulk of their players being forced to particapate for their clubs in the French Federation competition during the week, as well as fronting up in Super League.

And in June they were asked to represent their country in midweek, too.

The pundits feared the worst.

Rugby League Express voiced its concerns in the Upfront column on the Monday before the tournament opener in Carcassonne.

"Even though international football is vital for Rugby League, as it is for any other sport, we have to ask whether it is wise to hold these matches on midweek evenings in June."

The fears turned out to be justified.

For the first game aginst Wales, France were rocked by the withdrawal of their captain Pierre Chamorin, who had aggravated a shoulder injury playing for his club Saint-Esteve in the French Championship final on May 26th.

No less than eight of the starting thirteen for the game in Carcasonne played for Paris Saint-Germain the previous Sunday in a 52-10 mauling at the hands of Champions to be, St Helens.

So it was left to the enigmatic Patrick Entat to lead from the front against the Welsh, with young gun Fabien Devecchi - one of the French players to develop as a true Super League performer as the season wore on - replacing Chamorin at stand-off.

Wales coach Clive Griffiths had problems of his own.

The bedrock of his side, which had performed so excellently in the World Cup, had disintegrated.

Allan Bateman was playing with Cronulla in the Australian League; Scott Gibbs was struggling to recover from a shoulder injury; Kevin Ellis and Richie Eyres had both been sidelined by a long running contractual disputes with their respective clubs; and the jewel in his crown, Jonathan Davies, had been lured back to Welsh Rugby Union in a big money deal.

Then the previous Friday night John Devereux broke an ankle playing for his club, Widnes, at Rochdale.

In came Warrington's Jason Lee and Gareth Davies to join other new cap Jason Critchley of Keighley, Salford's Ian Watson and St Helens Chris Morley. Gerald Cordle, who had played no club rugby in the first team that year, was drafted in on the wing.

The gamble appeared to have been a mistake, when Cordle failed to deal with a fifth-minute kick into the corner of the in-goal area, and French winger Arnaud Cervello pounced to give the home side a shock lead.

Wales were struggling in the evening heat of the Midi, but in Warrington's brilliant young stand-off Iestyn Harris they had a player to win at any level of international football. As Super League Week's reporter Paul Vaughan wrote from Carcassonne,

146

England got off to a winning start
by easily disposing of a disappointing French side at Gateshead

Harris played a pivotal role in winning the game for the reigning European Champions.

"When Wales lost Jonathan Davies last year there were some people who reckoned that it was the end of Wales' great international adventure.

"After all, there aren't too many teams with such limited resources who could call on talents quite like his.

"But then again there aren't too many teams who can call on such an able successor as Iestyn Harris".

Harris, still two weeks short of his 20th bithday, gave a faultless display in an eventual 34-14 win.

The young star pulled his Welsh troops out of a sticky situation.

Three times he dummied and cut through for tries. The first came in direct reply to Cervello's try. With his own conversion, this gave Wales the lead they never lost.

The second came seven minutes after the break, and the last, nine minutes later, was a real treat, Harris mesmerising the French with a series of dummies and sidesteps to score.

There were tries, too, for Jason Critchley, who made an impressive debut, Richard Webster, who was put in by Watson, and former Welsh student player Gareth Davies.

There was a mighty effort in the strength-sapping conditions from the Welsh pack, none more so than from Mark Jones, who put in one of his best performances in League,

147

particularly after the withdrawal of skipper David Young with ankle ligament damage after a half hour.

France looked totally exhausted and dispirited, despite competing well and being rewarded with tries for Wigan Alliance player Gael Tallec and Cervello who, in another stroke of bad luck, twisted an ankle while scoring in the dying seconds of the game.

No-one had seriously expected the French to beat the Welsh, and a disappointing crowd of 4,382 at the Stade Albert Domec - in the traditional heartland of Rugby League in France - reflected the current status of the national side in the eyes of the Triezistes.

A week later - with a 54-22 hammering of Paris SG by Castleford at the Charlety Stadium sandwiched in between - the French faced up to the awesome task of taking on England at Gateshead International Stadium.

English coach Phil Larder had already courted controversy by leaving out Wigan's Shaun Edwards from his initial 21-man squad, in favour of St Helens' in-form Bobbie Goulding.

"At the end of the day it came down to a straight choice between Bobbie and Shaun," admitted Larder. "...in the end Bobbie just shaded it."

But Larder enmphasised that Edwards' international carreer was not over: "It's not the end for Shaun by any means," he said.

This proved to be prophetic, as Goulding cracked his collar bone during the Spring Bank Holiday win over Castleford at Knowsley Road, a game in which he kicked eleven goals on his way to the fastest ever century of goals in the history of the game.

And despite the earlier snub, Edwards accepted Larder's invitation to take his place.

The episode meant that Edwards would be playing under his teammate Andy Farrell, who had been named a captain of the side when Larder first named his squad.

Farrell became the youngest skipper of a national side, when he led out England at Gateshead. He was just 21 years and 14 days old.

"What more can a player achieve after the Great Britain captaincy?" he asked at the time.

Larder's only injury problem for the game was at full-back, when Wigan young gun Kris Radlinski was forced to withdraw with an ankle injury.

Salford's Steve Blakeley was also drafted in to replace Castleford's Tony Smith, also out injured. Blakeley got a start at stand-off outside Edwards.

Radlinski's replacement was St Helens' Steve Prescott, whose original omision had stunned many observers.

Prescott didn't let anyone down, as he set a new points-scoring record for England with 20 points, kicking seven goals and going over for two tries in a 73-6 romp.

"England - as expected" ran the Super League Week headline. Perhaps it should have read: "as feared."

For French scrum-half and capatin Patrick Entat it was a sad way to bow out of the international scene.

The European Championships

His retirement fom international football, announced in advance of the game, marked the end of an era in French rugby league.

Entat, 31, had been the mainstay of France's international side for almost a decade, and France's most capped player of the present era (with 36 international appearances since his debut in 1986).

"It was disappointing for me," sald Entat immediately after the game. "When you think about your last game you want it to be something beautiful. But all the time I've been playing I've been very happy to be in the French team.

"Unfortunately we're going through a bad time at the moment. I don't know what's happened, but it's in our heads. You can put up with losing by 30 or 40 points, but nothing like that. It's like some players don't want to play. That's terrible.

"But now my international career is over, and it's time for me to concentrate on Paris Saint-Germain. I'm quite happy just to do that."

Entat stood out in a truly uninspiring performance by the French.

England's backline was the best it could possibly call on - including Robinson, Newlove, Connolly and Offiah. Connolly scored a hat-trick, Newlove two tries, Robinson one, and Offiah collected four plus an improbable drop-goal twelve minutes into the game, ten minutes after he had opened the scoring with a burst of pace that had the French grasping thin air.

It was the biggest defeat that England had inflicted on France, and a

England's Jason Robinson
left the French defence grasping at air

149

The European Championships

point more than Great Britain's biggest score against them, at Headingley in 1993.

If the European Championship of 1996 had worked for anyone, then French Rugby League could not be included.

Once again the bold experiment of taking international games to the north east had paid dividends in the midst of a country gripped with Euro '96 mania, with more than 6,000 appreciative League fans turning out for a rare glimpse of live League. In the context of this summer's competition it would be hard to see a bigger crowd attending at a stadium even in League's heartland.

If the competition from soccer had been understimated when the timing of the European Championship had been decided, events had taken a turn for the worse for the organisers by the time of the decider in Cardiff two weeks later.

The same night of the Wales-England game, the English soccer team, with considerably more media attention, played Germany in the semi-final of the soccer cup.

After a week of dire predictions the RFL was visibly relieved to draw a gate of nearly five and a half thousand.

It was a sign of the pulling power of League in South Wales, as the Welsh people flocked to Cardiff Arms Park hoping for a repeat of Wales' 18-16 defeat of England the previous year.

Their expectations were raised when the news broke from Australia that Allan Bateman would make the long trip home to help the cause. This went some way to alleviating the loss of Anthony Sullivan, who picked up a deadleg in the Wigan-Saints game the previous Friday night.

Ian Watson kept his place at scrum-half, with the fit again Gareth Stephens on the subs bench. Wigan's Neil Cowie came in at number ten in place of David Young. Chris Morley's display at Carcasonne three weeks earlier earned him the loose-forward shirt, with Rowland Phillips starting as substitute.

Larder lost Paul Newlove, who suffered a chest infection, and Martin Offiah and Karl Harrison, both injured, and chose Keighley Cougars' Daryl Powell in preference to Steve Blakeley at stand-off.

In the end, England ran out 26-12 winners to wrest the European Championship from the Welsh, but it wasn't without a hard fight.

Larder had asked for a tough match to help him in his preparations for the Lions tour at the end of the season and that is what he got, Steve Prescott's runaway try in the 76th minute finally ended Wales' hopes of winning the game.

Iestyn Harris - voted man of the series by the press - had given the Welsh the lead when he broke down the right and looped a pass inside to full debutant Chris Morley.

The battle between the two hookers, Wales' Keiron Cunningham and Sheffield's John Lawless, had been billed as the contest for the Great Britain number nine jumper, but the showdown was ended before it got going, when Lawless had to retire in the 20th minute with a back injury.

The incident played a major part in deciding the outcome of the game. Lawless was

England captain Andy Farrell charges through the Welsh line
as he leads his side to the European Championship

replaced by Goulding, who had recovered from his injury, and the genial Saints' star turned the match England's way.

It was his 48th minute try that pulled England away. He ran from dummy half to dash over under the posts. His conversion gave England an eight point lead.

Wales replied with a superb length of the field try, with Paul Atcheson sending Critchley on a thrilling run to the line. Harris converted to make the gap a mere two points.

But Edwards was on hand to finish off Connolly's break, and Prescott scored to secure an England Championship.

Clive Griffiths, the Welsh coach, experienced bitter-sweet feelings after the game.

"We were disappointed that we didn't win," he said. "But England will know they've been in a game. That was the cream of British Rugby League, and we competed with some players who have come straight out of A-team football.

"We had some injuries early on which affected the team, and that, together with the fact that we could not pick some of our best players, did not make it easy. But all credit to the boys on the park tonight. They rose to the occasion, and proved they could mix and match it with the best.

"It took four pieces of individual brilliance to break us down, and everything else they threw at us we knocked back."

151

The European Championships

THE GAMES

FRANCE 14 .... WALES 34
at Stade Albert Domec, Carcassonne,
Wednesday 5th June

FRANCE
1 Fred Banquet
2 Pascal Bomati
3 Eric Vergniol
4 Jean-Marc Garcia
5 Arnaud Cervello
6 Fabien Devecchi
7 Patrick Entat
8 Hadj Boudebza
9 Patrick Torreilles
10 Frederic Teixido
11 Gael Tallec
12 Didier Cabestany
13 Pascal Jampy
Subs
14 Regis Pastre-Courtine
    for Teixido (30)
17 Laurent Cambre for Jampy (50)
15 Jerome Bisson for Vergniol (63)
16 Laurent Lucchese
    for Pastre-Courtine (63)
Teixido for Cabestany (53)
Jampy for Boudebza (75)

Tries: Cervello (6,79), Tallec (39)
Goal: Torreilles

WALES
1 Paul Atcheson
2 Gerald Cordle
3 Gareth Davies
4 Jason Critchley
5 Anthony Sullivan
6 Iestyn Harris
7 Ian Watson
8 Mark Jones
9 Keiron Cunningharn
10 David Young
11 Paul Moriarty
12 Rowland Phillips
13 Mark Perrett
Subs
14 Chris Morley for Perrett (40)
15 Richard Webster for Young (30)
16 Martin Hall for Watson (50)
Watson for Phillips (65)
17 Jason Lee for Davies (69BB)
Davies for Lee (73BB)
Phillips for Moriarty (78)
Lee for Cordle (78)

Tries: Harris (12,47,56), Atcheson (16),
Webster (35), Davies (76)
Goals: Harris 5

League Express Men of the Match
France: Pascal Bomati
Wales: Iestyn Harris

Penalty Count: 6-8

Half-time: 10-16
Referee: Russell Smith (Castleford)
Attendance: 4,382

ENGLAND 73 .... FRANCE 6
at Gateshead International Stadium,
Wednesday 12th June

ENGLAND
1 Steve Prescott
2 Jason Robinson
3 Gary Connolly
4 Paul Newlove
5 Martin Offiah
6 Steve Blakeley
7 Shaun Edwards
8 Karl Harrison
9 Johnny Lawless
10 Paul Broadbent
11 Chris Joynt
12 Steve McNamara
13 Paul Sculthorpe
Subs
14 Matt Calland for Newlove (62)
15 Paul Rowley for Lawless (61)
16 Adrian Morley for McNamara (73)
17 Steve Molloy for Harrison (30)
Harrison for Broadbent (67)

Tries: Offiah (3,40,52,60), Newlove
(6,53), Blakeley (23), Prescott (28,50),
Connolly (20,44,77), Robinson (55),
Sculthorpe (66)
Goals: Prescott 7, McNamara
Drop-goal: Offiah

FRANCE
1 Laurent Lucchese
2 Pascal Bomati
3 Frederic Banquet
4 Jean-Marc Garcia
5 Arnaud Cervello
6 Fabien Devecchi
7 Patrick Entat
8 Hadj Boudebza
9 Patrick Torreilles
10 Frederic Teixido
11 Pascal Jampy
12 Didier Cabestany
13 Jacques Pech
Subs
14 Darren Adams for Boudebza (24)
15 Eric van Brussell for Bomati (21)
16 Jerome Bisson for Banquet (53)
17 Bagdad Yaha for Cervello (36)

Try: van Brussell (72)
Goal: Torreilles

League Express Men of the Match
England: Shaun Edwards
France: Patrick Entat

Penalty Count: 3-0

Half-time: 33-0
Referee: Bill Harrigan (Australia)
Attendance: 6,235

WALES 12 .... ENGLAND 26
at Cardiff Arms Park,
Wednesday 26th June

WALES
1 Paul Atcheson (Oldham)
2 Diccon Edwards (Castleford)
3 Allan Bateman (Cronulla)
4 Gareth Davies (Warrington)
5 Jason Critchley (Keighley)
6 Iestyn Harris (Warrington)
7 Ian Watson (Salford)
8 Mark Jones (Warrington)
9 Keiron Cunningham (St Helens)
10 Neil Cowie (Wigan)
11 Paul Moriarty (South Wales)
12 Mark Perrett (Halifax)
13 Chris Morley (St Helens)
Subs
14 Martin Hall (Wigan) for Perrett (54)
15 Richard Webster (Salford)
    for Jones (23)
16 Gareth Stephens (Hull)
    for Watson (75)
17 Rowland Phillips (Workington)
    for Cowie (9)

Tries: Morley (9), Critchley (50)
Goals: Harris 2

ENGLAND
1 Steve Prescott (St Helens)
2 Jason Robinson (Wigan)
3 Gary Connolly (Wigan)
4 Nathan McAvoy (Salford)
5 John Bentley (Halifax)
6 Daryl Powell (Keighley)
7 Shaun Edwards (Wigan)
8 Paul Broadbent (Sheffield)
9 Johnny Lawless (Sheffield)
10 Steve Molloy (Featherstone)
11 Chris Joynt (St Helens)
12 Paul Sculthorpe (Warrington)
13 Andy Farrell (Wigan)
Subs
14 Bobbie Goulding (St Helens)
    for Lawless (21)
15 Steve Blakeley (Salford)
    for Powell (25)
16 Barrie McDermott (Leeds)
    for Molloy (29)
17 Mick Cassidy (Wigan) for Joynt (72)

Tries: Joynt (28), Goulding (48),
Edwards (67), Prescott (76).
Goals: Goulding (5)

Penalty Count: 1-6

League Express Men of the Match
Wales: Iestyn Harris
England: Bobbie Goulding

Referee Bill Harrigan (Australia)
Half-time 6-8
Attendance 5,425

THE SEASON DOWN UNDER

Malcolm Andrews

There is no doubt that historians will look back on 1996 as the second most significant season in Australian Rugby League. The first was, of course, 1907, when a group of rebels threw off Rugby Union's shackles, joining those who had rebelled in northern England eight years earlier.

The latest upheaval reached its climax on Friday, October 5, 1996, when three Appeal Court judges in Sydney gave Rupert Murdoch's Super League the go-ahead to start its own breakaway from the traditional game, and implement plans for a truly global game, with matches between the top clubs of both Australia and Europe.

What a difference eight months would make! Back in February, the season down-under got underway amid bitter acrimony, with the Australian Rugby League holding all the aces. It finished with an almost fairy-tale ending for St George, which made it through to the Grand Final despite starting the year facing extinction. Then five days later there was the stunning court victory for Super League, and the possibility that in 1997 there would be two competitions vying for the attention of the fans in Australia.

It almost happened in 1996.

Super League had announced a draw for its own competition involving the eight rebel clubs and two new teams, the Hunter Mariners, based in Newcastle, and the Adelaide Rams. And they organised the World Nines in the Fijian capital of Suva with 16 nations taking part. Meanwhile the ARL released its own draw involving all 20 of the clubs which had played in 1995. As it turned out this was the only competition to take place.

The day before the World Nines, Judge James Burchett, gave his ruling in the Super League court case. It proved to be a resounding victory to the ARL. This was never more clear than when he handed down his final orders the following week. They were Draconian.

- No Super League involving the Australian teams anywhere in the world until the year 2000.
- Super League players and coaches banned from playing or coaching anywhere in the world except in the ARL competition.
- Players and coaches not be paid by Super League unless they turned out in the ARL competition.
- Super League clubs to hand over to the ARL all clothing, jumpers, mascots, videos and advertising material.

153

The Season Down Under

- All Super League contracts be legally considered as being held in trust for the ARL (which meant the ARL got every benefit from the contract, while Super League had to pay for them).

Two days later the Full Bench of the Federal Court granted stays on five of Justice Burchett's orders until the appeal was held. This meant that the players and the coaches could not be forced into the ARL competition, and their Super League payments would continue.

The players refused to play for the ARL, and the Super League clubs were forced to forfeit their first round matches. Almost immediately the 311 players announced they would start their own competition, with the help of English Rugby League supremo Maurice Lindsay. It would be called Global League.

Their plans were quickly thwarted by the courts. They were forced into capitulation by the Full Bench of the Federal Court, which made yet another ruling - a return to the provision that if they didn't play in the ARL competition they would not receive the money promised to them by Rupert Murdoch's News Corporation.

And so all 20 teams were back in action - even if a couple of the rebel players (Gorden Tallis and Ian Roberts) never made it onto the field all year.

As it transpired, the full bench of the Appeal Court overruled almost all of Justice Burchett's orders. When the decision was announced he was in Turkey on holiday, prompting ARL chairman Ken Arthurson to note: "I wish I was in Turkey or Tanganyika or anywhere but here. I can't believe for the life of me that we could win 100-nil in the eyes of one judge, and in the eyes of three others virtually lose 100-nil."

Within hours Australian Super League chiefs were meeting with RFL supremo Maurice Lindsay to try to work out the feasibility of a revolutionary global competition, which would see European clubs jetting down under and Aussie sides making reciprocal visits to England and France. The mini-tours would last two or three weeks, and include three or four games.

"It is an opportunity for all of our European Super League clubs to play against the great Australian sides and develop our game," Lindsay explained. "It will accelerate the growth of our game."

The lightning trips were being considered for several reasons:
- They would give the game a higher profile in Europe.
- British coaches and players would get a chance to learn from the best in Australia and eventually match wits with them.
- Australian players on ARL loyalty contracts would be more tempted to jump ship by the lure of overseas travel and international competition.

Lindsay admitted that there could be some lopsided scores in the early days.

"People ask what about Oldham playing the Brisbane Broncos," he said. "I accept that there could be some awful thrashings in the first year or two. That's the price you pay to get ahead.

And just remember, Canberra got some awful thrashings when they first joined the Australian Premiership race."

Lindsay admitted Rugby Union's Super 12s, featuring state and provincial sides from Australia, New Zealand and South Africa, had influenced the decision on the world club series: "They (the Rugby Union chiefs) should be congratulated on their Super 12s. But ours will be bigger and better."

It was perhaps predictable that Manly would win the Optus Cup. But it was very nearly a fairytale finish for the St George Dragons, 100-1 outsiders at the start of the season.

The season was dominated by a Manly side which many critics believe is the best defensive

154

1996 saw another outstanding season for Optus Cup winners Manly
for whom Daniel Gartner is pictured in action

outfit in the 90-year history of the game in Australia. In 25 matches the Sea Eagles only conceded 213 points (an average of just 8.5 a game).

During the last 160 minutes of the season, Manly let in just one try. Yet the Sea Eagles were equally as devastating in attack with 609 points (at an average of 24.4).

One would expect this from a side with 15 internationals - Mark Carroll, Daniel Gartner, David Gillespie, Des Hasler, Solomon Haumono, Terry Hill, John Hopoate, Craig Innes, Nik Kosef, Cliff Lyons, Steve Menzies, Danny Moore, Matthew Ridge, Jim Serdaris and Geoff Toovey - and the Australian coach Bob Fulton.

Although beaten 20-8 in the Grand Final, the St George players could look back on the 1996 season with pride.

The club was in disarray at the start of the year. The Dragons' coach-elect Rod Reddy had defected to the Adelaide Rams. And several of their stars threatened to sit out the season (all except Gorden Tallis eventually relented).

But under new coach David Waite they came home under a wet sail, finishing seventh in the final table before disposing of Canberra (16-14), the Sydney City Roosters (36-16) and North Sydney (29-12) to reach the Grand Final. Sadly, that's when the dream run came to an end, with Manly turning in a sensational defensive effort to take out the inaugural Optus Cup and, with it, the traditional JJ Giltinan Shield.

Another surprise packet in 1996 was Western Suburbs. They were mainly untried young rookies, with a couple of veterans, Paul Langmack and Andrew Leeds, giving them some substance. They were given little hope, but, inspired by coach Tom Raudonikis, they scraped into the top eight and only lost out to Cronulla in the dying minutes of their quarter-final.

There were also some surprising efforts from the unfashionable sides.

The Season Down Under

Super League will accelerate the growth of Rugby League said Maurice Lindsay

The Tigers, with Ellery Hanley, Paul Sironen and Tim Brasher the only name players in their ranks, were still in the Premiership hunt until the last round. The credit for this good showing must lie with coach Wayne Pearce.

The Gold Coast almost folded before the season began. But, once their future was clear, the renamed Chargers were fairly competitive, although they won only five matches. One of their stars was Kiwi Dave Watson, who had a checkered career in Britain, before taking up the captaincy of the Chargers.

Their Queensland cousins, the Crushers, had a disastrous season, taking out the wooden spoon. And as 1996 drew to a close their future was very much up in the air, with $9 million in debts and their creditors demanding payment. These creditors included the players themselves. They were only paid for three of the 22 games.

Another disappointment was Newcastle. The Mal Reilly-coached club had a side containing no less than eight internationals - Jamie Ainscough, Brad Godden, Paul Harragon, Lee Jackson, Andrew and Matthew Johns, Adam Muir and Robbie O'Davis. But it failed to make the top eight play-offs, and ended the year with debts of around $3 million.

The ARL adopted one of the Super League ideas when it scheduled the top game of each round for Monday night. The matches were played before bumper crowds, and in almost every game the result hung in the balance until the closing minutes of play. Twice in Monday Night Football the Roosters drew new club record crowds to the Sydney Football Stadium. The second, when they were lined up against Manly, was the biggest for any match during the year.

Without a doubt the star of the season was Brisbane Broncos' halfback Allan Langer. The Broncos were knocked out of the Optus Cup in the semi-finals, but through no fault of Alfie. Throughout the year when Brisbane had been in trouble it was inevitably a piece of Langer genius which saved the day. It was no surprise that he won almost every individual award except the Rothmans Medal. And the judging in that award (made by the referees) has always

156

Mal Reilly's Newcastle Knights had a disappointing season.
They failed to make the top eight play-offs and ended the year with debts of around $3 million

come in for criticism. Not far behind him was his old Test match partner, stand-off Laurie Daley. Daley held Canberra together after a succession of disastrous injuries to their top players.

Hooker Steve Walters missed the first half of the season. Half Ricky Stuart and loose-forward Bradley Clyde suffered injuries which sidelined them for most of the year. Then there were internationals Jason Croker, David Furner and Ruben Wiki, and boom young Rugby Union convert Ben Kennedy, who also missed a significant part of the season.

Throw in suspensions to Kiwi Test forwards Quentin Pongia and John Lomax, and it seems remarkable that Canberra still made it through to the play-offs.

Daley (and departing coach Tim Sheens) can take credit for that. Next season Mal Meninga will be in the hot seat as the Raiders' coach.

Norths' half and captain Jason Taylor won the Rothmans. Without him, the Bears may not have figured so prominently. Sadly, their long period in the wilderness continues.

Norths have not won a Premiership since 1922, when they were regarded as having one of the best club combinations ever. From their backline, five made the 1921-22 Kangaroo squad which toured Britain.

They included winger Harold Horder, who headed the pointscoring on tour with 127 (35 tries and 11 goals), fellow winger Cec Blinkhorn was second with 117 points from 39 tries (still a Kangaroo record), and halfback Duncan Thompson finished fourth with 107.

Taylor topped the pointscoring table in the Optus Cup with 237. But had Matthew Ridge been there from the start he would have given him a fight.

The Kiwi captain refused to play with Manly until the ninth round, because he wanted to

157

The Season Down Under

join the Auckland Warriors. But he relented, and was a vital cog in the Manly machine which ground its way the Premiership. Ridge's 165 points was the equivalent of 242 points, had he been on the field from the start of the year.

The State of Origin matches saw the return of Super League players (overlooked in the previous year's bitterness), and NSW gained sweet revenge for the 1995 whitewash with a 3-nil victory over the Maroons. The Blues created a record when they played the same squad in every match. Cronulla second-rower Craig Greenhill set an unwanted record, when he became the first player ever sent off in an Origin clash.

The Super League struggle virtually wiped out the international calendar. The ARL had to cancel a Test series against New Zealand when the Super League players refused to play. But a 'Test' against a rebel group of Fijian players went ahead, using players loyal to the ARL. Predictably, the Australians thrashed the part-timers 84-14.

A week after the Grand Final another 'Test' squad, led by Manly's Geoff Toovey, went to Port Moresby to play against a group which had broken away from the Super League-aligned PNGRL. In an intriguing concession, Kumul captain and Roosters halfback Adrian Lam, signed to the ARL, was allowed to play a Test against the touring Great Britain side a week before captaining the second Papua New Guinea combination, the Palais, against the Australians. He scored a try in the opening minutes of the latter game, to give the home side a 6-0 lead, but the professionalism of the Australians soon told, with the tourists winning 52-6.

AUSTRALIAN SCOREBOARD

INTERNATIONALS

AUSTRALIA 84
NATIONAL RUGBY LEAGUE (FIJI)........14

Australia: T - B Dallas 4, S Menzies 2, A Johns 2, T Brasher, B Fittler, M Johns, D Fairleigh, R Wishart, P Harragon, T Hill: G - A Johns 12
NRL: T - N Nailagoliva, M Kunahau: G - S Taga 3
Half-time: 50-2
Referee: David Manson
Attendance: 19,234 at Marathon Stadium (July 12)

PAPUA NEW GUINEA PALAIS 6
AUSTRALIA 52

Palais: T - A Lam; G - T Karu
Australia: T - T Brasher 2, R Wishart 2, M Buettner 2, W Bartrim 2, A Johns; G - A Johns 8
Half-time: 26-6
Referee: Kelvin Jeffes
Attendance: 8,000 at Lloyd Robson Oval, Port Moresby (October 6)

STATE OF ORIGIN SERIES

QUEENSLAND 6
NEW SOUTH WALES 14

Queensland: T - A Langer; G - W Bartrim
NSW: T - A Ettingshausen, S Menzies; G - A Johns 3
Half-time: 0-10
Referee: David Manson
Attendance: 39,348 at Suncorp Stadium (May 20)

NEW SOUTH WALES 18
QUEENSLAND 6

NSW: T - B Mullins 2, R Wishart; G - A Johns 3
Queensland: T - S Renouf; G - J O'Neill
Half-time: 8-6
Referee: David Manson
Attendance: 41,955 at Sydney Football Stadium (June 3)

QUEENSLAND 14
NEW SOUTH WALES 15

Queensland: T - M Coyne, B Dallas: G - W Carne 3
NSW: T - A Ettingshausen, B Mullins: - R Wishart 2, A Johns; DG - B Fittler
Half-time: 2-6
Referee: David Mason
Attendance: 38,217 at Suncorp Stadium (June 17)

Man of the Series: Geoff Toovey (NSW)

OPTUS CUP FINAL TABLE

	P	W	D	L	F	A	Pts
Manly	22	18	-	4	549	191	36
Broncos	21	17	-	4	607	263	34
Norths	22	15	2	5	598	325	32
Roosters	22	15	1	6	521	321	31
Cronulla	21	14	2	5	399	268	30
Canberra	21	13	1	7	538	384	27
St George*	21	12	1	8	443	360	27
Wests	22	12	1	9	394	434	25
Newcastle*	21	10	1	10	416	388	23
Canterbury	21	11	-	0	375	378	22
Warriors*	21	10	-	11	412	427	22
Tigers	22	11	-	11	319	459	22
Parramatta*	21	9	1	11	404	415	21
Illawarra	22	8	-	14	407	440	16
Penrith	21	7	1	13	363	464	15
Western R	21	6	1	14	313	420	13
Cowboys	21	6	-	15	288	643	12
Gold Coast	22	5	1	16	359	521	11
Souths	22	5	1	16	314	634	11
Crushers	22	4	-	18	220	496	8

Two points for a win on forfeit

AUSTRALIAN SCOREBOARD

QUARTER FINALS

CRONULLA SHARKS 20
WESTERN SUBURBS MAGPIES 12
Cronulla: T - P Green 2, P Donaghy;
G - M Rogers 4
Wests: T - P Bell, D Willis; G - A Leeds 2
Half-time: 2-6
Referee: David Manson
Attendance: 22,433 at Parramatta Stadium
(September 6)

CANBERRA RAIDERS 14
ST GEORGE DRAGONS 16
Canberra: B Mullins, S Collins;
G - D Furner 3
St George: W Bartrim, M Bell;
G - W Bartrim 4
Half-time: 8-8
Referee: Kelvin Jeffes
Attendance: 28,185 at Sydney Football
Stadium (September 7)

BRISBANE BRONCOS 16
NORTH SYDNEY BEARS 21
Broncos: T - A Langer 2, R Ross:
G - W Carne 2
Norths: T - M Buettner 2, G Florimo;
G - J Taylor 4; DG - J Taylor
Half-time: 6-13
Referee: Eddie Ward
Attendance: 25,989 at Suncorp Stadium
(September 7)

MANLY SEA EAGLES 16
SYDNEY CITY ROOSTERS 14
Manly: T - J Hopoate, S Menzies, C Innes;
G - M Ridge 2
Roosters: T - B Fittler; G - I Cleary 5
Half-time: 6-4
Referee: Paul McBlane
Attendance: 31,327 at Sydney Football
Stadium (September 8)

SEMI-FINALS

CRONULLA SHARKS 22
BRISBANE BRONCOS 16
Cronulla: T - A Ettingshausen, D Peachey,
R Barnett; G: S Rogers 5
Broncos: T - T Carroll 2, R Ross;
G - D Lockyer 2
Half-time: 14-8
Referee: Kelvin Jeffes
Attendance: 27,665 at Sydney Football
Stadium (September 14)

The Optus Cup

ST GEORGE DRAGONS 36
SYDNEY CITY ROOSTERS 16
St George: T - M Bell 2, A Brunker 2, M
Coyne, A Mundine; G - W Bartrim 6
Roosters: T - D Junee 2, A Lam;
G - I Cleary 2
Half-time: 16-4
Referee: David Manson
Attendance: 37,858 at Sydney Football
Stadium (September 15)

PRELIMINARY FINALS

NORTH SYDNEY BEARS 12
ST GEORGE DRAGONS 29
Norths: T - M Seers, M Soden;
G - J Taylor 2
St George: T - D Raper, A Mundine, W
Bartrim, N Brown, M Bell: G - W Bartrim
4; DG - N Goldthorpe
Half-time: 6-7
Referee: Kelvin Jeffes
Attendance: 37,779 at Sydney Football
Stadium (September 21)

MANLY SEA EAGLES 24
CRONULLA SHARKS 0
Manly: T - S Menzies 2, C Lyons, D
Moore; G - C Innes 3, M Ridge
Half-time: 6-0
Referee: David Manson
Attendance: 41,000 at Sydney Football
Stadium (September 22)

GRAND FINAL

MANLY SEA EAGLES 20
ST GEORGE DRAGONS 8
Manly: T - C Innes, S Menzies, D Moore;
G - M Ridge 3, C Innes
St George: T - N Zisti; G - W Bartrim 2
Half-time: 14-2
Referee: David Manson
Clive Churchill Medal (Man of the Match):
Geoff Toovey (Manly)
Attendance: 40,895 at the Sydney Football
Stadium (September 29)

SEASON'S TOP POINTSCORERS

	T	G	D	Pts
Jason Taylor (Norths)	4	110	1	237
Ivan Cleary (Roosters)	2	83	-	182
Wayne Bartrim (St George)	7	71	-	170
Matthew Ridge (Manly)	7	68	1	165
Ryan Girdler (Penrith)	8	65	-	162
Rod Wishart (Illawarra)	14	52	-	160
Mat Rogers (Cronulla)	8	59	-	150

SEASON'S TOP TRYSCORERS

Noa Nadruku (Canberra) 21
Steve Menzies (Manly) 20
Steve Renouf (Broncos) 19
Ben Ikin (Norths)................................. 15
Darren Junee (Roosters) 15
Darren Smith (Broncos) 14
Brett Dallas (Norths) 14
Rod Wishart (Illawarra) 14

THE INDIVIDUAL AWARDS

Rothmans Medal:
Jason Taylor (Norths)
Dally M Award:
Allan Langer (Broncos)
Rugby League Week Player of the Year:
Allan Langer (Broncos)
Sports Weekly Player of the Year:
Allan Langer (Broncos)
Sky Radio Network Player of the Year:
Allan Langer (Broncos)
Norwich Rising Star:
Ben Kennedy (Canberra)

3
STATISTICAL REVIEW

BRADFORD BULLS

DATE	FIXTURE	RESULT	SCORERS	LGE	ATT
31/3/96	Castleford(h)	W30-18	t:Donougher(3),Paul(2),Calland g:Loughlin(3)	N/A	10,027
5/4/96	Sheffield(a)	L40-24	t:Calland(2),Nickle,Lowes g:Cook(4)	6th	5,202
8/4/96	London(h)	W31-24	t:Paul(2),Dwyer,Fairbank g:Cook(7) dg:Cook	5th	7,192
14/4/96	St Helens(a)	L26-20	t:Calland(3),Scales g:McNamara(2)	7th	10,010
19/4/96	Wigan(a)	L22-6	t:Loughlin g:Cook	8th	9,872
27/4/96	St Helens(a)	L40-32(CCF)	t:Scales,Paul(3),Dwyer g:Cook(6)	N/A	75,994
5/5/96	Warrington(h)	W36-14	t:Loughlin,Scales,Calland,Paul,Bradley,Medley,Knox g:Cook(4)	7th	9,278
10/5/96	Oldham(a)	W30-10	t:Scales(2),Loughlin,McDermott,Dwyer,Bradley g:McNamara(2),Cook	6th	4,228
19/5/96	Paris(h)	W60-32	t:Fairbank(2),Hassan,Donougher,Dwyer,Loughlin,Paul,Medley,Scales, Tomlinson,Bradley g:McNamara(8)	5th	8,194
24/5/96	Leeds(h)	W54-8	t:Lowes(2),Spruce(2),McDermott,Scales,McNamara,Fairbank,Bradley g:McNamara(9)	3rd	10,229
2/6/96	Workington(h)	W52-4	t:Calland(2),Hassan,Paul,Spruce,Tamani,Lowes,Medley,Tomlinson, Cook g:Cook(6)	3rd	8,658
9/6/96	Halifax(a)	W22-20	t:Spruce,Paul,Lowes,Calland g:McNamara(3)	3rd	7,187
16/6/96	Castleford(a)	L26-23	t:Donougher,Spruce,Cook,Dwyer g:McNamara(3) dg:McNamara	3rd	6,275
23/6/96	Sheffield(h)	W64-22	t:McDermott,Spruce,Loughlin,Paul(2),Scales(2),Lowes,Donougher, Medley,Tomlinson g:McNamara(7),Cook	3rd	8,359
29/6/96	London(a)	W22-16	t:Scales,Paul,Dwyer g:McNamara(5)	3rd	3,814
5/7/96	St Helens(h)	W50-22	t:Bradley(2),Loughlin,Nickle,Tamani,Donougher,Spruce,Scales,Knox g:McNamara(7)	3rd	11,467
12/7/96	Wigan(h)	W20-12	t:Medley,Dwyer,Scales(2) g:McNamara(2)	3rd	17,360
20/7/96	Warrington(a)	W30-20	t:Calland,McDermott,Dwyer,Bradley g:McNamara(7)	3rd	8,423
28/7/96	Oldham(h)	W56-0	t:Paul(3),Bradley,Tomlinson,Lowes,Nickle,Tamani(2),Loughlin g:McNamara(8)	3rd	9,849
4/8/96	Leeds(a)	W56-18	t:Paul(3),Loughlin(2),Cook,Lowes,McDermott,Nickle,Medley g:McNamara(6),Cook(2)	3rd	10,505
11/8/96	Workington(a)	W28-14	t:Spruce,Donougher,Cook,Paul,Lowes g:McNamara(4)	3rd	2,430
18/8/96	Halifax(h)	L27-26	t:Spruce(2),Bradley,Nickle,Calland g:McNamara(2),Cook	3rd	13,196
24/8/96	Paris(a)	W27-14	t:Bradley,Dwyer,Lowes(2),Spruce g:McNamara(3) dg:McNamara	3rd	6,152
31/8/96	Wigan(a)	L42-36(PSF)	t:Bradley(3),Paul(2),Calland,Tomlinson g:McNamara(4)	N/A	9,878

SCORERS...League games only

	APP	T	G	DG	PTS
Graeme Bradley	21(1)	10	0	0	40
Matt Calland	22	12	0	0	48
Paul Cook	8(6)	4	27	1	71
Jeremy Donougher	18(1)	8	0	0	32
Bernard Dwyer	18(3)	8	0	0	32
Karl Fairbank	17(2)	4	0	0	16
Carlos Hassan	6(4)	2	0	0	8
Simon Knox	2(9)	2	0	0	8
Paul Loughlin	17(3)	9	3	0	42
James Lowes	22	11	0	0	44
Brian McDermott	22	5	0	0	20
Steve McNamara	20	1	78	2	162
Paul Medley	1(17)	6	0	0	24
Sonny Nickle	9(9)	5	0	0	20
Robbie Paul	22	18	0	0	72
Jonathan Scales	19	12	0	0	48
Stuart Spruce	14	12	0	0	48
Joe Tamani	11(3)	4	0	0	16
Glen Tomlinson	7(11)	4	0	0	16

LEAGUE RECORD
P22-W17-D0-L05
(3rd, SL)
F767, A409, Diff+358
34 points.

ATTENDANCES
Best - v Wigan (17,360)
Worst - v London (7,192)
Total - 113,809
Average - 10,346
(Up by 5,753 on
Centenary season)

TOP TACKLER
James Lowes - 649

TOP BUSTS
Robbie Paul - 80

TOP METRE GAINER
Brian McDermott - 2328

Joe Tamani -
four tries

162

Brian McDermott

There were so many highlights in 1996.

From a Bradford supporters point of view, the wins against St Helens and Wigan in successive weeks will live in the memories for a long time to come.

At that point in the season we'd have given any team in the world a good run.

That seems like big talk but it's true. We were working with each other so well and the build up was just right.

Saints were never in the game and we played with great flair. The week after against Wigan we showed we could dig deep and drew on grit and determination.

The crowds have been brilliant, and that 17,500 for the Wigan game was amazing. I get more nervous now playing at Odsal than anywhere else.

I wouldn't swop Wembley for anything else, although I'd like to change my silver medal for a gold one. We'd played Saints in the league the week before the Final and to be 14 points up, we couldn't believe it.

When I look back it was disappointing. We didn't ease off, in fact we stepped up a gear. To lose like that was like having your heart ripped out - I just could not speak to anybody for days.

But it wasn't really a low point. On the field that came at Castleford. It was a hot still day and I struggled with the heat and it was a disappointing defeat.

The real low point was when Smithy (coach Brian Smith) told us he was leaving.

He told us on the Saturday morning, the day after we beat Saints. I thought he was going to tell us he wasn't going. A lot of the lads were stunned. Nobody said a word.

But Matthew Elliott teaches the same kind of coaching principles and it is up to the players to give him as much respect as they gave to Brian Smith.

He's put so much work in with individual players over the last year, I think he's already got a lot of respect anyway.

As for players of the year, Robbie Paul is an outstanding individual, he's got the world at his feet. I think you have got to mention Graeme Bradley, too. When he first came to the club, I thought, what an earth has this guy come over for - he couldn't even do sit ups. But I think his performances on the field speak for themselves.

But every single player has upgraded their game.

We were very rarely been outmuscled in the pack - credit to the Castleford pack, they got the better of us that day.

CASTLEFORD TIGERS

DATE	FIXTURE	RESULT	SCORERS	LGE	ATT
31/3/96	Bradford(a)	L30-18	t:T Smith(2),Crooks g:Botica(3)	N/A	10,027
5/4/96	Leeds(h)	W26-23	t:Botica,J Flowers,Gay,Russell,Schick g:Botica(3)	7th	7,179
9/4/96	Halifax(a)	W34-30	t:Smales(2),J Flowers,Goddard,T Smith,Tuuta g:Goddard(4),Botica	6th	4,791
14/4/96	Wigan(h)	L28-10	t:T Smith g:Goddard(3)	9th	7,985
20/4/96	Oldham(h)	L24-20	t:Flynn,Sampson,Smales g:Botica(4)	9th	4,396
3/5/96	Sheffield(a)	L20-12	t:C Smith,Schick g:Botica(2)	9th	5,486
12/5/96	Workington(h)	W50-16	t:Flynn(2),Tonks,Schick,Harland,Steadman,Tuuta,T Smith g:Botica(9)	8th	3,605
19/5/96	London(h)	L21-20	t:J Flowers,C Smith,Middleton g:Botica(3),Crooks	8th	3,489
27/5/96	St Helens(a)	L62-24	t:Steadman,Schick,T Smith,Middleton g:Botica(4)	9th	8,239
31/5/96	Warrington(h)	L22-17	t:Paramore,Edwards,Flynn g:Botica(2) dg:Botica	9th	2,874
7/6/96	Paris(a)	W54-22	t:Flynn,Chapman,Botica,Schick,Steadman,C Smith,Anderson,J Flowers,Maskill g:Botica(8),Maskill	8th	6,618
16/6/96	Bradford(h)	W26-23	t:J Flowers,Flynn,Botica,Chapman g:Botica(5)	7th	6,275
22/6/96	Leeds(a)	L25-18	t:Flynn,Chapman,J Flowers g:Botica(3)	8th	6,242
30/6/96	Halifax(h)	L24-20	t:J Flowers(2),Anderson g:Botica(4)	9th	4,194
5/7/96	Wigan(a)	L26-25	t:Crooks,T Smith,Tuuta,Paramore g:Botica(4) dg:Botica	9th	8,180
14/7/96	Oldham(a)	W30-20	t:T Smith,Middleton,Flynn,C Smith,Paramore g:Botica(5)	9th	3,480
21/7/96	Sheffield(h)	W36-31	t:Schick,C Smith(3), Middleton,Chapman g:Botica(6)	9th	4,524
28/7/96	Workington(a)	W46-20	t:Middleton,C Smith(2),Smales(2),Richardson,Harland g:Botica(9)	7th	1,622
2/8/96	St Helens(h)	L20-16	t:J Flowers,T Smith g:Botica(4)	9th	6,143
10/8/96	Warrington(a)	L38-24	t:Flynn,Botica,Schick,T Smith,Goddard g:Botica(2)	9th	4,277
17/8/96	Paris(h)	W22-18	t:Gay,Chapman,Botica,J Flowers g:Botica(3)	8th	4,473
25/8/96	London(a)	L56-0	No Scorers	9th	3,500

SCORERS...League games only

	APP	T	G	DG	PTS
Grant Anderson	10(1)	2	0	0	8
Frano Botica	21	5	84	2	190
David Chapman	13(1)	5	0	0	20
Lee Crooks	19(1)	2	1	0	10
Diccon Edwards	10(2)	1	0	0	4
Jason Flowers	16(5)	10	0	0	40
Adrian Flynn	17(1)	9	0	0	36
Richard Gay	4(6)	2	0	0	8
Richard Goddard	8(3)	2	7	0	22
Lee Harland	12(3)	2	0	0	8
Colin Maskill	8	1	1	0	6
Simon Middleton	8(3)	5	0	0	20
Junior Paramore	5(5)	3	0	0	12
Shaun Richardson	1(6)	1	0	0	4
Richard Russell	10(2)	1	0	0	4
Dean Sampson	8(9)	1	0	0	4
Andrew Schick	19(2)	7	0	0	28
Ian Smales	10(4)	5	0	0	20
Chris Smith	20	9	0	0	36
Tony Smith	18(1)	10	0	0	40
Graham Steadman	6(5)	3	0	0	12
Ian Tonks	1(2)	1	0	0	4
Brendon Tuuta	21	3	0	0	12

LEAGUE RECORD
P22-W9-D0-L13
(9th, SL)
F548, A599, Diff -51
18 points.

ATTENDANCES
Best - v Wigan (7,985)
Worst - v Warrington (2,874)
Total - 55,137
Average - 5,012
(Up by 940 on
Centenary season)

TOP TACKLER
Nathan Sykes - 576

TOP BUSTS
Chris Smith - 77

TOP METRE GAINER
Andrew Schick - 2233

Frano Botica -
top points scorer

Tony Smith

It was a very disappointing end to the season from a team point of view.

We finished in ninth position in the table but there were so many games we could have won that we didn't. Up until the last game of the season there was only St Helens that had really beaten us fair and square.

But that last game at London Broncos wasn't a good way to finish the season. I was lucky because I got on the tour and I'll have other games to think about over the off-season. But for every body else it's always the last game you've played that sticks in your mind. It was a terrible performance.

People say it was because we had nothing to play for and that the Broncos had to win it to get into the top four play-offs but that is a load a rubbish. As professionals, under the public glare, you need to perform well whenever you play.

We really did throw a lot of games away. One that springs to mind is the game against Wigan at Wheldon Road which we were in a position to win.

We also had a couple of games that were taken away from us, for example that game against Warrington. And that incident against Wigan where I was sin-binned in injury time for not handing the ball over - it wasn't even the last tackle. The video clearly shows that. The referee (Aussie Stephen Clark) didn't have another game after that.

That was our biggest let down.

As a team, our best performance was against Bradford at Wheldon Road - and I wasn't playing (Smith was recovering from an operation on his hand). It was their first defeat since Wembley. Next up would be the win against Paris over there.

But we only showed at times what we were capable of doing.

When we really dug in and played for each other we showed what we could do - look at the game early on at Halifax. We must have been twenty down at one point but we came through, so we have got character and we've got some good players.

We set off at the start of the season thinking we could get into the top four but looking back now we needed to add a couple of more signings to have a chance.

The young lads in the Academy are really good but whether they are ready to come into first grade yet, I don't know. The crowds have been disappointing but I think the fans were frustrated by so many players leaving and not being replaced.

A couple of signings could change all that for 1997.

HALIFAX BLUE SOX

DATE	FIXTURE	RESULT	SCORERS	LGE	ATT
30/3/96	London(h)	L24-22	t:Baldwin,Schuster,Umaga,M Jackson g:Schuster(3)	N/A	4,773
5/4/96	Oldham(a)	L34-22	t:Dean(2),Ekoku,Hallas g:Umaga(3)	11th	3,932
9/4/96	Castleford(h)	L34-30	t:Moana(2),P Anderson,Dean,Umaga g:Schuster(5)	10th	4,791
12/4/96	Warrington(a)	L16-10	t:Amone,W Jackson g:Schuster	10th	3,721
21/4/96	St Helens(h)	L30-28	t:Schuster(2),Baldwin,Perrett g:Schuster(6)	11th	6,260
6/5/96	Workington(a)	D18-18	t:Bentley(2),M Jackson g:Schuster(3)	11th	2,214
14/5/96	Wigan(h)	L50-4	t:Tuilagi	11th	5,269
19/5/96	Leeds(a)	W32-18	t:Dean(2),Umaga,Rowley,Bentley g:Schuster(6)	11th	10,028
27/5/96	Paris(a)	W38-10	t:Amone(3),Gillespie(2),Bentley,Hallas,Highton g:Schuster(3)	10th	5,832
2/6/96	Sheffield(h)	W33-30	t:Baldwin(2),Seal,Perrett(2),Ekoku g:Schuster(4) dg:Rowley	7th	4,287
9/6/96	Bradford(a)	L22-20	t:Ekoku,Amone,Briggs g:Schuster(4)	9th	7,187
16/6/96	London(a)	W52-24	t:Bentley(2),Umaga,Schuster,Gillespie,Tuilagi,Moana g:Schuster(8)	8th	3,200
23/6/96	Oldham(h)	L20-14	t:Ekoku,Schuster,Hallas g:Schuster	9th	4,591
30/6/96	Castleford(a)	W24-20	t:Bentley(2),M Jackson,Moana,Rowley g:Schuster(2)	8th	4,194
7/7/96	Warrington(h)	W25-18	t:Bentley,Moana(2) g:Schuster(6) dg:Schuster	8th	4,247
14/7/96	St Helens(a)	L58-20	t:Bentley,Schuster,Hallas g:Schuster(4)	8th	9,283
21/7/96	Workington(h)	W74-14	t:Umaga(5),Baldwin(2),Hallas,Tuilagi,Brewer,Dean,Bentley(2) g:Schuster(11)	7th	4,374
26/7/96	Wigan(a)	L34-26	t:Schuster,Dean,Baldwin,Tuilagi g:Schuster(5)	8th	8,221
4/8/96	Paris(h)	W56-10	t:Tuilagi,Moana(2),Rowley(2),Munro(2),Bentley(2),Umaga g:Schuster(8)	7th	4,819
11/8/96	Sheffield(a)	L42-28	t:Bentley,Baldwin(2),Amone g:Schuster(6)	7th	3,201
18/8/96	Bradford(a)	W27-26	t:Umaga(2),Perrett,Schuster g:Schuster(5) dg:Schuster	7th	13,196
25/8/96	Leeds(h)	W64-24	t:Bentley(4),Dean(2),Umaga,Ekoku,Brewer,Moana,Amone g:Schuster(10)	6th	5,287

SCORERS...League games only

	APP	T	G	DG	PTS
Asa Amone	17(4)	7	0	0	28
Paul Anderson	5(1)	1	0	0	4
Simon Baldwin	18(1)	9	0	0	36
John Bentley	18(1)	21	0	0	84
Johnny Brewer	4(2)	2	0	0	8
Carl Briggs	5(3)	1	0	0	4
Craig Dean	14(3)	9	0	0	36
Abi Ekoku	15(1)	5	0	0	20
Carl Gillespie	11(9)	3	0	0	12
Graeme Hallas	11(4)	5	0	0	20
Paul Highton	3(10)	1	0	0	4
Michael Jackson	9(4)	3	0	0	12
Wayne Jackson	6(1)	1	0	0	4
Martin Moana	13(3)	9	0	0	36
Damien Munro	2	2	0	0	8
Mark Perrett	15(3)	4	0	0	16
Paul Rowley	20(1)	4	0	1	17
John Schuster	21	8	101	2	236
Danny Seal	2(5)	1	0	0	4
Fereti Tuilagi	15(3)	5	0	0	20
Mike Umaga	18(1)	13	3	0	58

LEAGUE RECORD
P22-W10-D1-L11
(6th, SL)
F667, A576, Diff +91
21 points.

ATTENDANCES
Best - v Bradford (7,187)
Worst - v Warrington (4,247)
Total - 55,885
Average - 5,080
(Up by 423 on
Centenary season)

TOP TACKLER
Paul Rowley - 482

TOP BUSTS
Paul Rowley - 79

TOP METRE GAINER
John Bentley - 2764

John Bentley -
21 tries

Craig Dean

The thing that sticks in my mind the most was those opening seven games when we couldn't get a win.

The league table didn't look that promising by the middle of May.

We thought we should have won a lot of those games but we seemed to be losing every one by just a couple of points.

Even in the big midweek defeat by Wigan at Thrum Hall, we played okay. Once you dig yourself into a hole it is very hard to get out of it.

We always knew we would start winning games but the luck didn't go our way.

I missed four or five games with a shoulder injury which was a bit disappointing, but once the season got going it went well for us.

We kept plugging away and we knew that a win was going to come but to be honest we expected it a lot sooner.

Once we started winning it was like setting a ball rolling.

And when we beat Bradford at Bradford at the end of the season, that was the big one for us. John Schuster dropped a late goal to win - it was made sweeter by it being their first home defeat of the season.

For me personally the low point came before the season even started when we lost to Leeds in the quarter-final of the Challenge Cup.

All the imports had a big impact at Thrum Hall, especially Martin Moana. And Paul Rowley and Karl Harrison had big seasons up front. Everybody played okay it's just that we couldn't win in those early weeks.

The news of the move from Thrum Hall could be very exciting. I know some of the fans are upset but it's all for the good of the game and of the club.

I was disappointed with the level of the support - I suppose it was because of that opening run of defeats, but if we can get off to a good start in 1997, I'm sure that the fan-base will grow, especially if the stadium development takes place in time.

LEEDS

DATE	FIXTURE	RESULT	SCORERS	LGE	ATT
31/3/96	Warrington(h)	L22-18	t:Iro,Mann,Fozzard g:Holroyd(3)	N/A	10,036
5/4/96	Castleford(a)	L26-23	t:Shaw(2),Cummins,Iro g:Holroyd(3) dg:A Gibbons	10th	7,179
8/4/96	St Helens(h)	L46-24	t:Cummins(2),Fallon,Hassan g:Holroyd(3),Cummins	11th	11,848
13/4/96	Oldham(a)	L25-16	t:Fallon,Iro(2) g:Holroyd(2)	11th	3,350
21/4/96	Sheffield(h)	W36-22	t:Fallon,Holroyd(2),Mercer,D Gibbons(2),A Gibbons g:Holroyd(3),Cummins	10th	9,039
5/5/96	London(h)	L27-20	t:Cummins,Iro,Mercer g:Holroyd(4)	10th	9,000
10/5/96	Paris(a)	W40-14	t:Fallon(2),Morley(2),Iro(2),Cummins,Holroyd g:Holroyd(4)	10th	15,107
19/5/96	Halifax(h)	L32-18	t:A Gibbons,Holroyd,Shaw g:Holroyd(3)	10th	10,028
24/5/96	Bradford(a)	L54-8	t:Cummins,Hall	10th	10,229
1/6/96	Wigan(h)	L40-20	t:Holroyd(2),Mann,Cummins g:Holroyd(2)	11th	9,508
9/6/96	Workington(a)	W48-18	t:Kemp(2),Holroyd(2),Golden,Morley,Mercer,Clark g:Holroyd(8)	10th	2,949
14/6/96	Warrington(a)	L36-12	t:Harmon,Hassan g:Holroyd(2)	10th	5,580
22/6/96	Castleford(h)	W25-18	t:McDermott,Hall,Mercer,Golden g:Holroyd(4) dg:Holroyd	10th	6,242
30/6/96	St Helens(a)	L42-16	t:Fozzard,McDermott,Mercer g:Holroyd,Tuipuloto	10th	8,702
7/7/96	Oldham(h)	L28-26	t:Tait,Clark(2),Hall g:Holroyd(5)	10th	6,754
14/7/96	Sheffield(a)	L34-31	t:Golden(2),Mercer,Hulme,Tuipuloto g:Holroyd(5) dg:Holroyd	10th	4,265
21/7/96	London(a)	L33-16	t:Hulme,St Hilaire,Forshaw g:Holroyd(2)	10th	3,900
28/7/96	Paris(h)	W34-12	t:Holroyd(2),Kemp,Shaw,Bell g:Holroyd(7)	10th	6,479
4/8/96	Bradford(h)	L56-18	t:Hughes(2),Handley(2) g:Tuipuloto	10th	10,505
9/8/96	Wigan(a)	L68-14	t:Forshaw(2) g:Holroyd(3)	10th	7,814
18/8/96	Workington(h)	W68-28	t:Hughes(2),Mercer,Holroyd,Shaw(2),Golden,Brown,Iro(2),McDermott,Fozzard g:Holroyd(10)	10th	4,956
25/8/96	Halifax(a)	L64-24	t:Forshaw(2),Hassan,Shaw g:Holroyd(2),Brown(2)	10th	5,287

SCORERS...League games only

	APP	T	G	DG	PTS
Dean Bell	1	1	0	0	4
Gavin Brown	3(2)	1	2	0	8
Dean Clark	11(2)	3	0	0	12
Francis Cummins	12	7	2	0	32
Jim Fallon	10	5	0	0	20
Mike Forshaw	11(3)	5	0	0	20
Nick Fozzard	6(12)	3	0	0	12
Anthony Gibbons	9(4)	2	0	1	9
David Gibbons	3(4)	2	0	0	8
Marvin Golden	11(3)	5	0	0	20
Carl Hall	7(2)	3	0	0	12
Paddy Handley	1(1)	2	0	0	8
Neil Harmon	10	1	0	0	4
Phil Hassan	17(4)	3	0	0	12
Graham Holroyd	20(1)	11	76	2	198
Adam Hughes	4(1)	4	0	0	16
David Hulme	8(1)	2	0	0	8
Kevin Iro	16	9	0	0	36
Tony Kemp	6(1)	3	0	0	12
George Mann	11(4)	2	0	0	8
Barrie McDermott	15(7)	3	0	0	12
Gary Mercer	17(2)	7	0	0	28
Adrian Morley	16(1)	3	0	0	12
Mick Shaw	12(2)	7	0	0	28
Marcus St Hilaire	6	1	0	0	4
Alan Tait	3(3)	1	0	0	4
Sateki Tuipuloto	6(3)	1	2	0	8

LEAGUE RECORD
P22-W6-D0-L16
(10th, SL)
F555, A745, Diff -190
12 points.

ATTENDANCES
Best - v St Helens (11,848)
Worst - v Workington (4,956)
Total - 94,395
Average - 8,581
(Down by 3,013 on
Centenary season)

TOP TACKLER
Gary Mercer - 420

TOP BUSTS
Barrie McDermott - 86

TOP METRE GAINER
Barrie McDermott - 2294

Barrie McDermott -
three tries

168

Adrian Morley

We lost a lot of experienced players and it was a case of blooding a lot of the young players.

And some of them came through. The young lads have really played well.

There's a lot of players for the future at Headingley - Gavin Brown didn't play that many games but when he did he played really well.

Dean Bell has been forced to throw everybody in at the deep end because we lost five or six world class players in a short space of time. That is going to affect any team.

It was a big burden on the young players but I think they have come through alright.

The trip to France to play Paris Saint-Germain was memorable. For a start it was my birthday.

It wasn't in my mind but I scored a couple of tries and it was a pretty good night all round.

We had plenty of lows.

In most games we seemed to be able to get ourselves into winning positions and then let it slip.

The game near the end of the season at Wigan was a good example. We had them at 14-4 after half an hour but then let them run away with it. We just didn't seem able to concentrate for the full eighty minutes.

We looked the better side at Bradford for twenty minutes, too, but then we let it slip and took another hammering.

David Hulme's arrival mid-season was a boost. He's a great worker and tackler and never stops talking in the middle of the park.

This season I just wanted to cement my place in the team at Leeds and everything happened so quickly - too quickly really.

Dean Bell has been a great help, he's always pulling us to one side and talking to me.

Towards the end of the season I thought Barrie McDermott was playing at the top of his game.

Realistically we still need to buy three more players. If we do, the potential of Leeds is enormous. The club has very high standards. I'm sure we can lift it again next year.

LONDON BRONCOS

DATE	FIXTURE	RESULT	SCORERS	LGE	ATT
30/3/96	Halifax(a)	W24-22	t:Rea,Pitt,Carroll,Shaw g:Barwick(4)	N/A	4,773
4/4/96	Paris(h)	W38-22	t:Myer,McCrae(2),Tollett(2),Dynevor,Paul g:Barwick(4),Dynevor	3rd	9,638
8/4/96	Bradford(a)	L31-24	t:Roskell(2),Gill,Tollett g:Dynevor(4)	4th	7,192
14/4/96	Sheffield(a)	L34-18	t:Gill,Matterson,Smith g:Matterson(3)	8th	3,888
21/4/96	Workington(h)	W58-0	t:Bryant,Roskell,Matterson,Bawden,Rea,Tollett,Mestrov,Pitt,Cochrane g:Matterson(11)	5th	4,138
5/5/96	Leeds(a)	W27-20	t:Gill(2),Tollett(2),Rea g:Matterson,Dynevor(2) dg:McCrae	3rd	9,000
12/5/96	St Helens(a)	L24-22	t:Barwick(2),Minto,Roskell g:Barwick(3)	4th	7,225
19/5/96	Castleford(a)	W21-20	t:Tollett,Minto,Barwick,Gill g:Barwick(2) dg:Barwick	3rd	3,489
25/5/96	Warrington(a)	L28-24	t:Matterson,Roskell,Barwick,Shaw g:Barwick(4)	5th	3,772
2/6/96	Oldham(a)	W28-22	t:Barwick,Maguire,Strutton,Matterson g:Barwick(5),Matterson	5th	4,629
9/6/96	Wigan(a)	D18-18	t:Minto,Matterson,Strutton g:Matterson(3)	5th	9,189
16/6/96	Halifax(h)	L52-24	t:Maguire(2),Rosolen,Minto g:Maguire(4)	5th	3,200
23/6/96	Workington(a)	W34-6	t:R Allen(2),Tollett,Rosolen,Mestrov,Pitt g:Matterson(3),Maguire(2)	5th	1,400
29/6/96	Bradford(h)	L22-16	t:Rea,Dynevor(2) g:Matterson(2)	5th	3,814
6/7/96	Sheffield(h)	W45-8	t:Barwick(3),Rosolen,Maguire(2),Tollett,R Allen g:Maguire(6) dg:Pitt	5th	3,572
13/7/96	Paris(a)	L24-18	t:Maguire,Barwick(2),Langer g:Barwick	5th	9,840
21/7/96	Leeds(h)	W33-16	t:Tollett,Rosolen,Barwick,Shaw,Bawden g:Barwick(6) dg:Barwick	5th	3,900
27/7/96	St Helens(h)	L32-28	t:Bawden,Roskell(2),Rosolen g:Barwick(6)	5th	6,286
4/8/96	Warrington(h)	W20-13	t:McCrae,Barwick,Pitt g:Barwick(4)	4th	6,903
11/8/96	Oldham(a)	W22-14	t:Offiah(2),Mestrov,Krause g:Barwick(3)	4th	2,327
17/8/96	Wigan(h)	L34-13	t:T Martin,Offiah g:Barwick(2) dg:T Martin	5th	10,014
25/8/96	Castleford(h)	W56-0	t:Barwick(4),Dynevor(2),Gill(2),Krause,T Martin,Maguire g:Barwick(6)	4th	3,500
1/9/96	St Helens(a)	L25-14(PSF)	t:Strutton(2) g:Barwick(3)	N/A	9,250

SCORERS...League games only

	APP	T	G	DG	PTS
Ray Allen	5(3)	3	0	0	12
Greg Barwick	15	16	50	2	166
Russell Bawden	8(12)	3	0	0	12
Justin Bryant	7(8)	1	0	0	4
Bernard Carroll	2(1)	1	0	0	4
Evan Cochrane	5(1)	1	0	0	4
Leo Dynevor	8(11)	5	7	0	34
Peter Gill	16	7	0	0	28
David Krause	5	2	0	0	8
Kevin Langer	12(4)	2	0	0	8
Mark Maguire	10(3)	7	12	0	52
Tony Martin	8	2	0	1	9
Terry Matterson	12	5	24	0	68
Duncan McCrae	11(2)	3	0	1	13
Tony Mestrov	21(1)	3	0	0	12
John Minto	13	4	0	0	16
Kieran Myer	4	1	0	0	4
Martin Offiah	4	3	0	0	12
Junior Paul	3	1	0	0	4
Darryl Pitt	2(16)	4	0	1	17
Tony Rea	22	4	0	0	16
Scott Roskell	12	7	0	0	28
Steve Rosolen	10(6)	5	0	0	20
Darren Shaw	19(2)	3	0	0	12
Danny Smith	2(1)	1	0	0	4
Graham Strutton	9(1)	2	0	0	8
Tulsen Tollett	22	9	0	0	36

LEAGUE RECORD
P22-W12-D1-L9
(4th, SL)
F611, A462, Diff +149
25 points.

ATTENDANCES
Best - v Wigan (10,014)
Worst - v Halifax (3,200)
Total - 59,594
Average - 5,418
(Up by 3,032 on
Centenary season)

TOP TACKLER
Tony Rea - 741

TOP BUSTS
Russell Bawden - 51

TOP METRE GAINER
Tony Mestrov - 3722

Martin Offiah -
three tries since his
move from Wigan

Tulsen Tollett

It was a good season for us, one in which we cemented our place in Super League and proved to everyone that we deserved to be in there.

The highlight would have to be the 18-18 draw at Wigan, but making the top four was our major target. Our goal was to make the top six, and once we had established ourselves there we pushed on to make the top four.

We knew we had the players to do it. We were a little inconsistent but the injuries we picked up didn't help.

Without doubt the lowpoint was the defeat in Paris. We went with perhaps a lacksadaisical attitude and were a little overconfident. Too many of us were looking forward to seeing the sights rather than doing the job on the field.

The two games against St Helens were disappointing also. At Knowsley Road we were 22-8 ahead but fell asleep for ten minutes. It was a similar situation at The Valley, where a couple of dubious decisions went against us.

Tony Mestrov and Peter Gill had an outstanding year. Mestrov didn't miss a game for us and took us forward the whole time. Tony Rea had a great season too, but Gill was the one who I would pick out as being our top performer.

As for the future, we hope to build on fourth place and with a bit of luck and a couple of new players there is no reason why we can't challenge for the major honours.

A lot has happened during the year to make the club more professional. Most of the squad has been retained and of course we have Martin Offiah on board now who will be a great promotional aide.

I know the plan is to move towards making the Broncos a team of mainly English players, and we need to sort out a permanent ground we can call home.

If that happens, I predict the Broncos will be a major force in the British game for many years to come.

OLDHAM BEARS

DATE	FIXTURE	RESULT	SCORERS	LGE	ATT
30/3/96	Wigan(h)	L56-16	t:Abram,Myler,Maloney g:Maloney(2)	N/A	7,709
5/4/96	Halifax(h)	W34-22	t:Abram(2),Atcheson,Crompton,Myler,Patmore g:Maloney(5)	9th	3,932
8/4/96	Paris(a)	D24-24	t:Abram,Maloney,Munro,Patmore g:Maloney(4)	9th	6,327
13/4/96	Leeds(h)	W25-16	t:Atcheson,Patmore,Crompton(2) g:Maloney(4) dg:Crompton	6th	3,350
20/4/96	Castleford(a)	W24-20	t:Maloney,Abram,Atcheson(2) g:Maloney(4)	4th	4,396
5/5/96	St Helens(a)	L66-18	t:Faimalo,Abram,Davidson g:Maloney,Topping(2)	6th	10,181
10/5/96	Bradford(h)	L30-10	t:Bradbury,Munro g:Maloney	7th	4,228
19/5/96	Sheffield(a)	L23-10	t:Munro g:Topping(2),Gartland	7th	3,200
26/5/96	Workington(h)	L29-27	t:Belle(2),Clark,Atcheson g:Maloney(5) dg:Crompton	8th	2,228
2/6/96	London(a)	L28-22	t:Faimalo,Topping,Myler,Davidson g:Maloney,Topping(2)	8th	4,629
9/6/96	Warrington(h)	W35-24	t:Abram,Sherratt,Myler,Bradbury,Belle g:Topping(7) dg:Crompton	7th	3,243
16/6/96	Wigan(a)	L44-16	t:Atcheson(2),Crompton g:Topping(2)	9th	7,226
23/6/96	Halifax(a)	W20-14	t:Crompton,Bradbury(2),Clarke g:Topping,Maloney	7th	4,591
28/6/96	Paris(h)	W24-6	t:Crompton,Belle,Faimalo(2),Clarke g:Maloney(2)	7th	2,548
7/7/96	Leeds(a)	W28-26	t:Munro(2),Maloney(2),Temu g:Maloney(2),Topping(2)	6th	6,754
14/7/96	Castleford(h)	L30-20	t:Hill,Ranson,Atcheson,Crompton g:Maloney(2)	7th	3,480
19/7/96	St Helens(h)	L54-18	t:Ranson,McKinney,Belle g:Maloney(3)	8th	4,354
28/7/96	Bradford(a)	L56-0	No Scorers	9th	9,849
4/8/96	Workington(a)	W30-24	t:Atcheson,Maloney,Bradbury(2),Belle,Abram g:Maloney(3)	8th	1,759
11/8/96	London(h)	L22-14	t:Davidson,Crompton,Belle g:Maloney	8th	2,327
16/8/96	Warrington(a)	L42-24	t:Belle,Neal(2),Crompton g:Maloney(3),Crook	9th	3,800
25/8/96	Sheffield(h)	W34-25	t:Ranson(3),Atcheson(2),Burns,Bradbury g:Maloney,Crook(2)	8th	2,515

SCORERS...League games only

	APP	T	G	DG	PTS
Darren Abram	14(1)	8	0	0	32
Paul Atcheson	21	11	0	0	44
Adrian Belle	19	8	0	0	32
David Bradbury	16(3)	7	0	0	28
Gary Burns	6	1	0	0	4
John Clarke	16	3	0	0	12
Martin Crompton	19	9	0	3	39
Paul Crook	4(9)	0	3	0	6
Paul Davidson	5(11)	3	0	0	12
Joe Faimalo	17(5)	4	0	0	16
Steve Gartland	1(1)	0	1	0	2
Howard Hill	7(6)	1	0	0	4
Francis Maloney	18(1)	6	45	0	114
Chris McKinney	(4)	1	0	0	4
Matt Munro	16(3)	5	0	0	20
Rob Myler	11	4	0	0	16
Mike Neal	2(2)	2	0	0	8
Andrew Patmore	8(5)	3	0	0	12
Scott Ranson	7	5	0	0	20
Ian Sherratt	5(3)	1	0	0	4
Jason Temu	15(1)	1	0	0	4
Paul Topping	16(5)	1	18	0	40

LEAGUE RECORD
P22-W9-D1-L12
(8th, SL)
F473, A681, Diff -208
19 points.

ATTENDANCES
Best - v Wigan (7,709)
Worst - v Workington (2,228)
Total - 39,914
Average - 3,629
(Up by 442 on
Centenary season)

TOP TACKLER
Joe Faimalo - 498

TOP BUSTS
David Bradbury - 72

TOP METRE GAINER
Joe Faimalo - 2349

Paul Topping -
one try and 18 goals

172

David Bradbury

Overall, everybody at the club should hold their heads up high and be very pleased with what we achieved at Oldham in Super League.

It was a mix of a season for us. We started very well and then obviously the injuries started to come in as they do for every team.

Unfortunately at Oldham we have only got a small squad, so when one or two players do go down it does affect the team.

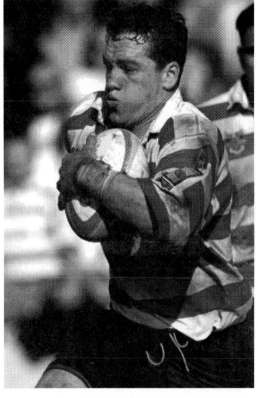

Andy Goodway has done a good job. The majority of the players, including myself, are the same players that were playing in the old division two a few years ago.

The low point had to be the defeat at home to Workington.

But in a way it was the big turning point of the season.

We'd had a few defeats before then but after that game one or two players had to take a look at themselves. They were getting good pay and were there to entertain the fans and they just weren't doing it.

So from then on they pulled their socks up and really got stuck in.

If we could have had a full team all season we would have competed with most teams. We competed with them all anyway except the top three teams.

I like to look back on the Warrington game as the most satisfying of the campaign - it was one of the best team performances. The defence was good and the attack was perfect. When times got rough we just stuck at it.

Throughout the season Martin Crompton led us so well. His attitude to the game and the team is absolutely fantastic. Joe Faimalo has been ever present all season - he gave 110% wherever he played. And at the back we had Paul Atcheson who in my opinion was unlucky to miss the tour.

I'll miss the Watersheddings. I loved playing there. There was nothing wrong with the playing surface, just the condition of the stands.

But Boundary Park is a beautiful little ground. The playing surface is perfect and it's better for the spectators. It won't be long until the supporters count Boundary Park as home.

173

PARIS ST GERMAIN

DATE	FIXTURE	RESULT	SCORERS	LGE	ATT
29/3/96	Sheffield(h)	W30-24	t:Banquet,Piskunov,Adams,Chamorin,Cervello(2) g:Torreilles(3)	N/A	17,873
4/4/96	London(a)	L38-22	t:Cervello,Turner,Bomati,Ramondou g:Torreilles(3)	8th	9,638
8/4/96	Oldham(h)	D24-24	t:Bomati,Cabestany,Entat,Lucchese g:Torreilles(4)	8th	6,327
13/4/96	Workington(h)	W34-12	t:Chamorin(3),Pastre-Courtine,Bomati,Kacala g:Torreilles(5)	5th	6,534
21/4/96	Warrington(a)	L48-24	t:Pastre-Courtine(3),Vergniol g:Torreilles(4)	7th	4,123
5/5/96	Wigan(a)	L76-8	t:Wulf g:Torreilles,Yaha	8th	10,675
10/5/96	Leeds(h)	L40-14	t:Cabestany,Banquet(2) g:Torreilles	9th	15,107
19/5/96	Bradford(a)	L60-32	t:Texeido,Banquet,Vergniol,Bomati(2),Yaha g:Chamorin(2),Torreilles(2)	9th	8,194
27/5/96	Halifax(h)	L38-10	t:Vergniol,Torreilles g:Torreilles	7th	5,832
2/6/96	St Helens(a)	L52-10	t:Cervello,Bomati g:Torreilles	11th	8,548
7/6/96	Castleford(h)	L54-22	t:Banquet(2),Brown(2) g:Yaha(3)	11th	6,618
15/6/96	Sheffield(a)	L52-18	t:Wulf,Yaha,Entat g:Smith(3)	11th	5,350
22/6/96	Warrington(h)	L26-24	t:Smith,Banquet,Lucchese,Bloomfield,Bomati g:Smith(2)	11th	5,254
28/6/96	Oldham(a)	L24-6	t:Wulf g:Banquet	11th	2,548
7/7/96	Workington(a)	L14-10	t:Vergniol,Bird g:Banquet	11th	2,173
13/7/96	London(h)	W24-18	t:Devecchi,Wulf,Bloomfield,Wilson(2) g:Smith(2)	11th	9,840
20/7/96	Wigan(h)	L24-20	t:Bird,Chamorin(2),Bomati g:Smith,Banquet	11th	5,428
28/7/96	Leeds(a)	L34-12	t:Bird,Bloomfield g:Smith(2)	11th	6,479
4/8/96	Halifax(a)	L56-10	t:Vergniol,Griffiths g:Chamorin	11th	4,819
10/8/96	St Helens(h)	L32-12	t:Bird,Bomati g:Smith(2)	11th	4,050
17/8/96	Castleford(a)	L22-18	t:Bird,Vergniol,Devecchi,Bomati g:Banquet	11th	4,473
24/8/96	Bradford(h)	L27-14	t:Bird,Wilson g:Smith(3)	11th	6,152

SCORERS...League games only

	APP	T	G	DG	PTS
Darren Adams	9(1)	1	0	0	4
Frederic Banquet	16(2)	7	4	0	36
Dion Bird	9	6	0	0	24
Vea Bloomfield	4(14)	3	0	0	12
Pascal Bomati	17(1)	10	0	0	40
Todd Brown	8(1)	2	0	0	8
Didier Cabestany	18(2)	2	0	0	8
Arnaud Cervello	4	4	0	0	16
Pierre Chamorin	15	6	3	0	30
Fabien Devecchi	12(6)	2	0	0	8
Patrick Entat	22	2	0	0	8
Jonathan Griffiths	(4)	1	0	0	4
Gregory Kacala	7	1	0	0	4
Laurent Lucchese	13(5)	2	0	0	8
Regis Pastre-Courtine	4(3)	4	0	0	16
Mikhail Piskunov	1(1)	1	0	0	4
Jean-Luc Ramondou	1(1)	1	0	0	4
Danny Smith	10(2)	1	15	0	34
Frederic Texeido	2(2)	1	0	0	4
Patrick Torreilles	9(1)	1	25	0	54
Ian Turner	1(1)	1	0	0	4
Eric Vergniol	14(1)	6	0	0	24
George Wilson	7(2)	3	0	0	12
Vincent Wulf	13(4)	4	0	0	16
Baghdad Yaha	4(4)	2	4	0	16

LEAGUE RECORD
P22-W3-D1-L18
(11th, SL)
F398, A795, Diff -397
7 points.

ATTENDANCES
Best - v Sheffield (17,873)
Worst - v St Helens (4,050)
Total - 89,015
Average - 8,092

TOP TACKLER
Didier Cabestany - 477

TOP BUSTS
Laurent Lucchese/
Pascal Bomati - 31

TOP METRE GAINER
Jason Sands - 2012

Dion Bird -
six tries in
nine appearances

John Kear

I first joined up with Paris in June.

It was obvious to everybody by then that they were really struggling and their coach Michel Mazare was grateful for any help he could get.

There were ten weeks of the season left. They had got five league points to their name which had come in the opening rounds - at home to Sheffield, Workington and Oldham - but had really struggled away from home when they came up against the likes of St Helens and Wigan.

Pierre Chamorin

I was looking forward to getting involved in hands on coaching. I watched the Castleford (home) and Sheffield (away) games as an observer and they conceded 50 points in both games. It was obvious that there was no structure to the defence and their technique was quite indifferent.

And the players were very naive compared to the battle hardened pro's in England. They were used to playing for 20 minutes and then resting for the next twenty, which they could do in the French competition.

They were in a fair old state but throughout the player attitude was first class. The Aussies were young kids who were keen to learn and the French players were very receptive.

One of the most memorable games was my first one as an official part of the coaching team - the home game against Warrington. Paris were unlucky not to win that and the performance was a huge contrast to the hammering at Sheffield the week before.

But the big one for me was the last away game at Castleford on the next to the last week of the season.

They lost, but only just, but the improvement from when they had played Cas' at Charlety - which was the real crisis point for the team - was unbelievable.

They finally proved that they could play away from home. They overcame a block about playing in England that had stuck with them all through 1996.

Dion Bird was first class and of the French players young Bomati improved all year and Pierre Chamorin, who is a bit more experienced, needs to be the cornerstone of the side in the future.

The experiment of introducing a Paris side into Super League definitely worked. It wasn't easy but we had to make it work. We could make South Wales work too, and if we are serious about expanding, we can't afford to miss the opportunity.

SHEFFIELD EAGLES

DATE	FIXTURE	RESULT	SCORERS	LGE	ATT
29/3/96	Paris(a)	L30-24	t:Lawford,Hay,Crowther,Carr,Senior g:Crowther,Aston	N/A	17,873
5/4/96	Bradford(h)	W40-24	t:Lawless,Broadbent,Sheridan,Senior,Hay,Aston g:Aston(8)	5th	5,202
8/4/96	Workington(a)	W54-22	t:Garcia(2),Sodje(2),Cook,Farrell,Hay,McAllister,Senior,Sheridan g:Aston(7)	3rd	1,904
14/4/96	London(h)	W34-18	t:Senior(2),Garcia,Sheridan,McAllister,Broadbent g:Aston(5)	3rd	3,888
21/4/96	Leeds(a)	L36-22	t:Garcia,Lawless,Lawford,Hughes g:Aston(3)	6th	9,039
3/5/96	Castleford(h)	W20-12	t:Sodje,Farrell,Turner,Senior g:Aston(2)	4th	5,486
12/5/96	Warrington(a)	L36-26	t:Hay,Sodje,Lawless,Sheridan,Senior g:Aston(3)	5th	3,906
19/5/96	Oldham(h)	W23-10	t:Senior,Sodje,Garcia,Sheridan g:Aston(3) dg:Sheridan	4th	3,200
29/5/96	Wigan(a)	L50-6	t:Lawless g:Lawford	6th	9,158
2/6/96	Halifax(a)	L33-30	t:Garcia(2),Sovatabua,Crowther(2) g:Aston(5)	6th	4,287
8/6/96	St Helens(h)	L43-32	t:Senior,Dixon,Sovatabua,Hughes,Crowther g:Aston(6)	6th	6,708
15/6/96	Paris(h)	W52-18	t:Grimley,Farrell(2),Sodje(2),Stott(3),Senior(2) g:Aston(6)	6th	5,350
23/6/96	Bradford(a)	L64-22	t:Farrell,Crowther,Garcia,Senior g:Aston(3)	6th	8,359
29/6/96	Workington(h)	W32-16	t:Chapman(2),Hughes,Senior,Crowther,Garcia g:Aston(4)	6th	3,468
6/7/96	London(a)	L45-8	t:Broadbent g:Aston(2)	7th	3,572
14/7/96	Leeds(h)	W34-31	t:McAllister,Stott(2),Garcia,Turner,Senior g:Aston(5)	6th	4,265
21/7/96	Castleford(a)	L36-31	t:Sovatabua(2),Cook,Senior,Laughton g:Aston(5) dg:Lawford	6th	4,524
28/7/96	Warrington(h)	W28-22	t:Crowther,Stott,Aston,Sovatabua,Hay g:Aston(4)	6th	4,000
3/8/96	Wigan(h)	L54-12	t:Lawless,Garcia g:Aston(2)	6th	5,103
11/8/96	Halifax(h)	W42-28	t:Hughes,Garcia,Stott(2),Carr,Senior,Lawless g:Aston(7)	6th	3,201
18/8/96	St Helens(a)	L68-2	g:Aston	6th	9,021
25/8/96	Oldham(a)	L34-25	t:Lawless,Senior,McAllister,Garcia g:Aston(4) dg:Aston	7th	2,515

SCORERS...League games only

	APP	T	G	DG	PTS
Mark Aston	20(1)	2	86	1	181
Paul Broadbent	21(1)	3	0	0	12
Paul Carr	11(1)	2	0	0	8
Richard Chapman	1	2	0	0	8
Mick Cook	9(10)	2	0	0	8
Matt Crowther	10(3)	7	1	0	30
Paul Dixon	5(6)	1	0	0	4
Anthony Farrell	14(5)	5	0	0	20
Jean-Marc Garcia	21	13	0	0	52
Danny Grimley	4(1)	1	0	0	4
Andy Hay	16(1)	5	0	0	20
Ian Hughes	9(8)	4	0	0	16
Dale Laughton	10(8)	1	0	0	4
Dean Lawford	9(5)	2	1	1	11
Johnny Lawless	18(1)	7	0	0	28
Danny McAllister	15(6)	4	0	0	16
Keith Senior	21(1)	17	0	0	68
Ryan Sheridan	9(3)	5	0	1	21
Bright Sodje	13	7	0	0	28
Waisale Sovatabua	16	5	0	0	20
Lynton Stott	17(3)	8	0	0	32
Darren Turner	3(11)	2	0	0	8

LEAGUE RECORD
P22-W10-D0-L12
(7th, SL)
F599, A730, Diff -131
20 points.

ATTENDANCES
Best - v St Helens (6,708)
Worst - v Oldham (3,200)
Total - 49,871
Average - 4,534
(Up by 1,428 on
Centenary season)

TOP TACKLER
Paul Broadbent - 555

TOP BUSTS
Johnny Lawless - 64

TOP METRE GAINER
Paul Broadbent - 3357

Johnny Lawless -
top busts

Paul Broadbent

Big things were expected from us because we had such a good Centenary season.

We started badly with that defeat in Paris, but it was always going to be their night. It was their big opening and despite their poor form during the rest of the year they were really fired up and deserved their win, so I wouldn't call that a lowpoint.

What was disappointing was our inconsistency. We had some very heavy defeats, such as those by Wigan and London, but they didn't all come together. One week we'd be going really well, then we'd get a good thumping and the next week we'd be back up there. It was very frustrating.

And every time we were off form we seemed to be playing away. I don't really believe in the home and away factor and I tend to think it was more of a coincidence. We had this win-lose-win-lose cycle that no-one could really understand.

We had some pretty good wins along the way though. The win against Bradford was a notable victory and a really good night. We dug deep and showed a lot of guts and determination. We also beat Workington on the Monday of that week, and were probably playing our best football at that time.

If we are to improve, I think we need to add one or two top players. It's always been a trademark of Sheffield to bring on youngsters and we usually come up with the goods. We have a lot of very talented youngsters in the team now and if we can supplement that with

one or two top class players, especially in the backs, I think we can be a side capable of challenging for top honours.

What we don't have is anyone who the opposition is really worried about every time he gets the ball. We have a good steady side that's pretty strong as a unit, but no-one like a Connolly or Tuigamala who can put a bit of panic into the opposition.

That's not to knock our players, but we do need more of a killer instinct.

177

ST HELENS

DATE	FIXTURE	RESULT	SCORERS	LGE	ATT
31/3/96	Workington(a)	W62-0	t:Hammond,Newlove(3),Arnold(4),Prescott,Veivers,Perelini g:Goulding(9)	N/A	3,641
5/4/96	Wigan(h)	W41-26	t:Arnold(3),Cunningham,Martyn,Northey,Pickavance g:Goulding(6) dg:Goulding	1st	15,883
8/4/96	Leeds(a)	W46-24	t:Arnold(2),Cunningham,Hunte,Martyn,Newlove,Northey g:Goulding(9)	1st	11,848
14/4/96	Bradford(h)	W26-20	t:Arnold,Gibbs,Perelini,Newlove g:Goulding(5)	1st	10,010
21/4/96	Halifax(a)	W30-28	t:Hammond,Newlove(3),Arnold g:Goulding(5)	1st	6,260
27/4/96	Bradford(a)	W40-32(CCF)	t:Prescott(2),Arnold(2),Cunningham,Booth,Pickavance,Perelini g:Goulding(4)	N/A	75,994
5/5/96	Oldham(h)	W66-18	t:Hammond(2),Hunte,Perelini,Newlove(3),Goulding,Sullivan(2),McVey,Martyn g:Goulding(8),McVey	1st	10,181
12/5/96	London(h)	W24-22	t:Booth,Gibbs,Martyn,Newlove g:Goulding(4)	1st	7,225
17/5/96	Warrington(a)	W25-24	t:Prescott,Newlove,Pickavance g:Goulding(6) dg:Goulding	1st	6,508
27/5/96	Castleford(h)	W62-24	t:Arnold,Martyn,Perelini,Prescott(2),Newlove(2),Morley,Matautia,Haigh g:Goulding(11)	1st	8,239
2/6/96	Paris(h)	W52-10	t:McVey(2),Prescott,Arnold,Hammond,Matautia,Newlove(2),Haigh,Joynt g:Prescott(4),Martyn(2)	1st	8,548
8/6/96	Sheffield(a)	W43-32	t:Cunningham,Hunte(2),Hammond,Sullivan(2),Newlove g:Prescott(7) dg:Hammond	1st	6,708
16/6/96	Workington(h)	W60-16	t:Cunningham,Joynt,Matautia,Prescott,Hunte,Arnold(2),Goulding,Sullivan(3) g:Goulding(8)	1st	7,237
21/6/96	Wigan(a)	L35-19	t:Goulding,Newlove,Morley g:Goulding(3) dg:Goulding	1st	20,429
30/6/96	Leeds(h)	W42-16	t:McVey(2),Arnold,Cunningham,Hammond,Hayes,Newlove,Perelini g:Prescott(3),Goulding(2)	1st	8,702
5/7/96	Bradford(a)	L50-22	t:Newlove(2),Cunningham(2) g:Prescott(3)	2nd	11,467
14/7/96	Halifax(h)	W58-20	t:Arnold,Cunningham(3),Joynt,Newlove,Goulding,Hunte(2),Hayes,Hammond g:Goulding(7)	1st	9,283
19/7/96	Oldham(a)	W54-18	t:Arnold(2),Perelini(2),Hammond(2),Hayes(2),Hunte,Newlove g:Goulding(7)	1st	4,354
27/7/96	London(a)	W32-28	t:Hayes,Perelini(2),Newlove,Matautia,Gibbs g:Goulding(4)	1st	6,286
2/8/96	Castleford(a)	W20-16	t:Sullivan(2),Martyn,Newlove g:Goulding(2)	1st	6,143
10/8/96	Paris(a)	W32-12	t:Hunte,Sullivan(2),Perelini,Cunningham,Prescott g:Goulding(4)	1st	4,050
18/8/96	Sheffield(h)	W68-2	t:Sullivan(3),Prescott(4),Hammond(3),Haigh,Hunte g:Goulding(10)	1st	9,021
26/8/96	Warrington(h)	W66-14	t:Hunte(3),Martyn(2),Sullivan(2),Newlove(2),McVey,Goulding,Hayes,Fogerty g:Goulding(7)	1st	18,098
1/9/96	London(h)	W25-14(PSF)	t:Hayes,Goulding,Sullivan(2) g:Goulding(4) dg:Goulding	N/A	9,250
8/9/96	Wigan(a)	L44-14(PF)	t:Newlove,Martyn g:Goulding(3)	N/A	35,013

SCORERS...League games only

	APP	T	G	DG	PTS
Danny Arnold	18(1)	19	0	0	76
Simon Booth	9(1)	1	0	0	4
Keiron Cunningham	22	11	0	0	44
Adam Fogerty	13	1	0	0	4
Scott Gibbs	9	3	0	0	12
Bobbie Goulding	19	5	117	3	257
Andy Haigh	1(9)	3	0	0	12
Karle Hammond	22	13	0	1	53
Joey Hayes	7(2)	6	0	0	24
Alan Hunte	17(2)	13	0	0	52
Chris Joynt	18	3	0	0	12
Tommy Martyn	11(9)	8	2	0	36
Vila Matautia	3(13)	4	0	0	16
Derek McVey	17(3)	6	1	0	26
Chris Morley	9(10)	2	0	0	8
Paul Newlove	20	28	0	0	112
Andy Northey	6(4)	2	0	0	8
Apollo Perelini	18(2)	10	0	0	40
Ian Pickavance	6(16)	2	0	0	8
Steve Prescott	20	11	17	0	78
Anthony Sullivan	15	16	0	0	64
Phil Veivers	(1)	1	0	0	4

LEAGUE RECORD
P22-W20-D0-L2
(Champions, SL)
F950, A455, Diff +495
40 points.

ATTENDANCES
Best - v Warrington (18,098)
Worst - v London (7,225)
Total - 112,427
Average - 10,221
(Up by 3,078 on
Centenary season)

TOP TACKLER
Keiron Cunningham - 547

TOP BUSTS
Keiron Cunningham - 131

TOP METRE GAINER
Keiron Cunningham - 2800

Keiron Cunningham -
547 tackles, 131 busts,
2800 metres, 11 tries

Karle Hammond

The season started off with a bang, with the run in the Challenge Cup running alongside.

We were always confident that we could do well and shake off the "bridesmaids" tag.

We had a lot of strength in depth and that meant that everybody had to keep their form to play at Wembley, which meant we didn't relax in the games leading up to the final.

There was a lot of feeling in the squad that this would be our year.

You are in the game to win trophies and a couple of great signings at the start of the season did the trick.

Paul Newlove and Derek McVey proved to be key players. Nobody had heard of Derek McVey before he came over but he showed the way for a lot of other players.

Playing at Wembley was a highlight. I'd always dreamed of playing there and it was everything I ever expected and more.

But the run into the Super League was amazing. All those games away from home were just incredible. We'd got our butts kicked at Bradford. But that made us realise that we were not invincible.

Any team can get beat, no matter how well they are going. That hammering spurred us on, and we had to do it tough. Not many would have backed us to go through the rest of the season undefeated.

There were a few nailbiters to come - London and Castleford spring to mind.

The two home games at the end were a great way to finish.

The aim now is to repeat the trick next season. We know that, in any other year, two defeats and a draw would have been enough to give Wigan the title. It just shows what character St Helens has got, from the players and coaches through to the administration.

We stuck in when times were hard and I guess the summer league just suited Saints.

WARRINGTON

DATE	FIXTURE	RESULT	SCORERS	LGE	ATT
31/3/96	Leeds(a)	W22-18	t:Mafi,Harris,Knott g:Harris(5)	N/A	10,036
5/4/96	Workington(h)	W45-30	t:Kohe-Love(2),Bennett,Forster,Henare,Mafi,Penny g:Harris(8) dg:Harris	2nd	4,511
8/4/96	Wigan(a)	L42-12	t:Knott,Kohe-Love g:Harris(2)	7th	14,620
12/4/96	Halifax(h)	W16-10	t:Forster,Henare g:Harris(4)	4th	3,721
21/4/96	Paris(h)	W48-24	t:Kohe-Love(2),Hough,Shelford,Rudd,Knott(2),Penny g:Harris(4),Rudd,Knott(3)	3rd	4,123
5/5/96	Bradford(a)	L36-14	t:Knott,Roper,Henare g:Harris	5th	9,278
12/5/96	Sheffield(h)	W36-26	t:Knott,Harris(2),Swann,Penny g:Harris(8)	3rd	3,906
17/5/96	St Helens(h)	L25-24	t:Kohe-Love,Henare,Jones,Roper g:Harris(4)	6th	6,508
25/5/96	London(h)	W28-24	t:Roper(2),Henare,Harris,Swann g:Harris(4)	4th	3,772
31/5/96	Castleford(a)	W22-17	t:Sculthorpe,Henare,Roper,Rudd g:Harris(3)	4th	2,874
9/6/96	Oldham(a)	L35-24	t:Henare,Kohe-Love(2),Roper,Swann g:Harris(2)	4th	3,243
14/6/96	Leeds(h)	W36-12	t:Roper(2),Cullen,Knott,Hilton,Finau g:Harris(6)	4th	5,580
22/6/96	Paris(a)	W26-24	t:Roper(2),Watson,Swann,Sculthorpe g:Harris(3)	4th	5,254
30/6/96	Wigan(h)	L21-0	No Scorers	4th	8,103
7/7/96	Halifax(a)	L25-18	t:Hulme,Sculthorpe,Henare(2) g:Rudd	4th	4,247
14/7/96	Workington(a)	W49-4	t:Roper,Rudd(2),Forster(2),Jones,Henare,Penny,Barrow g:Harris(6) dg:Harris	4th	2,269
20/7/96	Bradford(h)	L30-20	t:Henare,Rudd,Mafi,Penny g:Rudd,Roper	4th	8,423
28/7/96	Sheffield(a)	L28-22	t:Forster,Kohe-Love,Knott,Mafi g:Harris(3)	4th	4,000
4/8/96	London(a)	L20-13	t:Roper,Mafi g:Knott(2) dg:Shelford	5th	6,903
10/8/96	Castleford(h)	W38-24	t:Henare(2),Cullen,Shelford,Sculthorpe,Hulme,Mafi g:Knott(5)	5th	4,277
16/8/96	Oldham(h)	W42-24	t:Finau(2),Watson,Cullen,Henare(3),Knott g:Knott(5)	4th	3,800
26/8/96	St Helens(a)	L66-14	t:Forster,Henare,Mafi g:Knott	5th	18,098

SCORERS...League games only

	APP	T	G	DG	PTS
Paul Barrow	1(9)	1	0	0	4
Andy Bennett	6(5)	1	0	0	4
Paul Cullen	19	3	0	0	12
Salesi Finau	4(9)	3	0	0	12
Mark Forster	22	6	0	0	24
Iestyn Harris	16	4	63	2	144
Richard Henare	18(1)	17	0	0	68
Mark Hilton	18	1	0	0	4
John Hough	6	1	0	0	4
Paul Hulme	10(1)	2	0	0	8
Mark Jones	8(11)	2	0	0	8
Ian Knott	11(5)	9	16	0	68
Toa Kohe-Love	21(1)	9	0	0	36
Mateaki Mafi	6(8)	7	0	0	28
Lee Penny	13(1)	5	0	0	20
Jonathan Roper	15(2)	12	1	0	50
Chris Rudd	13(9)	5	3	0	26
Paul Sculthorpe	22	4	0	0	16
Kelly Shelford	7(3)	2	0	1	9
Willie Swann	15(1)	4	0	0	16
Kris Watson	11(2)	2	0	0	8

LEAGUE RECORD
P22-W12-D0-L10
(5th, SL)
F569, A565, Diff +4
24 points.

ATTENDANCES
Best - v Bradford (8,423)
Worst - v Halifax (3,721)
Total - 56,724
Average - 5,157
(Up by 235 on
Centenary season)

TOP TACKLER
Paul Sculthorpe - 728

TOP BUSTS
Iestyn Harris - 85

TOP METRE GAINER
Paul Sculthorpe - 2730

Richard Henare -
Wire's top try scorer

Paul Sculthorpe

It was disappointing to finish outside the play-off spot.

We thought we were a better team than fifth. Top-four was always our aim.

We had a lot of games that we should have won but we lost them in the last few minutes. Against top teams, like St Helens and Bradford, we really threw those games away.

We were beating Saints with four minutes to go and seven points clear. You would have expected us to win from there. Talk about last minute stuff!

But we won a few close ones too.

The win against London at Wilderspool really sticks in my mind. London were going to be our big challengers for the play-offs and it was a good one to win, even though they took us at the end of the season.

Jon Roper's try near the end clinched it for us. It was a great win.

The low points of the season were Oldham and Halifax away.

They were the games that lost us our chance. We just went over there too confident. You can't afford to do that.

When we did come up against the big teams, that is when we performed.

The game that really decided it was the one down in London. We didn't play that badly but they just edged it.

I was happy with the way 1996 went for me. I finished second in the Super League list of tacklers which I was pleased about, it's obviously such a big part of the game.

And then to make it into the Great Britain squad and then the Test team, capped off a great year for me.

Jon Roper had a good year too, especially after coming back from a serious injury, and he deserved his place in the Lions' squad. Mark Hilton would have been here too if he hadn't done his shoulder.

And Richard Henare's confidence grew and grew as the season ran on.

So, all in all, not an ideal end to the season, we just missed out on our target, but we played in some great games along the way.

WIGAN

DATE	FIXTURE	RESULT	SCORERS	LGE	ATT
30/3/96	Oldham(a)	W56-16	t:Offiah(2),Connolly(3),Hall,Paul,Radlinski(2),Edwards(2) g:Farrell(6)	N/A	7,709
5/4/96	St Helens(a)	L41-26	t:Hall(2),O'Connor,Smyth,Tuigamala g:Paul(3)	4th	15,883
8/4/96	Warrington(h)	W42-12	t:Edwards(2),Haughton,Johnson,Paul,Radlinski,Smyth g:Farrell(6),Paul	2nd	14,620
14/4/96	Castleford(a)	W28-10	t:Farrell,Robinson,Smyth,Paul,Connolly g:Farrell(4)	2nd	7,985
19/4/96	Bradford(h)	W22-6	t:Paul,Craig,Haughton,Murdock g:Farrell(3)	2nd	9,872
5/5/96	Paris(h)	W76-8	t:Cassidy,Connolly(2),Farrell,Haughton(2),Murdock,Paul(3),Radlinski,Smyth(3) g:Farrell(4),Paul(6)	2nd	10,675
14/5/96	Halifax(a)	W50-4	t:Cassidy,Smyth(2),Edwards,Connolly,Robinson(2),Murdock,Haughton g:Farrell(5),Hall(2)	2nd	5,269
18/5/96	Workington(a)	W64-16	t:Farrell(2),Craig,Robinson(2),Hall,Edwards,Offiah,Tuigamala(2),Murdock g:Farrell(8),Paul,Tuigamala	2nd	3,176
29/5/96	Sheffield(h)	W50-6	t:Offiah(3),Connolly,Hall,Cassidy,Paul,Smyth,Johnson g:Farrell(7)	2nd	9,158
1/6/96	Leeds(a)	W40-20	t:Robinson,Smyth(2),Paul,Offiah,Murdock g:Farrell(8)	2nd	9,508
9/6/96	London(h)	D18-18	t:Robinson,Tuigamala,Murdock g:Farrell(3)	2nd	9,189
16/6/96	Oldham(h)	W44-16	t:Haughton,Smyth(2),Robinson(3),Connolly,Quinnell,Ellison g:Farrell(2),Edwards(2)	2nd	7,226
21/6/96	St Helens(h)	W35-19	t:Smyth,Robinson(2),Tuigamala,Murdock,Haughton g:Paul(3),Hall(2) dg:Robinson	2nd	20,429
30/6/96	Warrington(a)	W21-0	t:Paul(2),Smyth(2) g:Connolly(2) dg:Wright	2nd	8,103
5/7/96	Castleford(h)	W26-25	t:Robinson(2),Tuigamala,Johnson g:Farrell(5)	1st	8,180
12/7/96	Bradford(a)	L20-12	t:Ellison,Paul g:Farrell(2)	2nd	17,360
20/7/96	Paris(a)	W24-20	t:Robinson,Tuigamala,Radlinski,Johnson g:Farrell(4)	2nd	5,428
26/7/96	Halifax(h)	W34-26	t:Radlinski,Ellison,Connolly,Tuigamala,Paul,Murdock g:Farrell(5)	2nd	8,221
3/8/96	Sheffield(a)	W54-12	t:Paul(2),Robinson,Haughton,Connolly,Murdock,Edwards,Hall,Ellison g:Farrell(9)	2nd	5,103
9/8/96	Leeds(h)	W68-14	t:Robinson(5),Tuigamala,Murdock,Connolly(2),Cowie,Edwards(2),Radlinski g:Farrell(8)	2nd	7,814
17/8/96	London(a)	W34-13	t:Paul(2),Edwards,Robinson,Johnson,Tuigamala g:Farrell(5)	2nd	10,014
24/8/96	Workington(h)	W78-4	t:Paul(3),Barrow(3),Robinson(2),Haughton(2),Edwards(2),Farrell,Ellison,Tuigamala g:Farrell(9)	2nd	6,466
31/8/96	Bradford(h)	W42-36(PSF)	t:Edwards(4),Radlinski,Ellison(2),Paul g:Farrell(5)	N/A	9,878
8/9/96	St Helens(a)	W44-14(PF)	t:Ellison(3),Connolly,Edwards,Haughton,Paul,Robinson,Murdock g:Farrell(4)	N/A	35,013

SCORERS...League games only

	APP	T	G	DG	PTS
Steve Barrow	(8)	3	0	0	12
Mick Cassidy	22	3	0	0	12
Gary Connolly	21	13	2	0	56
Neil Cowie	16(1)	1	0	0	4
Andrew Craig	5(5)	2	0	0	8
Shaun Edwards	17(3)	12	2	0	52
Danny Ellison	8(1)	5	0	0	20
Andy Farrell	22	5	103	0	226
Martin Hall	22	6	4	0	32
Simon Haughton	15(7)	10	0	0	40
Andrew Johnson	4(15)	5	0	0	20
Craig Murdock	8(12)	10	0	0	40
Terry O'Connor	21	1	0	0	4
Martin Offiah	8	7	0	0	28
Henry Paul	19	20	14	0	108
Scott Quinnell	6(3)	1	0	0	4
Kris Radlinski	17	7	0	0	28
Jason Robinson	21	24	0	1	97
Rob Smyth	11(5)	16	0	0	64
Va'aiga Tuigamala	21	11	1	0	46
Nigel Wright	(2)	0	0	1	1

LEAGUE RECORD
P22-W19-D1-L2
(2nd, SL)
F902, A326, Diff +576
39 points.

ATTENDANCES
Best - v St Helens (20,429)
Worst - v Workington (6,466)
Total - 111,670
Average - 10,152
(Down by 1,795 on
Centenary season)

TOP TACKLER
Mick Cassidy - 644

TOP BUSTS
Jason Robinson - 190

TOP METRE GAINER
Andy Farrell - 3229

Jason Robinson -
24 tries in 21 appearances

182

Kris Radlinski

Obviously we would have liked to have won the first Super League. We are disappointed we just missed out.

But if you look at our record, we only lost two games. It was still a tremendous season and towards the end we knew we were the best team in the competition.

In the past we would have won the championship with only two defeats.

But the turning point was undoubtedly the game against London. They just came to spoil the party on that day and we just couldn't handle their tactics.

Credit to them but that game cost us the title.

The defeat at Bradford was a key game too. We knew it was going to be hard and, fair play to the Bulls, they played some tremendous rugby towards the end of that game at Odsal.

But after that we played some outstanding rugby, as we showed in the Premiership Final. The team spirit was tremendous and we really played well.

That game was definitely the high point of the season. We were awesome.

Everything that we planned came off. It's a great place to play, I always enjoy it at Old Trafford. There was a bigger crowd this year which made for a better atmosphere.

The defeat at St Helens on the second weekend of the season was probably the lowest point. We'd started off really well but it all went to pieces that day. It made for an exciting season though and I can't wait to play them again next season.

Jason Robinson and Henry Paul both had unbelievable seasons, a different class, but Gary Connolly was even better - he had his best year ever.

And there's a lot of youngsters coming through too. They are starting to look the part and you can look forward to seeing some fine young players in the not too distant future.

All the lads want to win that title back more than ever.

All those successes in the past are history.

It's a new era now and all the lads want our name on that Super League trophy.

WORKINGTON TOWN

DATE	FIXTURE	RESULT	SCORERS	LGE	ATT
31/3/96	St Helens(h)	L62-0	No Scorers	N/A	3,641
5/4/96	Warrington(a)	L45-30	t:Chilton(2),Armstrong,Campbell,Palmada g:Marwood(5)	12th	4,511
8/4/96	Sheffield(h)	L54-22	t:Allen,Phillips,L Smith g:Marwood(5)	12th	1,904
13/4/96	Paris(a)	L34-12	t:Wallace,Burns g:Marwood(2)	12th	6,534
21/4/96	London(a)	L58-0	No Scorers	12th	4,138
6/5/95	Halifax(h)	D18-18	t:L Smith,Wallace,Kitchin g:Marwood(3)	12th	2,214
12/5/96	Castleford(a)	L50-16	t:Nairn,Penrice,Kitchin g:Marwood(2)	12th	3,605
18/5/96	Wigan(h)	L64-16	t:L Smith,Holgate,Allen g:Marwood(2)	12th	3,176
26/5/96	Oldham(a)	W29-27	t:Palmada,L Smith,Wallace,Filipo g:Marwood(3),Kitchin(3) dg:Kitchin	12th	2,228
2/6/96	Bradford(a)	L52-4	t:Allen	12th	8,658
9/6/96	Leeds(h)	L48-18	t:Johnson,Chilton,Filipo g:Kitchin(3)	12th	2,949
16/6/96	St Helens(a)	L60-16	t:Allen,Keenan,Holgate g:J Smith,Carter	12th	7,237
23/6/96	London(h)	L34-6	t:Chilton g:Kitchin	12th	1,400
29/6/96	Sheffield(a)	L32-16	t:Nairn,T Smith g:Kitchin(4)	12th	3,468
7/7/96	Paris(h)	W14-10	t:Filipo g:Kitchin(5)	12th	2,173
14/7/96	Warrington(h)	L49-4	t:Allen	12th	2,269
21/7/96	Halifax(a)	L74-14	t:Chilton,Kitchin,Armswood g:Kitchin	12th	4,374
28/7/96	Castleford(h)	L46-20	t:Johnson,Grima,Allen g:Watson(4)	12th	1,622
4/8/96	Oldham(h)	L30-24	t:Penrice,Nairn,Watson,Holgate g:Watson(4)	12th	1,759
11/8/96	Bradford(h)	L28-14	t:Bethwaite,Chilton g:Watson(3)	12th	2,430
18/8/96	Leeds(a)	L68-28	t:Nairn,Johnson,Fatinowna(2),Grima g:Watson(4)	12th	4,956
24/8/96	Wigan(a)	L78-4	t:Johnson	12th	6,466

SCORERS...League games only

	APP	T	G	DG	PTS
John Allen	20(1)	6	0	0	24
Colin Armstrong	11(2)	1	0	0	4
Richard Armswood	5(1)	1	0	0	4
Mike Bethwaite	17(3)	1	0	0	4
Paul Burns	5(2)	1	0	0	4
Logan Campbell	7(1)	1	0	0	4
Darren Carter	10(3)	0	1	0	2
Lee Chilton	10(3)	6	0	0	24
Abram Fatinowna	5	2	0	0	8
Lafaele Filipo	15(4)	3	0	0	12
Andrew Grima	2(9)	2	0	0	8
Stephen Holgate	19	3	0	0	12
Mark Johnson	12	4	0	0	16
Mark Keenan	3(4)	1	0	0	4
Wayne Kitchin	11(6)	3	17	1	47
Dean Marwood	9(6)	0	22	0	44
Brad Nairn	14	4	0	0	16
Jason Palmada	12	2	0	0	8
Paul Penrice	11(2)	2	0	0	8
Rowland Phillips	22	1	0	0	4
Jamie Smith	5(3)	0	1	0	2
Leigh Smith	9	4	0	0	16
Tony Smith	9	1	0	0	4
Mark Wallace	14(1)	3	0	0	12
Ian Watson	4(1)	1	15	0	34

LEAGUE RECORD
P22-W2-D1-L19
(12th, SL)
F325, A1021, Diff -696
5 points.

ATTENDANCES
Best - v St Helens (3,641)
Worst - v London (1,400)
Total - 25,537
Average - 2,322
(Down by 739 on
Centenary season)

TOP TACKLER
Rowland Phillips - 482

TOP BUSTS
Rowland Phillips - 73

TOP METRE GAINER
Rowland Phillips - 2831

Lafaele Filipo -
three tries for Town

Rowland Phillips

It's very difficult to pick out that many high points from our season but probably the away win at Oldham was the pinnacle.

We came back from the dead that day.

All in all, I think everybody at Workington thought it was a pretty sub-standard season for the club.

The real lows came near the end of the season.

After we beat Paris - we played pretty well that day - we had Oldham and Castleford to come at Derwent Park.

And, on the back of the Paris win, we thought they were two games we could take.

But we let the games slip, and I got sent off against Castleford, which was doubly disappointing.

Those defeats were the final nail in our Super League coffin.

The real plus for the club is Ross O'Reilly. He's got the ability to run the club from boardroom level down to the groundstaff. Unfortunately, only a few times in the season we clicked on to what he wanted us to do.

We had short periods of good play but we didn't have the experience or the self-confidence to extend those periods to a half, three-quarters or the whole game. We lost concentration, as a team, not as individuals.

The Player of the Year at the club was John Allen. He played in the centre though he had been a second-row with BARLA. He never got bettered and in fact he probably won all the battles he had. He is going to be a very big name in the future.

Stephen Holgate had a good year again and Mike Bethwaite had a consistent season in the hooking spot.

But there's a lot of good youngsters coming through at the club.

Personally, I had an enjoyable year but in years to come nobody will look at my individual stats, they will look at Workington Town finishing at the bottom of the Super League.

We've hit a low and we have got to claw it back. A good off season with Ross will make a big difference.

BATLEY BULLDOGS

DATE	FIXTURE	RESULT	SCORERS	LGE	ATT
31/3/96	Whitehaven(h)	W20-13	t:Moxon,Child,Turpin,Stainburn g:Stainburn(2)	N\A	1,015
5/4/96	Dewsbury(a)	D6-6	t:Tomlinson g:Irvine	4th	2,500
8/4/96	Wakefield(h)	L28-6	t:Stainburn g:Holmes	5th	1,545
14/4/96	Rochdale(a)	D16-16	t:Tomlinson,Heron,Middleton g:Holmes(2)	6th	1,078
21/4/96	Huddersfield(h)	L23-10	t:Walton,Holmes g:Holmes	8th	2,057
5/5/96	Featherstone(a)	L56-10	t:McWilliam,Moxon g:Holmes	8th	1,847
19/5/96	Keighley(h)	L34-8	t:Tomlinson g:Holmes(2)	9th	2,148
26/5/96	Widnes(h)	L22-12	t:Irvine,Holmes g:Holmes(2)	9th	981
2/6/96	Hull(a)	L68-12	t:Barnett,Walker g:Holmes(2)	9th	2,100
9/6/96	Salford(h)	L56-18	t:Heron,Barnett,Holmes g:Holmes(3)	10th	1,262
16/6/96	Whitehaven(a)	L27-6	t:Appleby g:Holmes	10th	990
23/6/96	Dewsbury(h)	L29-24	t:Price(2),Thornton,Moxon,Summerill g:Holmes(2)	10th	1,378
29/6/96	Wakefield(a)	L26-4	t:Simpson	10th	1,461
7/7/96	Rochdale(h)	L26-12	t:Mirfin,Price g:Holmes(2)	11th	943
14/7/96	Huddersfield(a)	L56-6	t:Moxon g:Summerill	11th	3,337
21/7/96	Featherstone(h)	L32-0	No Scorers	11th	1,051
4/8/96	Widnes(a)	L46-20	t:Kuiti,Child,Moxon g:Parkinson(3),Holmes	11th	1,683
11/8/96	Hull(h)	W20-4	t:Price(2),Simpson,Thornton g:Walker(2)	11th	1,200
18/8/96	Salford(a)	L60-6	t:Simpson g:Walker	11th	2,444
25/8/96	Keighley(a)	L40-14	t:Tomlinson(2),Walker g:Walker	11th	3,866

SCORERS...League games only

	APP	T	G	DG	PTS
Darren Appleby	10	1	0	0	4
Gary Barnett	16(2)	2	0	0	8
Darren Child	13(6)	2	0	0	8
Dave Heron	10(2)	2	0	0	8
Phil Holmes	13(2)	3	20	0	52
Jimmy Irvine	6(1)	1	1	0	6
Mike Kuiti	10	1	0	0	4
Chris McWilliam	9	1	0	0	4
Graham Middleton	5(5)	1	0	0	4
Phil Mirfin	7(7)	1	0	0	4
Darren Moxon	16(1)	5	0	0	20
Andy Parkinson	18	0	3	0	6
Richard Price	10	5	0	0	20
Roger Simpson	10	3	0	0	12
John Stainburn	4	2	2	0	12
Darren Summerill	7	1	1	0	6
Gary Thornton	10(3)	2	0	0	8
Max Tomlinson	15(2)	5	0	0	20
David Turpin	2	1	0	0	4
Steve Walker	13(5)	2	4	0	16
Tony Walton	5(2)	1	0	0	4

LEAGUE RECORD
P20-W2-D2-L16
(11th, Div 1)
F230, A668, Diff -438
6 points.

ATTENDANCES
Best - v Keighley (2,148)
Worst - v Rochdale (943)
Total - 13,580
Average - 1,358
(Up by 53 on
Centenary season)

Gary Thornton -
two tries for the Bulldogs

DEWSBURY

DATE	FIXTURE	RESULT	SCORERS	LGE	ATT
31/3/96	Keighley(a)	L54-2	g:Eaton	N\A	4,700
5/4/96	Batley(h)	D6-6	g:Eaton(3)	7th	2,500
8/4/96	Featherstone(a)	L52-12	t:Bell,McAllister,Williams	9th	2,539
14/4/96	Hull(h)	W12-10	t:Austerfield,Eaton g:Eaton(2)	7th	1,224
21/4/96	Rochdale(a)	W24-22	t:Austerfield(2),Williamson,Brent g:Eaton(4)	5th	1,057
12/5/96	Whitehaven(h)	L16-14	t:Delaney,Conway g:Eaton(3)	7th	923
19/5/96	Widnes(a)	L36-24	t:Crouthers,Woodcock,Kelly,Conway g:Eaton(4)	7th	2,330
24/5/96	Salford(a)	L54-0	No Scorers	7th	2,611
3/6/96	Huddersfield(h)	L25-20	t:Bell,Delaney,McKelvie,Austerfield g:Eaton(2)	8th	1,645
9/6/96	Wakefield(a)	L50-14	t:Hiscock,Brent,McKelvie g:Eaton	8th	1,680
16/6/96	Keighley(h)	W14-6	t:Williams,Eaton g:Eaton(3)	8th	1,960
23/6/96	Batley(a)	W29-24	t:McKelvie(2),Hiscock,Williamson,Williams g:Eaton(4) dg:Eaton	8th	1,378
1/7/96	Featherstone(h)	L38-2	g:Eaton	8th	1,232
7/7/96	Hull(a)	L22-6	t:Bell g:Eaton	8th	2,245
14/7/96	Rochdale(h)	W34-7	t:Williams,Hiscock,Lord(2),Bell g:Eaton(7)	8th	1,006
28/7/96	Whitehaven(a)	L36-8	t:Worthy,Bell	8th	901
4/8/96	Salford(h)	L46-6	t:Delaney g:Eaton	8th	1,303
11/8/96	Huddersfield(a)	L44-6	t:Crouthers g:Bramald	8th	2,304
18/8/96	Wakefield(h)	L54-6	t:Worthy g:Eaton	9th	1,305
25/8/96	Widnes(h)	W25-16	t:Woodcock,Bell,Crouthers,Hiscock g:Eaton(4) dg:Kelly	8th	926

SCORERS...League games only

	APP	T	G	DG	PTS
Shaun Austerfield	15	4	0	0	16
Glen Bell	10(6)	6	0	0	24
Matthew Bramald	7(3)	0	1	0	2
Andrew Brent	5(8)	2	0	0	8
Mark Conway	11(5)	2	0	0	8
Kevin Crouthers	6(4)	3	0	0	12
Paul Delaney	17	3	0	0	12
Barry Eaton	19	2	42	1	93
Craig Hiscock	12	4	0	0	16
Neil Kelly	4(5)	1	0	1	5
Paul Lord	9(2)	2	0	0	8
Terry McAllister	1(11)	1	0	0	4
Danny McKelvie	20	4	0	0	16
Shayne Williams	14	4	0	0	16
Leon Williamson	17	2	0	0	8
Robert Woodcock	16	2	0	0	8
Paul Worthy	10(1)	2	0	0	8

LEAGUE RECORD
P20-W6-D1-L13
(8th, Div 1)
F264, A618, Diff -354
13 points.

ATTENDANCES
Best - v Batley (2,500)
Worst - v Whitehaven (923)
Total - 14,024
Average - 1,402
(Up by 78 on
Centenary season)

Shayne Williams -
four tries

187

FEATHERSTONE

DATE	FIXTURE	RESULT	SCORERS	LGE	ATT
31/3/96	Rochdale(h)	W33-24	t:Roebuck,Tuffs,Rombo(2),Miller g:Pearson(6) dg:Fox	N\A	2,164
5/4/96	Wakefield(a)	W22-8	t:Pearson(2),Simpson,Wilson g:Pearson(3)	3rd	2,598
8/4/96	Dewsbury(h)	W52-12	t:Wilson(3),Simpson(2),Gunn,Hughes,Pearson,Roebuck,Rombo g:Pearson(5),Fox	1st	2,539
14/4/96	Widnes(a)	L25-8	t:Rombo g:Pearson(2)	3rd	2,816
21/4/96	Whitehaven(a)	W32-6	t:Pearson(2),Wilson,Gibson,Hughes g:Pearson(6)	1st	1,018
5/5/96	Batley(h)	W56-10	t:Hughes(2),Pearson,Gibson(2),Molloy(2),Lay,Simpson,Gunn g:Pearson(8)	1st	1,847
12/5/96	Keighley(a)	D22-22	t:Hughes,Powell,Rombo,Jackson g:Pearson(2) dg:Fox(2)	1st	5,197
19/5/96	Salford(a)	L32-10	t:Summers,Pearson g:Pearson	4th	3,130
26/5/96	Huddersfield(h)	W23-22	t:Simpson,Molloy,Rombo g:Pearson(5) dg:Fox	3rd	2,198
9/6/96	Hull(h)	L22-20	t:Gibson,Fox,Molloy g:Pearson(4)	5th	1,849
16/6/96	Rochdale(a)	W44-12	t:Rombo(2),Pearson(2),Tuffs,Gibson,Lay,Simpson g:Pearson(6)	4th	1,061
23/6/96	Wakefield(h)	D24-24	t:Pearson,Hughes,Rombo,Bibb,Roebuck g:Pearson(2)	3rd	2,187
1/7/96	Dewsbury(a)	W38-2	t:Fox(2),Hughes,Slater,Rombo,Simpson,Naidole g:Fox(3),Fallins(2)	3rd	1,232
7/7/96	Widnes(h)	W31-14	t:Summers(2),Simpson,Wilson g:Pearson(7) dg:Fox	3rd	1,567
14/7/96	Whitehaven(h)	W36-18	t:Rombo,Wilson,Pearson,Hughes,Stokes(2) g:Pearson(6)	2nd	1,457
21/7/96	Batley(a)	W32-0	t:Powell,Simpson,Rombo(2),Pearson(2) g:Pearson(4)	2nd	1,051
28/7/96	Keighley(h)	L48-26	t:Molloy(2),Powell,Rombo g:Pearson(5)	2nd	2,396
4/8/96	Huddersfield(a)	L34-10	t:Maskill,Pearson g:Pearson	3rd	2,605
18/8/96	Hull(a)	L26-9	t:Stokes g:Pearson(2) dg:Fox	5th	2,711
25/8/96	Salford(h)	W29-10	t:Hughes(2),Rombo,Summers g:Pearson(6) dg:Pearson	4th	1,673

SCORERS...League games only

	APP	T	G	DG	PTS
Chris Bibb	7(8)	1	0	0	4
Ty Fallins	(1)	0	2	0	4
Deryck Fox	20	3	4	6	26
Carl Gibson	10	5	0	0	20
Richard Gunn	4(15)	2	0	0	8
Darren Hughes	19(1)	10	0	0	40
Craig Jackson	3(11)	1	0	0	4
Steve Lay	7(8)	2	0	0	8
Colin Maskill	3(2)	1	0	0	4
Tony Miller	(5)	1	0	0	4
Steve Molloy	19	6	0	0	24
Joe Naidole	(10)	1	0	0	4
Martin Pearson	19	14	81	1	219
Roy Powell	20	3	0	0	12
Neil Roebuck	17	3	0	0	12
Eddie Rombo	20	15	0	0	60
Owen Simpson	16	9	0	0	36
Richard Slater	17	1	0	0	4
Jamie Stokes	2(2)	3	0	0	12
Neil Summers	10(2)	4	0	0	16
Simon Tuffs	18	2	0	0	8
Warren Wilson	12	7	0	0	28

LEAGUE RECORD
P20-W12-D2-L6
(4th, Div 1)
F557, A371, Diff +186
26 points.

ATTENDANCES
Best - v Dewsbury (2,539)
Worst - v Whitehaven (1,457)
Total - 19,877
Average - 1,988
(Down by 109 on
Centenary season)

Martin Pearson -
Featherstone's top
points scorer with 219

HUDDERSFIELD

DATE	FIXTURE	RESULT	SCORERS	LGE	ATT
31/3/96	Salford(h)	L26-21	t:Toole,Reynolds,Shelford,Hanger g:Schofield(2) dg:Mackey	N\A	4,043
5/4/96	Whitehaven(a)	W37-4	t:Austin,Barton,Hanger,Schofield,St Hilaire,Wilson g:Schofield(5),Kebbie dg:Mackey	6th	1,521
8/4/96	Rochdale(h)	W28-16	t:Austin(2),Kebbie(2),Hanger,Wilson g:Schofield(2)	3rd	3,008
14/4/96	Keighley(a)	L12-10	t:Austin,Barton g:Schofield	4th	5,855
21/4/96	Batley(a)	W23-10	t:Toole,Hanger,Austin,Marsden g:Booth(3) dg:Wilson	4th	2,057
25/4/96	Whitehaven(h)	W40-6	t:Coulter(3),Shelford(2),Mosley(2),Austin g:Booth(4)	1st	2,160
4/5/96	Hull(h)	W32-22	t:Wilson,Hanger,Austin,St Hilaire,Shelford,Milner g:Austin(4)	2nd	3,190
12/5/96	Widnes(a)	L21-6	t:Marsden g:Austin	4th	3,260
19/5/96	Wakefield(h)	W38-12	t:St Hilaire,Shelford,Hanger(2),Austin,Barton g:Austin(7)	3rd	4,298
26/5/96	Featherstone(a)	L23-22	t:Schofield(2),St Hilaire,Shelford g:Austin(3)	4th	2,198
3/6/96	Dewsbury(a)	W25-20	t:Toole(2),Hanger,Veivers,Austin g:Austin(2) dg:Mackey	3rd	1,645
16/6/96	Salford(a)	L26-20	t:Shelford(2),Richards g:Austin(4)	5th	4,107
30/6/96	Rochdale(a)	W36-10	t:Schofield(2),Wilson(2),Austin,Barton,Hanger g:Austin(4)	4th	1,197
7/7/96	Keighley(h)	W37-10	t:Mackey,Hanger(2),Wilson,Barton,Toole g:Schofield(5),Wilson dg:Schofield	4th	5,427
14/7/96	Batley(h)	W56-6	t:Hanger(4),Barton(2),Richards,King,Schofield,Veivers,Booth g:Booth(6)	4th	3,337
21/7/96	Hull(a)	L26-16	t:Reynolds,Mackey,St Hilaire g:Booth(2)	5th	3,553
28/7/96	Widnes(h)	L20-14	t:Bunyan,Shelford,Milner g:Booth	5th	2,644
4/8/96	Featherstone(h)	W34-10	t:Shelford(2),Toole,Bunyan,Wilson,Booth,Mackey g:Booth(3)	5th	2,605
11/8/96	Dewsbury(h)	W44-6	t:Bunyan(2),Wilson(2),Booth,Veivers,Milner,Richards g:Booth(6)	3rd	2,304
25/8/96	Wakefield(a)	L22-18	t:Booth,Toole,Bunyan,Barton g:Booth	5th	2,403

SCORERS...League games only

	APP	T	G	DG	PTS
Greg Austin	12(1)	10	25	0	90
Ben Barton	13	8	0	0	32
Steve Booth	9(3)	4	26	0	68
James Bunyan	7(3)	5	0	0	20
Garry Coulter	4(8)	3	0	0	12
Dean Hanger	19	15	0	0	60
Brimah Kebbie	3	2	1	0	10
Dave King	11(9)	1	0	0	4
Greg Mackey	20	3	0	3	15
Bob Marsden	5(4)	2	0	0	8
Lee Milner	10(10)	3	0	0	12
James Mosley	3(1)	2	0	0	8
Simon Reynolds	7(2)	2	0	0	8
Basil Richards	14(6)	3	0	0	12
Garry Schofield	16	6	15	1	55
Darrall Shelford	20	11	0	0	44
Lee St Hilaire	18(2)	5	0	0	20
Adrian Toole	20	7	0	0	28
Phil Veivers	13(1)	3	0	0	12
Alan Wilson	19	9	1	1	39

LEAGUE RECORD
P20-W12-D0-L8
(5th, Div 1)
F557, A308, Diff +249
24 points.

ATTENDANCES
Best - v Keighley (5,855)
Worst - v Whitehaven (2,160)
Total - 33,444
Average - 3,344
(Up by 917 on
Centenary season)

Phil Veivers -
has scored three tries
for the Giants since his
mid-season move from
St Helens

189

HULL

DATE	FIXTURE	RESULT	SCORERS	LGE	ATT
31/3/96	Wakefield(h)	W52-2	t:Vaikona(4),Webber,Divorty,Deakin,Windley g:Gray(10)	N\A	3,811
8/4/96	Keighley(a)	L34-30	t:Webber(3),Carter,Fisher,Moffatt g:Gray(3)	6th	6,069
14/4/96	Dewsbury(a)	L12-10	t:Webber g:Gray(3)	8th	1,224
21/4/96	Widnes(h)	W22-18	t:Fisher(2),Jackson,Craven g:Gray(3)	7th	3,092
4/5/96	Huddersfield(a)	L32-22	t:Jackson,Fisher,Kitching,Webber g:Gray(3)	7th	3,190
12/5/96	Salford(h)	W30-28	t:Divorty(2),Aston,Bai,Fisher g:Hewitt(5)	6th	3,354
19/5/96	Whitehaven(a)	W22-19	t:Manning,Craven,Vaikona g:Hewitt(3),Fitzgerald(2)	6th	1,006
26/5/96	Rochdale(h)	W24-18	t:Vaikona,Moffatt,Bai,Divorty g:Hewitt(2),Fitzgerald(2)	6th	2,696
2/6/96	Batley(h)	W68-12	t:Vaikona(2),Jackson,Divorty,Kitching(2),Fitzgerald,Hewitt,Webber, Nolan(2),Aston g:Hewitt(9),Fitzgerald	4th	2,100
9/6/96	Featherstone(a)	W22-20	t:Fisher,Jackson,Moffatt g:Hewitt(5)	4th	1,849
16/6/96	Wakefield(a)	W24-17	t:Stephens,Fisher,Divorty,Vaikona g:Hewitt(4)	3rd	2,248
30/6/96	Keighley(h)	L26-14	t:Vaikona,Wilson g:Hewitt(3)	5th	4,198
7/7/96	Dewsbury(h)	W22-6	t:Manning,Fitzgerald,Divorty,Deakin g:Hewitt(3)	5th	2,245
14/7/96	Widnes(a)	W25-24	t:Vaikona(2),Fitzgerald g:Hewitt(6) dg:Webber	5th	2,092
21/7/96	Huddersfield(h)	W26-16	t:Webber,Liddiard,Deakin,Moffatt g:Hewitt(5)	3rd	3,553
28/7/96	Salford(a)	L23-14	t:Fitzgerald,Webber g:Hewitt(3)	4th	4,059
4/8/96	Rochdale(a)	W58-40	t:Liddiard(4),Craven,Divorty,Kitching,Vaikona,Moffatt,Fisher g:Hewitt(9)	4th	1,126
11/8/96	Batley(a)	L20-4	t:Kitching	5th	1,200
18/8/96	Featherstone(h)	W26-9	t:Vaikona,Jackson,Nolan,Fisher g:Hewitt(5)	3rd	2,711
25/8/96	Whitehaven(h)	W50-16	t:Gray(3),Nolan(2),Divorty,Fisher,Kitching,Radford g:Hewitt(5),Gray,Radford	3rd	2,316
1/9/96	Keighley(a)	L41-28(PSF)	t:Hewitt,Stephens,Aston,Divorty(2) g:Hewitt(4)	N/A	4,107

SCORERS...League games only

	APP	T	G	DG	PTS
Jon Aston	12(6)	2	0	0	8
Marcus Bai	7(1)	2	0	0	8
Darren Carter	5	1	0	0	4
Steve Craven	18(1)	3	0	0	12
Leigh Deakin	6(1)	3	0	0	12
Gary Divorty	19	9	0	0	36
Andy Fisher	19	10	0	0	40
Peter Fitzgerald	9(1)	4	5	0	26
Kevin Gray	8(3)	3	23	0	58
Mark Hewitt	15(3)	1	67	0	138
Chico Jackson	15	5	0	0	20
Chris Kitching	18(1)	6	0	0	24
Glen Liddiard	4	5	0	0	20
Terry Manning	10(1)	2	0	0	8
Dave Moffatt	13(5)	5	0	0	20
Rob Nolan	7(1)	5	0	0	20
Lee Radford	(4)	1	1	0	6
Gareth Stephens	15(1)	1	0	0	4
Tevita Vaikona	16	14	0	0	56
Dave Webber	19	9	0	1	37
Richard Wilson	5(5)	1	0	0	4
Johan Windley	4	1	0	0	4

LEAGUE RECORD
P20-W14-D0-L6
(3rd, Div 1)
F565, A392, Diff +173
28 points.

ATTENDANCES
Best - v Keighley (4,198)
Worst - v Batley (2,100)
Total - 30,076
Average - 3,008
(Up by 184 on
Centenary season)

Dave Webber -
37 points for
the Airlie Birds

190

KEIGHLEY COUGARS

DATE	FIXTURE	RESULT	SCORERS	LGE	ATT
31/3/96	Dewsbury(h)	W54-2	t:Critchley(3),Pinkney(3),Ramshaw(2),Eyres,Wood,Irving g:Wood(3),Robinson(2)	N\A	4,700
5/4/96	Rochdale(a)	W14-12	t:Dixon,Foster,Whakarau g:Dixon	1st	2,150
8/4/96	Hull(h)	W34-30	t:Pinkney(2),Critchley,King,Ramshaw,Stoop g:Dixon(5)	2nd	6,069
14/4/96	Huddersfield(a)	W12-10	t:Ramshaw,Pinkney g:Dixon(2)	1st	5,855
5/5/96	Whitehaven(h)	W38-10	t:Doorey,Pinkney(2),Dixon,Larder,Foster,Whakarau g:Dixon(5)	3rd	4,582
12/5/96	Featherstone(h)	D22-22	t:King,Whakarau,Doorey g:Dixon(5)	2nd	5,197
19/5/96	Batley(a)	W34-8	t:King(3),Critchley(2),Wray g:Wood(4),Robinson	1st	2,148
26/5/96	Wakefield(a)	W30-10	t:Dixon,Ramshaw,Critchley(4),Cantillon g:Wood	1st	2,861
2/6/96	Salford(h)	L45-8	t:Wood g:Dixon(2)	2nd	6,564
9/6/96	Widnes(a)	W12-6	t:Critchley,Ramshaw g:Dixon(2)	2nd	3,089
16/6/96	Dewsbury(a)	L14-6	t:Pinkney g:Wood	2nd	1,960
23/6/96	Rochdale(h)	W42-12	t:Pinkney(3),Critchley(2),Irving,Foster(2) g:Dixon(5)	2nd	3,552
30/6/96	Hull(a)	W26-14	t:Wood(2),Pinkney,King g:Dixon(3)	2nd	4,198
7/7/96	Huddersfield(h)	L37-10	t:Dixon,Wray g:Dixon	2nd	5,427
21/7/96	Whitehaven(a)	D14-14	t:Irving,Dixon,Critchley g:Dixon	4th	1,301
28/7/96	Featherstone(a)	W48-26	t:King(3),Critchley,Whakarau,Tawhai,Parsons,Powell,Fleary g:Irving(5),Dixon	3rd	2,396
4/8/96	Wakefield(h)	W46-14	t:King(4),Whakarau(2),Wood,Cantillon,Race g:Dixon(5)	2nd	4,789
11/8/96	Salford(a)	L21-4	t:Milner	2nd	5,317
18/8/96	Widnes(h)	W64-12	t:Critchley(6),King,Powell,Wood,Larder,Ramshaw,Robinson g:Dixon(8)	2nd	3,964
25/8/96	Batley(h)	W40-14	t:Irving(2),Powell,Billy(2),Parsons,Cantillon g:Irving(6)	2nd	3,866
1/9/96	Hull(h)	W41-28(PSF)	t:Wood,Irving,Critchley(2),Dixon(2),Cantillon g:Irving(6) dg:Ramshaw	N/A	4,107
8/9/96	Salford(a)	L19-6(PF)	t:Cantillon g:Irving	N/A	35,013

SCORERS...League games only

	APP	T	G	DG	PTS
Marlon Billy	(1)	2	0	0	8
Phil Cantillon	12(7)	3	0	0	12
Jason Critchley	18	21	0	0	84
Keith Dixon	16(1)	5	46	0	112
Grant Doorey	12(1)	2	0	0	8
Andy Eyres	2(1)	1	0	0	4
Darren Fleary	20	1	0	0	4
Matthew Foster	8(5)	4	0	0	16
Simon Irving	6	5	11	0	42
Andrew King	14(1)	14	0	0	56
David Larder	11(7)	2	0	0	8
Mark Milner	6(1)	1	0	0	4
Steve Parsons	6(6)	2	0	0	8
Nick Pinkney	14	14	0	0	56
Daryl Powell	16	3	0	0	12
Wayne Race	3(3)	1	0	0	4
Jason Ramshaw	10(3)	7	0	0	28
Chris Robinson	12(1)	1	3	0	10
Andre Stoop	4(1)	1	0	0	4
Latham Tawhai	7	1	0	0	4
Sonny Whakarau	16(2)	6	0	0	24
Martin Wood	18	6	9	0	42
Simon Wray	9(8)	2	0	0	8

LEAGUE RECORD
P20-W14-D2-L4
(2nd, Div 1)
F558, A333, Diff +225
30 points.

ATTENDANCES
Best - v Salford (6,564)
Worst - v Rochdale (3,552)
Total - 48,710
Average - 4,871
(Up by 1,084 on
Centenary season)

Andy King -
14 tries in 14 full
appearances for Keighley

ROCHDALE HORNETS

DATE	FIXTURE	RESULT	SCORERS	LGE	ATT
31/3/96	Featherstone(a)	L33-24	t:Sharp,Churm,Ryan,Flanagan g:Booth(4)	N\A	2,164
5/4/96	Keighley(h)	L14-12	t:Churm,Pachniuk g:Agar,Booth	8th	2,150
8/4/96	Huddersfield(a)	L28-16	t:Gibson,Marriott,Sharp g:Booth(2)	10th	3,008
14/4/96	Batley(h)	D16-16	t:Booth,Flanagan g:Booth(4)	10th	1,078
21/4/96	Dewsbury(h)	L24-22	t:Ratu,Pitt,Sharp,Churm g:Agar(3)	10th	1,057
5/5/96	Salford(a)	L36-16	t:O'Keefe(2),Crowther g:Booth,Agar	10th	2,645
12/5/96	Wakefield(a)	L46-6	t:Churm g:Agar	11th	2,023
26/5/96	Hull(a)	L24-18	t:Marriott(2),Miller,Greenwood g:Booth	11th	2,696
31/5/96	Widnes(h)	W33-16	t:Reid,Pachniuk,Agar,Poynton,Edwards g:Booth(6) dg:Edwards	10th	1,147
9/6/96	Whitehaven(h)	L33-24	t:Edwards(2),Fa'aoso,Mawdsley g:Booth(4)	11th	987
16/6/96	Featherstone(h)	L44-12	t:Booth,Agar g:Booth(2)	11th	1,061
23/6/96	Keighley(a)	L42-12	t:Sharp,Pitt g:Turner(2)	11th	3,552
30/6/96	Huddersfield(h)	L36-10	t:Mawdsley,Diggle g:Booth	11th	1,197
7/7/96	Batley(a)	W26-12	t:Edwards(2),Marriott,Pachniuk g:Agar(2),Pachniuk(3)	10th	943
14/7/96	Dewsbury(a)	L34-7	t:Pachniuk g:Agar dg:Edwards	10th	1,006
21/7/96	Salford(h)	L42-6	t:Diggle g:Agar	10th	1,838
27/7/96	Wakefield(h)	L28-24	t:Fa'aoso,Mackie,Pucill,Alvarez g:Pachniuk(4)	10th	1,065
4/8/96	Hull(h)	L58-40	t:Flanagan(2),Durant,Morrison,Pitt,Edwards g:Pachniuk(8)	10th	1,126
11/8/96	Widnes(a)	D6-6	t:Mackie g:Pachniuk	10th	1,825
18/8/96	Whitehaven(a)	L30-18	t:Sharp,Pachniuk,Durant,Farrell g:Pachniuk	10th	904

SCORERS...League games only

	APP	T	G	DG	PTS
Richard Agar	11(4)	2	10	0	28
Sean Alvarez	1(4)	1	0	0	4
Craig Booth	11	2	26	0	60
Chris Churm	6(2)	4	0	0	16
Stephen Crowther	1(1)	1	0	0	4
Craig Diggle	8(2)	2	0	0	8
Lee Durant	6(1)	2	0	0	8
Logan Edwards	9(1)	6	0	2	26
James Fa'aoso	5(1)	2	0	0	8
Mick Farrell	1(3)	1	0	0	4
Neil Flanagan	18	4	0	0	16
Steve Gibson	4(2)	1	0	0	4
Adam Greenwood	12(1)	1	0	0	4
Damien Mackie	6(2)	2	0	0	8
Karl Marriott	18	4	0	0	16
Steve Mawdsley	5(3)	2	0	0	8
Vince Miller	4	1	0	0	4
Tony Morrison	11	1	0	0	4
Paul O'Keefe	5(1)	2	0	0	8
Richard Pachniuk	16(1)	5	17	0	54
Darren Pitt	9(7)	3	0	0	12
Phil Poynton	2(2)	1	0	0	4
Andy Pucill	6(1)	1	0	0	4
Emon Ratu	6(4)	1	0	0	4
Wayne Reid	18	1	0	0	4
Matt Ryan	5	1	0	0	4
Henry Sharp	12(1)	5	0	0	20
Steve Turner	1(1)	0	2	0	4

LEAGUE RECORD
P20-W2-D2-L16
(10th, Div 1)
F348, A602, Diff -254
6 points.

ATTENDANCES
Best - v Keighley (2,150)
Worst - v Whitehaven (987)
Total - 12,706
Average - 1,271
(Down by 27 on
Centenary season)

Wayne Reid -
18 appearances for Hornets

192

SALFORD REDS

DATE	FIXTURE	RESULT	SCORERS	LGE	ATT
31/3/96	Huddersfield(a)	W26-21	t:Martin(2),Eccles,Young,McAvoy g:Blakeley(3)	N\A	4,043
5/4/96	Widnes(h)	W46-14	t:McAvoy(2),Blakeley,Coussons,Edwards,Martin,Rogers,Webster g:Blakeley(7)	2nd	4,219
14/4/96	Whitehaven(a)	W38-14	t:Eccles,McAvoy,Blakeley,Mansson,Forber,Sini g:Blakeley(7)	2nd	1,025
21/4/96	Wakefield(a)	W32-26	t:Forber(2),Martin,Edwards,McAvoy,Rogers g:Blakeley(4)	2nd	3,010
5/5/96	Rochdale(h)	W36-16	t:Edwards,McAvoy,Rogers(2),Eccles,Savelio,Hampson g:Blakeley(4)	4th	2,645
12/5/96	Hull(a)	L30-28	t:Blakeley(2),McAvoy,Lee g:Blakeley(6)	3rd	3,354
19/5/96	Featherstone(h)	W32-10	t:Sini,McAvoy(2),Panapa,Burgess,Savelio g:Blakeley(4)	2nd	3,130
24/5/96	Dewsbury(h)	W54-0	t:Rogers,Edwards(2),Sini(2),Blease,Panapa,Coussons,Lee,McAvoy g:Blakeley(7)	2nd	2,611
2/6/96	Keighley(a)	W45-8	t:Coussons,Sini(3),Blakeley,Panapa,Rogers,Naylor g:Blakeley(6) dg:Lee	1st	6,564
9/6/96	Batley(a)	W56-18	t:Coussons(3),Blakeley(2),Lee,Blease,Rogers,Sini g:Blakeley(10)	1st	1,262
16/6/96	Huddersfield(h)	W26-20	t:Panapa(2),Rogers,Naylor,Martin g:Blakeley(3)	1st	4,107
23/6/96	Widnes(a)	W32-20	t:McAvoy(2),Rogers,Panapa,Lee,Hampson g:Blakeley(4)	1st	2,823
7/7/96	Whitehaven(h)	W38-12	t:Hampson(2),Blakeley,Naylor,Rogers(2),McAvoy,Martin g:Blakeley,Hampson,Watson	1st	3,343
14/7/96	Wakefield(h)	W42-24	t:Rogers(3),Martin,Savelio,Sini(2),McAvoy g:Blakeley(5)	1st	3,072
21/7/96	Rochdale(a)	W42-6	t:McAvoy(2),Blakeley,Edwards,Hampson,Martin,Randall,Davys g:Blakeley(3),Hampson	1st	1,838
28/7/96	Hull(h)	W23-14	t:Edwards,Sini(2) g:Blakeley(5) dg:Lee	1st	4,059
4/8/96	Dewsbury(a)	W46-6	t:Naylor,Edwards(2),Randall(2),Burgess,Martin,Rogers g:Blakeley(4),Sini(3)	1st	1,303
11/8/96	Keighley(h)	W21-4	t:Sini(2),Rogers,Forber g:Blakeley,Hampson dg:Lee	1st	5,317
18/8/96	Batley(h)	W60-6	t:Naylor(2),Blease,Davys,Eccles,Laurence,Sini,Savelio,Forber,Burgess g:Hampson(4),Sini(6)	1st	2,444
25/8/96	Featherstone(a)	L29-10	t:Coussons,Forber g:Sini	1st	1,673
1/9/96	Hull KR(h)	W36-16(PSF)	t:Blakeley,Panapa,Sini,Lee(2),McAvoy g:Blakeley(5),Hampson	N/A	2,339
8/9/96	Keighley(a)	W19-6(PF)	t:Naylor(2),Blakeley g:Blakeley(3) dg:Blakeley	N/A	35,013

SCORERS...League games only

	APP	T	G	DG	PTS
Steve Blakeley	17(1)	9	84	0	204
Ian Blease	14(5)	3	0	0	12
Andy Burgess	4(12)	3	0	0	12
Phil Coussons	7(1)	7	0	0	28
Ali Davys	2(7)	2	0	0	8
Cliff Eccles	20	4	0	0	16
Peter Edwards	20	9	0	0	36
Paul Forber	18(2)	6	0	0	24
Steve Hampson	14	5	8	0	36
Jason Laurence	1(1)	1	0	0	4
Mark Lee	18	4	0	3	19
Paul Mansson	3(10)	1	0	0	4
Scott Martin	9(6)	9	0	0	36
Nathan McAvoy	17	16	0	0	64
Scott Naylor	17	6	0	0	24
Sam Panapa	15	6	0	0	24
Craig Randall	1(8)	3	0	0	12
Darren Rogers	19	16	0	0	64
Lukeni Savelio	14(5)	4	0	0	16
Fata Sini	15(1)	15	10	0	80
Ian Watson	(3)	0	1	0	2
Richard Webster	7(4)	1	0	0	4
David Young	4	1	0	0	4

LEAGUE RECORD
P20-W18-D0-L2
(Champions, Div 1)
F733, A298, Diff +435
36 points.

ATTENDANCES
Best - v Keighley (5,317)
Worst - v Batley (2,444)
Total - 34,947
Average - 3,495
(Up by 885 on
Centenary season)

Steve Blakeley -
Salford's top
points scorer

193

WAKEFIELD TRINITY

DATE	FIXTURE	RESULT	SCORERS	LGE	ATT
31/3/96	Hull(a)	L52-2	g:Corcoran	N\A	3,811
5/4/96	Featherstone(h)	L22-8	t:Horsley g:Corcoran,Davis	11th	2,598
8/4/96	Batley(a)	W28-6	t:Allen,Davis,Grigg,Nable g:Davis(6)	8th	1,545
21/4/96	Salford(h)	L32-26	t:Foai(3),Copestake,Allen g:Davis(3)	9th	3,010
5/5/96	Widnes(a)	L31-14	t:McDonald(2),Nable g:Davis	9th	2,612
12/5/96	Rochdale(h)	W46-6	t:Wray(2),Grigg,Kuiti,Davis(2),McDonald,Foai,Allen g:Davis(4),Foai	8th	2,023
19/5/96	Huddersfield(a)	L38-12	t:Foai(2) g:Davis(2)	8th	4,298
26/5/96	Keighley(h)	L30-10	t:Foai,Wray g:Davis	8th	2,861
2/6/96	Whitehaven(a)	W19-10	t:Foai,Holland,Ford,Grigg g:Davis dg:Davis	7th	1,024
9/6/96	Dewsbury(h)	W50-14	t:Wray,Grigg(4),Flynn(2),Clarkson,Webster,Corcoran g:Davis(5)	7th	1,680
16/6/96	Hull(h)	L24-17	t:Ramsden,Clarkson,Holland g:Davis(2) dg:Davis	7th	2,248
23/6/96	Featherstone(a)	D24-24	t:Ford,Wray,Grigg,Wilson g:Davis(4)	7th	2,187
29/6/96	Batley(h)	W26-4	t:Conway(2),Grigg,Clarkson g:Davis(5)	7th	1,461
14/7/96	Salford(a)	L42-24	t:Beecraft,Davis,Proctor,Law,Copestake g:Davis(2)	7th	3,072
21/7/96	Widnes(h)	W31-4	t:Davis(4),Holland,Grigg g:Davis(3) dg:Davis	7th	1,503
27/7/96	Rochdale(a)	W28-24	t:Copestake,Conway,Flynn,Davis g:Davis(6)	7th	1,065
4/8/96	Keighley(a)	L46-14	t:Powell,Wilson,Ford g:Davis	7th	4,789
11/8/96	Whitehaven(h)	W30-22	t:Davis(3),Grigg,Clarkson g:Davis(5)	7th	1,304
18/8/96	Dewsbury(a)	W54-6	t:McDonald(3),Davis(2),Wray,Clarkson,Ramsden,Powell,Foai g:Davis(7)	6th	1,305
25/8/96	Huddersfield(h)	W22-18	t:Grigg,Wray,Nable,Davis g:Davis(3)	6th	2,403

SCORERS...League games only

	APP	T	G	DG	PTS
Kieran Allen	6(2)	3	0	0	12
Dennis Beecraft	4(1)	1	0	0	4
Michael Clarkson	11(8)	5	0	0	20
Billy Conway	5(1)	3	0	0	12
Lamond Copestake	7(3)	3	0	0	12
Jamie Corcoran	7	1	2	0	8
Brad Davis	20	15	62	3	187
Wayne Flynn	16	3	0	0	12
Lino Foai	11(1)	9	1	0	38
Mike Ford	17	3	0	0	12
Carl Grigg	19(1)	12	0	0	48
Martin Holland	11	3	0	0	12
Ryan Horsley	(7)	1	0	0	4
Mike Kuiti	8	1	0	0	4
Martin Law	(9)	1	0	0	4
Wayne McDonald	16(2)	6	0	0	24
Adam Nable	17	3	0	0	12
Daio Powell	4	2	0	0	8
Andy Proctor	4(6)	1	0	0	4
Mick Ramsden	3(15)	2	0	0	8
Mark Webster	4(3)	1	0	0	4
Andy Wilson	10(1)	2	0	0	8
Jon Wray	14	7	0	0	28

LEAGUE RECORD
P20-W10-D1-L9
(6th, Div 1)
F485, A455, Diff +30
21 points.

ATTENDANCES
Best - v Salford (3,010)
Worst - v Whitehaven (1,304)
Total - 21,091
Average - 2,109
(Up by 285 on
Centenary season)

Mike Ford -
early season buy
from Warrington

WHITEHAVEN

DATE	FIXTURE	RESULT	SCORERS	LGE	ATT
31/3/96	Batley(a)	L20-13	t:Palmer,Doyle g:Anderson(2) dg:Kiddie	N\A	1,015
5/4/96	Huddersfield(h)	L37-4	t:Seeds	10th	1,521
8/4/96	Widnes(a)	L40-8	t:Seeds(2)	11th	2,746
14/4/96	Salford(h)	L38-14	t:Williams,Lewthwaite,Quirk g:Wisnesky	11th	1,025
21/4/96	Featherstone(h)	L32-6	t:Williams g:Maguire	11th	1,018
25/4/96	Huddersfield(a)	L40-6	t:Smith g:Wisnesky	11th	2,160
5/5/96	Keighley(a)	L38-10	t:Muliumu,Williams g:Anderson	11th	4,582
12/5/96	Dewsbury(a)	W16-14	t:Edwards,Kiddie,Seeds g:Fenlon,Anderson	10th	923
9/5/96	Hull(h)	L22-19	t:Kerry,Kiddie,Anderson g:Casey(3) dg:Kerry	10th	1,006
2/6/96	Wakefield(h)	L19-10	t:Williams,Palmer g:Kerry	11th	1,024
9/6/96	Rochdale(a)	W33-24	t:Seeds(2),Dover,Palmer,Doyle g:Casey(3),Maguire(3) dg:Maguire	9th	987
16/6/96	Batley(h)	W27-6	t:Kiddie(3),Palmer,Anderson g:Maguire(2),Casey dg:Maguire	9th	990
30/6/96	Widnes(h)	L22-14	t:Muliumu,Seeds g:Casey(3)	9th	1,121
7/7/96	Salford(a)	L38-12	t:Seeds,Quirk g:Casey(2)	9th	3,343
14/7/96	Featherstone(a)	L36-18	t:Palmada,Edwards,Kiddie g:Casey(3)	9th	1,457
21/7/96	Keighley(h)	D14-14	t:Doyle,Quirk g:Maguire(2) dg:Maguire(2)	9th	1,301
28/7/96	Dewsbury(h)	W36-8	t:Seeds(2),Quirk,Kiddie,Lewthwaite g:Maguire(8)	9th	901
11/8/96	Wakefield(a)	L30-22	t:Williams,Doyle,Quirk,Lewthwaite,Edwards g:Casey	9th	1,304
18/8/96	Rochdale(h)	W30-18	t:Muliumu,Kiddie,Williams,Palmer g:Maguire(6),Casey	8th	904
25/8/96	Hull(a)	L50-16	t:Lewthwaite,Edwards,Williams g:Maguire(2)	9th	2,316

SCORERS...League games only

	APP	T	G	DG	PTS
Lee Anderson	15(1)	2	4	0	16
Sean Casey	18(2)	0	17	0	34
Peter Dover	(1)	1	0	0	4
Cassino Doyle	15(2)	4	0	0	16
Shane Edwards	16	4	0	0	16
Anthony Fenlon	5(4)	0	1	0	2
Steve Kerry	2(3)	1	1	1	7
Lee Kiddie	18	8	0	1	33
Graham Lewthwaite	4(3)	4	0	0	16
Steve Maguire	13(6)	0	24	4	52
Siose Muliumu	17(1)	3	0	0	12
Jason Palmada	5(1)	1	0	0	4
Glyn Palmer	18	5	0	0	20
Les Quirk	9(1)	5	0	0	20
David Seeds	19	10	0	0	40
Peter Smith	8(4)	1	0	0	4
Darren Williams	19	7	0	0	28
Shane Wisnesky	4	0	2	0	4

LEAGUE RECORD
P20-W5-D1-L14
(9th, Div 1)
F328, A546, Diff -218
11 points.

ATTENDANCES
Best - v Huddersfield (1,521)
Worst - v Dewsbury (901)
Total - 10,811
Average - 1,081
(Down by 124 on
Centenary season)

Steve Maguire -
24 goals and four
drop goals

195

WIDNES

DATE	FIXTURE	RESULT	SCORERS	LGE	ATT
5/4/96	Salford(a)	L46-14	t:Devereux,Thorniley g:Tyrer(3)	9th	4,219
8/4/96	Whitehaven(h)	W40-8	t:Pechey(2),Tyrer(2),Devereux,McCurrie,Thorniley,Wright g:Tyrer(4)	7th	2,746
14/4/96	Featherstone(h)	W25-8	t:Hulme,Spruce,Thorniley,Pechey,Wright g:Tyrer(2) dg:Tyrer	5th	2,816
21/4/96	Hull(a)	L22-18	t:Broadbent,Tyrer,Thorniley g:Tyrer(3)	7th	3,092
5/5/96	Wakefield(h)	W31-14	t:Hulme(2),Spruce(2),Pechey g:Tyrer(5) dg:Tyrer	5th	2,612
12/5/96	Huddersfield(h)	W21-6	t:Cooper,Devereux,Collier g:Tyrer(4) dg:Tyrer	5th	3,260
19/5/96	Dewsbury(h)	W36-24	t:McCurrie(2),Cooper,Preston,Spruce,Myler,Wright g:Tyrer(4)	5th	2,330
26/5/96	Batley(a)	W22-12	t:Preston,McCurrie(2),Wright g:Tyrer(3)	5th	981
31/5/96	Rochdale(a)	L33-16	t:Broadbent,Collier,Preston g:Tyrer(2)	6th	1,147
9/6/96	Keighley(h)	L12-6	t:Preston g:Tyrer	6th	3,089
23/6/96	Salford(h)	L32-20	t:Broadbent,Hansen,Tyrer g:Tyrer(4)	6th	2,823
30/6/96	Whitehaven(a)	W22-14	t:Tyrer,Gartland,Smith g:Tyrer(5)	6th	1,121
7/7/96	Featherstone(a)	L31-14	t:Pechey,Smith,Cooper g:Tyrer	6th	1,567
14/7/96	Hull(h)	L25-24	t:Wright,Cooper,Thorniley,McCurrie g:Tyrer(4)	6th	2,092
21/7/96	Wakefield(a)	L31-4	t:Thorniley	6th	1,503
28/7/96	Huddersfield(a)	W20-14	t:Myler,Cunningham,Waring,Kendrick g:Tyrer(2)	6th	2,644
4/8/96	Batley(h)	W46-20	t:Broadbent,Gartland,Tyrer,Cooper(2),Kendrick,Smith,Pechey g:Tyrer(7)	6th	1,683
11/8/96	Rochdale(h)	D6-6	t:Smith g:Myler	6th	1,825
18/8/96	Keighley(a)	L64-12	t:Cooper,Broadbent g:Myler(2)	7th	3,964
25/8/96	Dewsbury(a)	L25-16	t:Hansen,Kendrick,Cooper g:Myler(2)	7th	926

SCORERS...League games only

	APP	T	G	DG	PTS
Gary Broadbent	16(1)	5	0	0	20
Andy Collier	8(6)	2	0	0	8
Shane Cooper	18(1)	8	0	0	32
Gareth Cunningham	5(6)	1	0	0	4
John Devereux	7	3	0	0	12
Paul Gartland	15	2	0	0	8
Lee Hansen	20	2	0	0	8
Paul Hulme	7(1)	3	0	0	12
Phil Kendrick	5	3	0	0	12
Steve McCurrie	13(1)	6	0	0	24
Danny Myler	8(8)	2	5	0	18
Mike Pechey	16(2)	6	0	0	24
Mark Preston	7(1)	4	0	0	16
Peter Smith	8	4	0	0	16
Stuart Spruce	5	4	0	0	16
Tony Thorniley	13(1)	6	0	0	24
Christian Tyrer	17	6	54	3	135
Phil Waring	8	1	0	0	4
Darren Wright	15	5	0	0	20

LEAGUE RECORD
P20-W9-D1-L10
(7th, Div 1)
F413, A447, Diff -34
19 points.

ATTENDANCES
Best - v Huddersfield (3,260)
Worst - v Batley (1,683)
Total - 25,276
Average - 2,528
(Down by 380 on
Centenary season)

Phil Waring -
Widnes' mid-season
signing from
St Helens

196

BARROW BRAVES

DATE	FIXTURE	RESULT	SCORERS	LGE	ATT
31/3/96	Doncaster(a)	L60-16	t:Wilson,Trainor(2) g:Atkinson(2)	N/A	1,106
5/4/96	Carlisle(h)	L30-10	t:Atkinson g:Atkinson(3)	11th	921
8/4/96	Prescot(a)	L20-8	t:Magnus g:Meade(2)	11th	358
12/4/96	South Wales(h)	W16-4	t:Spenceley,Magnus,Robinson g:Atkinson(2)	10th	460
21/4/96	Swinton (a)	L36-10	t:McRory,Atkinson g:Atkinson	10th	1,378
3/5/96	York(a)	L20-8	t:Chelton g:Atkinson(2)	11th	462
10/5/96	Hunslet(h)	L44-20	t:Whalley(2),Spenceley g:Atkinson(2),Keane(2)	11th	668
19/5/96	Hull KR(a)	L42-10	t:Atkinson,Chelton g:Atkinson	11th	1,564
24/5/96	Bramley(h)	W26-14	t:Magnus,Neale,Goulding,John g:Atkinson(4) dg:Shaw,Neale	10th	608
2/6/96	Chorley(a)	L16-11	t:Ashcroft g:Atkinson(3) dg:Atkinson	10th	375
7/6/96	Leigh(h)	L41-12	t:John,Atkinson g:Atkinson(2)	10th	705
14/6/96	Doncaster(h)	L21-20	t:Atkinson(2),Milburn,Chelton g:Atkinson(2)	11th	505
23/6/96	Carlisle(a)	L50-18	t:Luxon,Schubert,Atkinson g:Atkinson(3)	11th	517
28/6/96	Prescot(a)	W30-6	t:Hutton(2),Atkinson,Plithakis,Magnus g:Atkinson(5)	9th	540
7/7/96	South Wales(a)	L48-16	t:Kettlewell,Milburn,Thacker g:Atkinson(2)	10th	300
12/7/96	Swinton(h)	L32-18	t:Proctor,Burns,Kettlewell g:Atkinson(3)	10th	586
19/7/96	York(h)	W35-18	t:Goulding,Plithakis(2),Atkinson,Kettlewell,Regan g:Atkinson(5) dg:Errington	9th	611
28/7/96	Hunslet(a)	L50-6	t:Burns g:Atkinson	9th	910
2/8/96	Hull KR(h)	L18-10	t:Burns g:Atkinson(3)	10th	610
11/8/96	Bramley(a)	W20-10	t:Hutton,Regan,Atkinson g:Atkinson(4)	9th	200
16/8/96	Chorley(h)	L27-10	t:Errington g:Atkinson(3)	10th	716
25/8/96	Leigh(a)	L44-24	t:Atkinson,Regan,John,Bent g:Atkinson(4)	10th	812

SCORERS...League games only

	APP	T	G	DG	PTS
Steve Ashcroft	11(1)	1	0	0	4
Phil Atkinson	21	11	57	1	159
Peers Bent	21(1)	1	0	0	4
Paul Burns	7	3	0	0	12
Gavin Chelton	12(9)	3	0	0	12
Craig Errington	6(1)	1	0	1	5
Adrian Goulding	11(4)	2	0	0	8
Glen Hutton	5	3	0	0	12
Martin John	4(7)	3	0	0	12
Jason Keane	8(2)	0	2	0	4
Ronnie Kettlewell	7(1)	3	0	0	12
Jeff Luxon	16(2)	1	0	0	4
Shaun Magnus	17(2)	4	0	0	16
Brett McRory	3(3)	1	0	0	4
Adrian Meade	5	0	2	0	4
Peter Milburn	5	2	0	0	8
Steve Neale	3(5)	1	0	1	5
Ben Plithakis	15(1)	3	0	0	12
Steve Proctor	3(8)	1	0	0	4
Craig Regan	8(1)	3	0	0	12
Roy Robinson	1(1)	1	0	0	4
Gary Schubert	9	1	0	0	4
Neil Shaw	20	0	0	1	1
Gary Spenceley	16(1)	2	0	0	8
Stuart Thacker	(1)	1	0	0	4
Pat Trainor	13(1)	2	0	0	8
Andy Whalley	7	2	0	0	8
Darren Wilson	2	1	0	0	4

LEAGUE RECORD
P22-W5-D0-L17
(10th, Div 2)
F354, A651, Diff -297
10 points.

ATTENDANCES
Best - v Carlisle (921)
Worst - v South Wales (460)
Total - 6,930
Average - 630
(Down by 36 on
Centenary season)

Pat Trainor -
two tries

BRAMLEY

DATE	FIXTURE	RESULT	SCORERS	LGE	ATT
31/3/96	Leigh(h)	W16-14	t:Hill,Long g:Creasser(4)	N/A	900
5/4/96	Hunslet(a)	L31-0	No Scorers	6th	1,090
8/4/96	South Wales(a)	L22-18	t:Hampshire,Pickles,Robinson g:Creasser(3)	8th	552
14/4/96	Chorley(h)	W62-10	t:Pickles(2),Long(2),Robinson(2),G Freeman,Brown,D Hall,Rowse(2) g:Creasser(9)	6th	450
21/4/96	Carlisle(a)	L26-6	t:Brown g:Creasser	6th	600
5/5/96	Hull KR(a)	L56-18	t:Blankley(2),G Hall g:Creasser(3)	8th	1,661
12/5/96	Swinton(h)	L60-22	t:Olpherts,Garrett,Creasser,Currie g:Creasser(3)	9th	400
19/5/96	Prescot(h)	W22-13	t:Olpherts,G Freeman,Long,Stead g:Creasser(3)	8th	200
24/5/96	Barrow(a)	L26-14	t:Terry,Greenwood g:Creasser(3)	9th	608
2/6/96	Doncaster(a)	L26-24	t:Blankley,McKie(2),Garrett g:Creasser(4)	9th	849
9/6/96	York(h)	L38-8	t:Brown,Pickles	9th	400
16/6/96	Leigh(a)	L54-20	t:Creasser,W Freeman,Stead,Fisher g:Creasser(2)	9th	1,056
23/6/96	Hunslet(h)	L56-0	No Scorers	9th	800
30/6/96	South Wales(h)	L44-6	t:Currie g:Long	10th	300
7/7/96	Chorley(a)	W15-10	t:Blankley,McKie g:Long(3) dg:Long	9th	320
14/7/96	Carlisle(h)	L48-12	t:McKie,Creasser g:Creasser(2)	9th	200
21/7/96	Hull KR(h)	L66-16	t:McKie(2),Halmshaw g:Creasser(2)	10th	650
28/7/96	Swinton(a)	L62-4	t:W Freeman	10th	1,201
4/8/96	Prescot(a)	W28-26	t:McKie(2),Pickles(2),Brown g:Creasser(4)	9th	350
11/8/96	Barrow(h)	L20-10	t:Pitt,Pickles g:Creasser	11th	200
18/8/96	Doncaster(h)	L24-20	t:Pitt,Terry,Pickles g:Creasser(4)	11th	650
23/8/96	York(a)	L27-19	t:Pickles,Currie,Stead g:Creasser(3) dg:Blankley	11th	501

SCORERS...League games only

	APP	T	G	DG	PTS
Dean Blankley	22	4	0	1	17
Steve Brown	20(2)	4	0	0	16
Dean Creasser	20	3	51	0	114
Eugene Currie	11(5)	3	0	0	12
Julian Fisher	2(9)	1	0	0	4
Glen Freeman	13(3)	2	0	0	8
Wayne Freeman	18(3)	2	0	0	8
Paul Garrett	4(4)	2	0	0	8
Barry Greenwood	7(3)	1	0	0	4
Dean Hall	4(2)	1	0	0	4
Gary Hall	17	1	0	0	4
Nigel Halmshaw	4	1	0	0	4
Richard Hampshire	1(1)	1	0	0	4
Kenny Hill	2(2)	1	0	0	4
Gordon Long	21	4	4	1	25
Andy McKie	13	8	0	0	32
Eric Olpherts	4	2	0	0	8
Damieon Pickles	12(5)	9	0	0	36
David Pitt	6(1)	2	0	0	8
Craig Robinson	9	3	0	0	12
Martin Rowse	4	2	0	0	8
Richard Stead	11(11)	3	0	0	12
Taniorn Terry	5(1)	2	0	0	8

LEAGUE RECORD
P22-W5-D0-L17
(11th, Div 2)
F360, A759, Diff -399
10 points.

ATTENDANCES
Best - v Leigh (900)
Worst - v Prescot (200)
Total - 5,150
Average - 468
(Up by 22 on
Centenary season)

Dean Blankley -
17 points

198

CARLISLE

DATE	FIXTURE	RESULT	SCORERS	LGE	ATT
31/3/96	Chorley(h)	W66-16	t:Russell,Ruddy(2),Manihera,Cusack(3),Richardson(2),Lynch,Rhodes, Kavanagh g:Richardson(9)	N/A	500
5/4/96	Barrow(a)	W30-10	t:Russell(2),Lynch,Manihera,Ruddy g:Richardson(5)	3rd	921
8/4/96	Leigh(h)	W42-34	t:Manihera(2),Russell(2),Kavanagh,Lynch,Meteer g:Richardson(7)	3rd	650
14/4/96	York(a)	L16-14	t:Manihera,Richardson g:Richardson(3)	3rd	575
21/4/96	Bramley(h)	W26-6	t:Williams,Lynch(2),Graham,Kavanagh g:Richardson(3)	3rd	600
5/5/96	Doncaster(a)	W35-10	t:Williams,Manihera(2),Lynch,Russell(2) g:Richardson(5) dg:Williams	2nd	1,098
12/5/96	Prescot(h)	W38-6	t:Manihera,Richardson(2),Kavanagh,Cusack,Manning g:Richardson(7)	2nd	517
19/5/96	Swinton(a)	L30-22	t:Williams(2),Manihera g:Richardson(5)	4th	1,352
26/5/96	Hull KR(h)	L28-22	t:Richardson,Thurlow,Graham,G Ruddy g:Richardson(3)	4th	917
2/6/96	Hunslet(h)	L23-16	t:Russell(2) g:Richardson(4)	4th	720
8/6/96	South Wales(a)	L37-18	t:Williams,Russell,Ruddy,Richardson g:Richardson	5th	6,708
16/6/96	Chorley(a)	L28-14	t:Graham,Williams g:Richardson(3)	7th	250
23/6/96	Barrow(h)	W50-18	t:Thurlow(2),Warwick,Williams,Russell,Rhodes,Manihera,Scott,Nable g:Richardson(7)	5th	517
30/6/96	Leigh(a)	W27-20	t:Williams(2),J Charlton,Lynch,Rhodes g:Richardson(3) dg:Manihera	5th	1,005
7/7/96	York(h)	W20-19	t:Ruddy,Bell(2),Nable g:Richardson(2)	4th	589
14/7/96	Bramley(a)	W48-12	t:Richardson,Rhodes(3),Manihera(2),Russell,Bell g:Richardson(8)	4th	200
21/7/96	Doncaster(h)	W22-16	t:Richardson,Bell,Manihera,Ruddy g:Richardson(3)	4th	615
28/7/96	Prescot(h)	W56-24	t:Nable(2),G Charlton,Russell(3),Bell,Ruddy(2),Kavanagh g:Richardson(8)	4th	299
4/8/96	Swinton(h)	L32-12	t:Nable,Ruddy g:Richardson(2)	4th	743
11/8/96	Hull KR(a)	L43-12	t:Scott,Meteer g:Richardson(2)	4th	1,633
18/8/96	Hunslet(a)	L52-6	t:Thurlow g:Richardson	4th	710
25/8/96	South Wales(h)	W58-6	t:Russell(2),Cusack(2),Kavanagh,Rhodes(2),Williams,Lynch,Manihera g:Richardson(9)	4th	457

SCORERS...League games only

	APP	T	G	DG	PTS
Alistair Bell	4(2)	5	0	0	20
Gary Charlton	15(2)	1	0	0	4
Jason Charlton	9(5)	1	0	0	4
Sean Cusack	15(1)	6	0	0	24
George Graham	11(2)	3	0	0	12
Mike Kavanagh	14(2)	6	0	0	24
Matt Lynch	20	8	0	0	32
Tane Manihera	20	14	0	1	57
Phil Manning	(3)	1	0	0	4
Paul Meteer	6(8)	2	0	0	8
Matt Nable	16	5	0	0	20
Stuart Rhodes	19(1)	8	0	0	32
Willie Richardson	22	9	100	0	236
Warren Rudd	7(9)	1	0	0	4
Gary Ruddy	16(1)	9	0	0	36
Danny Russell	22	17	0	0	68
Tony Scott	(5)	2	0	0	8
Jason Thurlow	16(1)	4	0	0	16
Dave Warwick	3	1	0	0	4
Barry Williams	18	10	0	1	41

LEAGUE RECORD
P22-W13-D0-L09
(4th, Div 2)
F654, A486, Diff +168
26 points.

ATTENDANCES
Best - v Hull KR (917)
Worst - v South Wales (457)
Total - 6,825
Average - 620
(Up by 125 on
Centenary season)

Danny Russell -
17 tries

199

CHORLEY MAGPIES

DATE	FIXTURE	RESULT	SCORERS	LGE	ATT
31/3/96	Carlisle(a)	L66-16	t:Holden,Walsh,Stewart g:Holden(2)	N/A	500
5/4/96	Doncaster(h)	L62-22	t:Bretherton,M Smith,Stewart g:M Smith(4),Holden	12th	750
8/4/96	Swinton(a)	L54-6	t:Walsh g:A Ruane	12th	1,475
14/4/96	Bramley(a)	L62-10	t:Little,Billington g:D Ruane	12th	450
21/4/96	Hull KR(h)	L92-10	t:Bretherton,Barrow g:Barrow	12th	400
5/5/96	Prescot(a)	L30-24	t:Barrow(2),L Smith,Carden g:Barrow(4)	12th	350
12/5/96	South Wales(a)	L58-0	No Scorers	12th	749
19/5/96	Leigh(h)	W15-14	t:Honey(2),Fairhurst g:A Ruane dg:A Ruane	12th	500
24/5/96	York(a)	L32-4	t:Francis	11th	525
2/6/96	Barrow(h)	W16-11	t:Stewart,Wareing g:Francis(3),Stewart	12th	375
9/6/96	Hunslet(a)	L28-14	t:Stewart,Emery g:Francis(3)	12th	806
16/6/96	Carlisle(h)	W28-14	t:Molyneux,Gee,Drummond(2),Westwood g:Francis(3),Stewart	10th	250
21/6/96	Doncaster(a)	L19-16	t:Waring,Fell,Stewart g:Francis(2)	10th	793
30/6/96	Swinton(h)	L30-16	t:Emery,Sorensen,Gee g:Francis,McMahon	11th	600
7/7/96	Bramley(h)	L15-10	t:Gee,Finney g:McMahon	11th	320
14/7/96	Hull KR(a)	L44-16	t:Gee,Molyneux,Gleave g:Francis(2)	11th	1,745
21/7/96	Prescot(h)	W32-4	t:L Smith(2),Parker(2),Wareing(2) g:Stewart(3),Francis	11th	345
28/7/96	South Wales(h)	L18-16	t:Gee,Ashcroft,Wareing g:Stewart(2)	11th	346
4/8/96	Leigh(a)	L32-26	t:Wareing,Allday,Finney,L Smith g:Francis(3),Allday(2)	11th	1,038
11/8/96	York(h)	W19-14	t:Gee(2),Wareing g:Francis(3) dg:L Smith	10th	262
16/8/96	Barrow(a)	W27-10	t:Wareing(2),Drummond,Molyneux,Briscoe g:Allday,Francis(2) dg:Parker	9th	716
25/8/96	Hunslet(h)	L14-11	t:Parsley,Finney g:Stewart dg:Parker	9th	425

SCORERS...League games only

	APP	T	G	DG	PTS
Neil Allday	1(2)	1	3	0	10
Steve Ashcroft	5	1	0	0	4
Warren Barrow	4	3	5	0	22
Alan Billington	1	1	0	0	4
Chris Bretherton	15	2	0	0	8
Carl Briscoe	4(7)	1	0	0	4
Ian Carden	1(1)	1	0	0	4
Des Drummond	11	3	0	0	12
Paul Emery	14	2	0	0	8
Craig Fairhurst	10	1	0	0	4
David Fell	8(2)	1	0	0	4
Milton Finney	8(4)	3	0	0	12
Stewart Francis	12(1)	1	23	0	50
Stephen Gee	17	7	0	0	28
Mark Gleave	2(4)	1	0	0	4
Martin Holden	4	1	3	0	10
Chris Honey	7(3)	2	0	0	8
Duane Little	5	1	0	0	4
Steve McMahon	2	0	2	0	4
Neil Molyneux	15	3	0	0	12
Carl Parker	6(2)	2	0	2	10
Neil Parsley	5	1	0	0	4
Andy Ruane	5	0	2	1	5
Denis Ruane	4(1)	0	1	0	2
Kurt Sorensen	10(2)	1	0	0	4
Lyndon Smith	16	4	0	1	17
Mike Smith	1(1)	1	4	0	12
Mike Stewart	15	5	8	0	36
Joe Walsh	15(6)	2	0	0	8
Roy Wareing	13	9	0	0	36
Lee Westwood	5(15)	1	0	0	4

LEAGUE RECORD
P22-W6-D0-L16
(9th, Div 2)
F354, A723, Diff -369
12 points.

ATTENDANCES
Best - v Doncaster (750)
Worst - v Carlisle (250)
Total - 4,573
Average - 416
(Down by 85 on
Centenary season)

Des Drummond -
three tries

200

DONCASTER DRAGONS

DATE	FIXTURE	RESULT	SCORERS	LGE	ATT
31/3/96	Barrow(h)	W60-16	t:Goulbourne,Levein,Coult(2),Carlyle(2),Ballot,Picksley(2),Green g:Chappell(10)	N/A	1,106
5/4/96	Chorley(a)	W62-22	t:Roache(3),Carlyle(2),Chappell,Coult,Davidson,Green,Heptinstall,Lidbury, Roberts g:Chappell(6),Green	2nd	750
8/4/96	York(h)	W29-18	t:Carlyle,Chappell,Coult,Hewitt,Picksley g:Chappell(4),Green	2nd	1,449
14/4/96	Swinton(a)	L28-8	t:Roache,Roberts	4th	1,731
21/4/96	South Wales(a)	W22-12	t:Goulbourne,Picksley,Coult,Green g:Chappell(3)	4th	992
5/5/96	Carlisle(h)	L35-10	t:Carlyle,Coult g:Chappell	5th	1,098
12/5/96	Hull KR(h)	L48-16	t:Moore,Coult,Levein g:Chappell(2)	5th	1,348
19/5/96	Hunslet(a)	L42-18	t:Picksley,Coult(2) g:Chappell(3)	5th	1,205
26/5/96	Leigh(a)	L25-12	t:Carlyle,Green g:Chappell(2)	6th	1,019
2/6/96	Bramley(h)	W26-24	t:Lidbury,Hewitt,Coult,Moore,Roberts g:Green(3)	6th	849
9/6/96	Prescot(a)	W48-22	t:Ballot(2),Chrimes,Coult(2),Green,Roberts,Lidbury g:Green(8)	6th	671
14/6/96	Barrow(a)	W21-20	t:Coult(2),Carlyle,Ballot g:Green(2) dg:Green	4th	505
21/6/96	Chorley(h)	W19-16	t:Goulbourne,Roach(2) g:Green(3) dg:Chappell	4th	793
28/6/96	York(a)	W18-14	t:Lidbury,Roberts,Chrimes,Chappell g:Chappell	4th	832
7/7/96	Swinton(h)	L25-4	t:Lidbury	5th	899
14/7/96	South Wales(h)	W24-18	t:Coult,Chappell,Lidbury,Ballot g:Chappell(3) dg:Chappell,Moore	5th	753
21/7/96	Carlisle(a)	L22-16	t:Ballot,Chappell,Roache g:Chappell(2)	5th	615
28/7/96	Hull KR(a)	L52-0	No Scorers	6th	1,840
4/8/96	Hunslet(h)	L46-21	t:Picksley,Busby,Chappell g:Chappell(4) dg:Chappell	6th	723
11/8/96	Leigh(h)	W10-7	t:Moore g:Chappell(3)	6th	767
18/8/96	Bramley(a)	W24-20	t:Carlyle,Hewitt,Moore,Coult g:Chappell(4)	6th	650
25/8/96	Prescot(h)	W32-12	t:Picksley(3),Hewitt,Ballot,Fletcher g:Chappell(4)	5th	837

SCORERS...League games only

	APP	T	G	DG	PTS
Andy Ballot	18(1)	7	0	0	28
Lance Busby	13(3)	1	0	0	4
Brendan Carlyle	22	9	0	0	36
Tony Chappell	17(2)	7	52	3	135
David Chrimes	12(5)	2	0	0	8
Mick Coult	20	17	0	0	68
Jason Davidson	(2)	1	0	0	4
Ian Fletcher	9(3)	1	0	0	4
Alex Goulbourne	14(2)	3	0	0	12
Alex Green	22	4	17	2	52
Jason Heptinstall	(1)	1	0	0	4
Richard Hewitt	9(6)	4	0	0	16
Matt Levein	19(1)	2	0	0	8
Steve Lidbury	12(2)	5	0	0	20
John Moore	15(1)	4	0	1	17
Richard Picksley	14(1)	9	0	0	36
Mark Roache	11(4)	7	0	0	28
Howard Roberts	9(9)	5	0	0	20

LEAGUE RECORD
P22-W13-D0-L9
(5th, Div 2)
F500, A540, Diff -40
26 points.

ATTENDANCES
Best - v York (1,449)
Worst - v Hunslet (723)
Total - 10,622
Average - 966
(Down by 60 on
Centenary season)

Tony Chappell -
52 goals for
the Dragons

HULL KR

DATE	FIXTURE	RESULT	SCORERS	LGE	ATT
31/3/96	South Wales(a)	W70-8	t:Atkins(2),Gene(2),M Fletcher,C Harrison(2),Okul,D'Arcy(2),Crane(2),Hoe g:M Fletcher(9)	N/A	1,879
5/4/96	York(a)	W54-12	t:Brown(2),D'Arcy(2),Gene(2),Charles,Hoe,Wardrobe g:M Fletcher(8),Eastwood	1st	1,434
8/4/96	Hunslet(h)	W30-21	t:D'Arcy(2),Eastwood,Okul g:Eastwood(7)	1st	2,000
14/4/96	Prescot(h)	W50-12	t:Brown,Scott,Atkins(2),C Harrison,Hoe,Adams,D'Arcy,Stewart g:M Fletcher(6),Gene	1st	1,635
21/4/96	Chorley(a)	W92-10	t:C Harrison,Oliver(5),Atkins(2),P Fletcher,Dannatt,Hoe,Gene(2),Crane, M Fletcher,O'Brien,Charles g:M Fletcher(12)	1st	400
5/5/96	Bramley(h)	W56-18	t:Oliver(3),Stewart,Atkins(2),Hoe,D'Arcy(2),Crane g:M Fletcher(8)	1st	1,661
12/5/96	Doncaster(a)	W48-16	t:Hoe,M Fletcher,D'Arcy,Atkins(2),C Harrison,Stewart,Brown g:M Fletcher(6)	1st	1,348
19/5/96	Barrow(h)	W42-10	t:Brown(4),Gene(2),D'Arcy(2) g:M Fletcher(5)	1st	1,564
26/5/96	Carlisle(a)	W28-22	t:Gene(2),Brown,Dearlove g:M Fletcher(6)	1st	917
2/6/96	Leigh(a)	L21-18	t:Atkins(3) g:M Fletcher(3)	1st	1,448
9/6/96	Swinton(h)	W28-24	t:Gene,Atkins,Eastwood,Wilson,Everitt g:M Fletcher(4)	1st	1,721
16/6/96	South Wales(h)	W40-16	t:Atkins(3),P Fletcher(2),Everitt,O'Brien(2) g:M Fletcher(4)	1st	1,412
23/6/96	York(h)	W58-6	t:Hoe,Atkins,Gene(2),Crane(4),O'Brien,D Harrison g:M Fletcher(9)	1st	1,546
30/6/96	Hunslet(a)	W36-14	t:Gene(2),Goulbourne,M Fletcher,Stewart,Wilson g:M Fletcher(6)	1st	2,428
7/7/96	Prescot(a)	W68-4	t:Atkins,C Harrison,Goulbourne,Gene(2),D'Arcy(2),P Fletcher,O'Brien,Brown, Chamberlain,Crane g:M Fletcher(10)	1st	442
14/7/96	Chorley(h)	W44-16	t:Goulbourne,P Fletcher(2),Gene,D'Arcy,Wilson,Brown,Atkins g:M Fletcher(6)	1st	1,745
21/7/96	Bramley(a)	W66-16	t:D'Arcy(2),Wilson(2),P Fletcher(2),Atkins(2),Gene(2),Allen g:M Fletcher(11)	1st	650
28/7/96	Doncaster(h)	W52-0	t:Goulbourne(2),Rouse,Gene(3),Hutchinson,Wilson g:M Fletcher(10)	1st	1,840
2/8/96	Barrow(a)	W18-10	t:Wilson,Atkins,Rouse g: M Fletcher(3)	1st	610
11/8/96	Carlisle(h)	W43-12	t:Rouse(2),Goulbourne(2),Stewart,Allen,Wilson g:M Fletcher(7) dg:Gene	1st	1,633
18/8/96	Leigh(h)	W60-16	t:Rouse,P Fletcher,Goulbourne,Hoe,Gene(2),Atkins(3),Crane,D'Arcy g:M Fletcher(8)	1st	1,928
25/8/96	Swinton(a)	W12-10	t:Gene,D'Arcy g:M Fletcher(2)	1st	2,292
1/9/96	Salford(a)	L36-16(PSF)	t:Allen,Rouse,D'Arcy g:M Fletcher(2)	N/A	2,339

SCORERS...League games only

	APP	T	G	DG	PTS
Jon Adams	1	1	0	0	4
Kieran Allen	6	2	0	0	8
Garry Atkins	21	26	0	0	104
Gary Brown	17	11	0	0	44
Richard Chamberlain	(9)	1	0	0	4
Chris Charles	10(8)	2	0	0	8
Mick Crane	4(17)	10	0	0	40
Andy Dannatt	16	1	0	0	4
Rob D'Arcy	20	19	0	0	76
Andy Dearlove	4(2)	1	0	0	4
Paul Eastwood	9	2	8	0	24
Bob Everitt	2(1)	2	0	0	8
Mike Fletcher	21	4	143	0	302
Paul Fletcher	22	9	0	0	36
Stanley Gene	21(1)	26	1	1	107
Alfie Goulbourne	9(1)	8	0	0	32
Chris Harrison	14(1)	6	0	0	24
Des Harrison	1(6)	1	0	0	4
Sean Hoe	22	8	0	0	32
Darren Hutchinson	(5)	1	0	0	4
Richard O'Brien	(11)	5	0	0	20
John Okul	2(1)	2	0	0	8
Richard Oliver	2	8	0	0	32
Paul Rouse	5(1)	5	0	0	20
Paul Scott	9(3)	1	0	0	4
Sam Stewart	22	5	0	0	20
Neil Wardrobe	(3)	1	0	0	4
Rob Wilson	18(2)	8	0	0	32

LEAGUE RECORD
P22-W21-D0-L1
(Champions, Div 2)
F1009, A294, Diff +715
42 points.

ATTENDANCES
Best - v Hunslet (2,000)
Worst - v South Wales (1,412)
Total - 18,685
Average - 1,699
(Up by 61 on
Centenary season)

Mike Fletcher -
top scorer for Rovers

HUNSLET HAWKS

DATE	FIXTURE	RESULT	SCORERS	LGE	ATT
31/3/96	Prescot(a)	W36-10	t:Viller(2),Plange(2),Battye,Close,Maea g:Wilson(2),Close(2)	N/A	395
5/4/96	Bramley(h)	W31-0	t:Brook,Maea,Rushton,Wilson g:Wilson(7) dg:Close	4th	1,090
8/4/96	Hull KR(a)	L30-21	t:Plange(2),Brook g:Wilson(4) dg:Close	5th	2,000
14/4/96	Leigh(h)	W19-16	t:Plange(2),Hanlan g:Wilson(3) dg:Hanlan	5th	1,002
21/4/96	York(h)	W48-18	t:Brook,Coyle(2),Lambert(2),Lingard,Plange,Farrell,Hanlan g:Wilson(6)	5th	1,105
5/5/96	Swinton(a)	W25-16	t:Sterling,Wilson,Boothroyd,Southernwood g:Wilson(4) dg:Brook	3rd	1,476
10/5/96	Barrow(a)	W44-20	t:Hanlan,Plange(4),Lambert,Boothroyd,Murphy g:Wilson(6)	3rd	668
19/5/96	Doncaster(h)	W42-18	t:Sterling(3),Boothroyd,Brook,Plange(2),Irwin g:Wilson(5)	2nd	1,205
26/5/96	South Wales(a)	W26-19	t:Lingard,Southernwood,Close,Lumb(2) g:Wilson(3)	2nd	919
2/6/96	Carlisle(a)	W23-16	t:Sterling(2),Close,Wilson g:Wilson(2) dg:Close,Hanlan,Wilson	2nd	720
9/6/96	Chorley(h)	W28-14	t:Lambert,Pryce,Wilson,Murphy,Plange g:Wilson(4)	2nd	806
16/6/96	Prescot(h)	W52-12	t:Murphy,Southernwood,Maea(2),Rodger(2),Pryce,Wilson,Plange g:Wilson(8)	2nd	633
23/6/96	Bramley(a)	W56-0	t:Lambert,Murphy(3),Rodger,White(2),Richardson(2),Plange(2) g:Wilson(6)	2nd	800
30/6/96	Hull KR(h)	L36-14	t:Flowers,Lambert,Murphy g:Wilson	2nd	2,428
7/7/96	Leigh(a)	W44-12	t:Southernwood(3),Murphy(3),Maea,Plange g:Wilson(6)	2nd	1,071
12/7/96	York(a)	W34-12	t:Sterling(2),Lambert,Plange(2),Southernwood,Close g:Wilson(3)	2nd	722
19/7/96	Swinton(h)	L12-11	t:Coyle,Sterling g:Wilson dg:Hanlan	3rd	1,318
28/7/96	Barrow(h)	W50-6	t:Irwin(2),Murphy,Maea(2),Southernwood(2),Rodger,Flowers,Wilson g:Wilson(5)	3rd	910
4/8/96	Doncaster(a)	W46-21	t:Close,Brook,Irwin(2),Plange(3),Coyle g:Wilson(7)	3rd	723
11/8/96	South Wales(h)	L21-14	t:Southernwood,Wilson g:Wilson(3)	3rd	873
18/8/96	Carlisle(h)	W52-6	t:Murphy,Irwin,Sterling(4),Plange,Southernwood,Baker,Rushton g:Wilson(6)	3rd	710
25/8/96	Chorley(a)	W14-11	t:Murphy,Lambert,Irwin g:Wilson	3rd	425

SCORERS...League games only

	APP	T	G	DG	PTS
Richard Baker	5(3)	1	0	0	4
Neil Battye	1	1	0	0	4
Giles Boothroyd	11(2)	3	0	0	12
David Brook	14(5)	5	0	1	21
David Close	18	5	2	2	26
Mick Coyle	17(4)	4	0	0	16
Carlton Farrell	2(4)	1	0	0	4
Stewart Flowers	9(4)	2	0	0	8
Lee Hanlan	9(7)	3	0	4	16
Shaun Irwin	13	7	0	0	28
Matt Lambert	20(1)	8	0	0	32
Glyn Lingard	6(8)	2	0	0	8
Tim Lumb	(2)	1	0	0	4
Des Maea	13(9)	7	0	0	28
Tim Murphy	13(5)	13	0	0	52
David Plange	22	25	0	0	100
Steve Pryce	21(1)	2	0	0	8
Gary Richardson	1(2)	2	0	0	8
Brett Rodger	11	4	0	0	16
Nick Rushton	17(3)	2	0	0	8
Graham Southernwood	17(2)	11	0	0	44
Paul Sterling	12	13	0	0	52
Jason Viller	3(2)	2	0	0	8
Paul White	2(2)	2	0	0	8
Simon Wilson	22	7	93	1	215

LEAGUE RECORD
P22-W18-D0-L4
(3rd, Div 2)
F730, A326, Diff +404
36 points.

ATTENDANCES
Best - v Hull KR (2,428)
Worst - v Prescot (633)
Total - 12,080
Average - 1,098
(Up by 228 on
Centenary season)

Simon Wilson -
215 points for
the Hawks

LEIGH CENTURIONS

DATE	FIXTURE	RESULT	SCORERS	LGE	ATT
31/3/96	Bramley(a)	L16-14	t:Mason,Stazicker,Burgess g:Wilkinson	N/A	900
5/4/96	Swinton(h)	L46-24	t:Ball,Daniel,Hill,McGughan,Veikoso g:Wilkinson(2)	9th	1,933
8/4/96	Carlisle(a)	L42-34	t:Cain,Hadcroft,Hill,Ingram,Lyon,Mason g:Wilkinson(5)	10th	650
14/4/96	Hunslet(a)	L19-16	t:Purtill,O'Loughlin g:Purtill(4)	11th	1,002
21/4/96	Prescot(h)	W49-12	t:Mason,Daniel(2),Purtill,Quigley,Bannister,Liku,Hadcroft g:Purtill(8) dg:Mason	9th	1,124
5/5/96	South Wales(h)	L23-20	t:Daniel,Mason(2) g:Purtill(4)	10th	1,090
12/5/96	York(h)	W42-16	t:Mason,Lyon(2),Quigley,Hadcroft,Ball,Purtill g:Purtill(7)	8th	968
19/5/96	Chorley(a)	L15-14	t:Ingram,Hadcroft,Lyon g:Purtill	9th	500
26/5/96	Doncaster(h)	W25-12	t:Mason,Lyon(2),Daniel,Cheetham g:Purtill(2) dg:Mason	8th	1,019
2/6/96	Hull KR(h)	W21-18	t:Veikoso(2),Cheetham g:Purtill(4) dg:Brown	7th	1,448
7/6/96	Barrow(a)	W41-12	t:Ingram(3),Purtill(2),Perigo,Quigley g:Purtill(6) dg:Brown	7th	705
16/6/96	Bramley(h)	W54-20	t:Lyon(2),Hadcroft,Quigley,Purtill,Hill(2),Ingram g:Purtill(11)	6th	1,056
23/6/96	Swinton(a)	L30-14	t:Ingram(2) g:Purtill(3)	7th	1,848
30/6/96	Carlisle(h)	W27-20	t:Burgess(3),Cheetham g:Purtill(2)	8th	1,005
7/7/96	Hunslet(h)	L44-12	t:Ingram,Ball g:Purtill(2)	8th	1,071
14/7/96	Prescot(a)	W42-2	t:Ingram(3),Purtill,O'Loughlin,Quigley(2) g:Purtill(7)	7th	450
21/7/96	South Wales(a)	L30-22	t:Ingram(4) g:Purtill(3)	8th	742
26/7/96	York(a)	W31-6	t:Ingram,O'Loughlin,Purtill,Ball g:Purtill(7) dg:Mason	7th	503
4/8/96	Chorley(h)	W32-26	t:Veikoso(3),Ingram(2) g:Purtill(6)	7th	1,038
11/8/96	Doncaster(a)	L10-7	t:Purtill g:Purtill dg:Mason	7th	767
18/8/96	Hull KR(a)	L60-16	t:Ingram,Purtill g:Purtill(4)	7th	1,928
25/8/96	Barrow(h)	W44-24	t:Purtill,Burgess,Quigley(2),Ingram,Cheetham,Blakeley g:Purtill(8)	7th	812

SCORERS...League games only

	APP	T	G	DG	PTS
Rob Ball	20(1)	4	0	0	16
Shaun Bannister	7	1	0	0	4
Mike Blakeley	3	1	0	0	4
Shaun Brown	8(1)	0	0	2	2
Barry Burgess	9	5	0	0	20
Alex Cain	14(4)	1	0	0	4
Andy Cheetham	10(1)	4	0	0	16
Paul Daniel	17(1)	5	0	0	20
Alan Hadcroft	16(1)	5	0	0	20
David Hill	14(8)	4	0	0	16
David Ingram	13(8)	21	0	0	84
Tau Liku	9(1)	1	0	0	4
David Lyon	12(1)	8	0	0	32
Alan Mason	15(5)	8	0	4	36
Mark McGughan	10(3)	1	0	0	4
Jason O'Loughlin	15(6)	3	0	0	12
John Perigo	5(3)	1	0	0	4
Dean Purtill	18	11	90	0	224
Jonathan Quigley	19	8	0	0	32
Ged Stazicker	3(1)	1	0	0	4
Jimmy Veikoso	17	6	0	0	24
Chris Wilkinson	3	0	8	0	16

LEAGUE RECORD
P22-W10-D0-L12
(7th, Div 2)
F594, A510, Diff +84
20 points.

ATTENDANCES
Best - v Swinton (1,933)
Worst - v Barrow (812)
Total - 12,564
Average - 1,142
(Down by 53 on
Centenary season)

Paul Daniel -
five tries in 17
full appearances

204

PRESCOT PANTHERS

DATE	FIXTURE	RESULT	SCORERS	LGE	ATT
31/3/96	Hunslet(h)	L36-10	t:England,Fanning g:Fanning	N/A	395
5/4/96	South Wales(h)	L24-22	t:England(2),Deakin,Munro g:Fanning(3)	10th	477
8/4/96	Barrow(h)	W20-8	t:Deakin(2),Mort g:Fanning(4)	7th	358
14/4/96	Hull KR(a)	L50-12	t:Fanning,England g:Fanning(2)	9th	1,635
21/4/96	Leigh(a)	L49-12	t:England,Deakin g:Fanning(2)	11th	1,124
5/5/96	Chorley(h)	W30-24	t:Melling,Scholes(2),Diggle,Hamer g:Fanning(5)	9th	350
12/5/96	Carlisle(a)	L38-6	t:Deakin g:Fanning	10th	517
19/5/96	Bramley(a)	L22-13	t:Fanning g:Fanning(4) dg:Charlesworth	10th	200
26/5/96	Swinton(h)	L34-12	t:Deakin,England g:Fanning(2)	11th	570
31/5/96	York(a)	L30-10	t:Hale,Eastwood g:Fanning	11th	533
9/6/96	Doncaster(h)	L48-22	t:Bridge,Fanning,Boucher g:Fanning(5)	11th	671
16/6/96	Hunslet(a)	L52-12	t:Evans(2) g:Fanning(2)	12th	633
23/6/96	South Wales(a)	L50-18	t:Mort,Graziano,Melling g:Fanning(3)	12th	300
28/6/96	Barrow(a)	L30-6	t:Ledger g:Errington	12th	540
7/7/96	Hull KR(h)	L68-4	t:Callaghan	12th	442
14/7/96	Leigh(h)	L42-2	g:Fanning	12th	450
21/7/96	Chorley(a)	L32-4	t:Bell	12th	345
28/7/96	Carlisle(h)	L56-24	t:Scholes,Callaghan,Harris,Ledger g:Fanning(4)	12th	299
4/8/96	Bramley(h)	L28-26	t:Scholes,Wade,Ledger(2) g:Fanning(4) dg:Callaghan(2)	12th	350
11/8/96	Swinton(a)	L90-0	No Scorers	12th	1,244
18/8/96	York(h)	L44-24	t:Stephenson(2),Bellis,Pennington g:Callaghan(4)	12th	120
25/8/96	Doncaster(a)	L32-12	t:Chisnall,Smith g:Callaghan(2)	12th	837

SCORERS...League games only

	APP	T	G	DG	PTS
Kevin Bell	3	1	0	0	4
Craig Bellis	3(1)	1	0	0	4
Philip Boucher	3	1	0	0	4
Russ Bridge	17(1)	1	0	0	4
Ian Callaghan	19(1)	2	6	2	22
Lee Charlesworth	2	0	0	1	1
Darren Chisnall	2(5)	1	0	0	4
Mike Deakin	7(7)	6	0	0	24
Craig Diggle	3	1	0	0	4
Jonathan Eastwood	6	1	0	0	4
Alan England	11(3)	6	0	0	24
Craig Errington	4	0	1	0	2
Matt Evans	7(1)	2	0	0	8
Sean Fanning	19	4	44	0	104
Joe Graziano	8(1)	1	0	0	4
Chris Hale	2(1)	1	0	0	4
Dave Hamer	15(6)	1	0	0	4
Darren Harris	4	1	0	0	4
Barry Ledger	7	4	0	0	16
Alex Melling	7(2)	2	0	0	8
Craig Mort	14(2)	2	0	0	8
Dave Munro	3(1)	1	0	0	4
Tony Pennington	3(4)	1	0	0	4
Damien Scholes	10(3)	4	0	0	16
Simon Smith	3	1	0	0	4
Andy Stephenson	4(1)	2	0	0	8
Neil Wade	16(2)	1	0	0	4

LEAGUE RECORD
P22-W2-D0-L20
(12th, Div 2)
F301, A883, Diff -582
4 points.

ATTENDANCES
Best - v Doncaster (671)
Worst - v York (120)
Total - 4,482
Average - 407
(Up by 69 on
Centenary season)

Craig Errington -
one goal for
the Panthers

SOUTH WALES

DATE	FIXTURE	RESULT	SCORERS	LGE	ATT
31/3/96	Hull KR(h)	L70-8	t:Rees,Alvis	N/A	1,879
5/4/96	Prescot(a)	W24-22	t:Currier,Marshall,Perryment,Riley,Waddell g:Rees(2)	8th	477
8/4/96	Bramley(h)	W22-18	t:Churcher,Healey,Hatton,Marshall g:Healey(3)	6th	552
12/4/96	Barrow(a)	L16-4	t:Perryment	8th	460
21/4/96	Doncaster(h)	L22-12	t:Alvis,Marshall g:Rees(2)	8th	992
5/5/96	Leigh(a)	W23-20	t:Marshall,Currier,Kelly,Alvis g:Healey(3) dg:Hatton	7th	1,090
12/5/96	Chorley(h)	W58-0	t:Marshall(2),Warburton,Williamson(2),Morris(2),D Williams(2),Churcher g:Healey(9)	6th	749
19/5/96	York(a)	L54-26	t:Perryment,Williamson,D Williams,Moriarty,Wysocki g:Healey(3)	6th	466
26/5/96	Hunslet(h)	L26-19	t:Alvis,Wysocki,Hatton,Currier g:Bebb dg:Churcher	7th	919
2/6/96	Swinton(a)	L26-8	t:Currier g:Bebb(2)	8th	1,101
8/6/96	Carlisle(h)	W37-18	t:Currier(2),Wallington(2),Bebb,Cordle g:Bebb(6) dg:Wallington	8th	6,708
16/6/96	Hull KR(a)	L40-16	t:Cordle(2),Alvis g:Bebb(2)	8th	1,412
23/6/96	Prescot(h)	W50-18	t:Cordle,Currier,Hatton,Bebb,D Williams,Marshall,Mills,Wallington g:Bebb(9)	8th	300
30/6/96	Bramley(a)	W44-6	t:Currier(4),Marshall,Riley(2),Bebb g:Bebb(6)	6th	300
7/7/96	Barrow(h)	W48-16	t:Marshall,Bebb(2),Wallington,Currier,Jenkins,Hatton(2),Bernard(2) g:Bebb(4)	6th	300
14/7/96	Doncaster(a)	L24-18	t:Marshall,Currier,Riley g:Bebb(3)	6th	753
21/7/96	Leigh(h)	W30-22	t:Bebb,G Williams,Currier,Mawdsley,Jenkins g:Bebb(4) dg:Hatton(2)	6th	742
28/7/96	Chorley(a)	W18-16	t:Currier,Marshall,Bebb g:Bebb(2) dg:Wallington(2)	5th	346
4/8/96	York(h)	W20-16	t:Perryment,G Williams,Marshall,Riley g:Bebb(2)	5th	400
11/8/96	Hunslet(a)	W21-14	t:Perryment(2),Riley g:Bebb(3) dg:Hatton,Docherty(2)	5th	873
18/8/96	Swinton(a)	L26-16	t:Riley,Docherty,Currier g:Docherty(2)	5th	1,477
25/8/96	Carlisle(a)	L58-6	t:Currier g:Bebb	6th	457

SCORERS...League games only

	APP	T	G	DG	PTS
James Alvis	3(11)	5	0	0	20
Marcus Barnard	4(4)	2	0	0	8
Ioan Bebb	15	7	45	0	118
James Churcher	7(3)	2	0	1	9
Gerald Cordle	6	4	0	0	16
Andy Currier	22	14	0	0	56
John-Paul Docherty	5	1	2	2	10
Anthony Hatton	21	5	0	4	24
Mike Healey	6(2)	1	18	0	40
Nick Jenkins	9	2	0	0	8
Neil Kelly	3(2)	1	0	0	4
Shaun Marshall	20(1)	14	0	0	56
Neil Mawdsley	3(1)	1	0	0	4
John McAtee	3	1	0	0	4
Paul Mills	11	1	0	0	4
Paul Moriarty	5	1	0	0	4
Nigel Morris	4(1)	2	0	0	8
Ian Perryment	10(2)	6	0	0	24
Dai Rees	3	1	4	0	12
Mike Riley	22	7	0	0	28
Hugh Waddell	9(6)	1	0	0	4
Mark Wallington	11(3)	4	0	3	19
Steve Warburton	1(5)	1	0	0	4
David Williams	7(2)	4	0	0	16
Gerald Williams	18	2	0	0	8
Paul Williamson	2(1)	3	0	0	12
Mark Wysocki	4(2)	2	0	0	8

LEAGUE RECORD
P22-W12-D0-L10
(6th, Div 2)
F528, A548, Diff -20
24 points.

ATTENDANCES
Best - v Carlisle (6,708)
Worst - v Prescot (300)
Total - 14,642
Average - 1,331

Andy Currier -
ever present for
South Wales

206

SWINTON LIONS

DATE	FIXTURE	RESULT	SCORERS	LGE	ATT
31/3/96	York(a)	L23-18	t:Morrison,Ashcroft(2),Riley g:Birkett	N/A	803
5/4/96	Leigh(a)	W46-24	t:Ashcroft(2),Price-Jones(2),Birkett,Cannon,Gunning,Riley,Roach g:Birkett(5)	5th	1,933
8/4/96	Chorley(h)	W54-6	t:Welsby(3),Cannon(2),Ashcroft,Price-Jones,Roach,Rodger,Skeech, Wolfgramm g:Roach(3),Birkett(2)	4th	1,475
14/4/96	Doncaster(h)	W28-8	t:Welsby,Roach,Riley,Cannon,Barrow g:Pearce(4)	2nd	1,731
21/4/96	Barrow(h)	W36-10	t:Birkett,Roach,Sheals,Riley,Cannon,Welsby g:Pearce(6)	2nd	1,378
5/5/96	Hunslet(h)	L25-16	t:Cannon,Roach g:Pearce(4)	4th	1,476
12/5/96	Bramley(a)	W60-22	t:Riley(3),Casey,Birkett,Holliday,Pearce,Wolfgramm,Ashcroft,Welsby g:Pearce(10)	4th	400
19/5/96	Carlisle(h)	W30-22	t:Morrison,Gibson,Welsby,Barrow g:Pearce(7)	3rd	1,352
26/5/96	Prescot(a)	W34-12	t:Birkett,Cannon,Roach,Barrow,Welsby,Ashcroft,Wolfgramm g:Pearce(3)	3rd	570
2/6/96	South Wales(a)	W26-8	t:Roach(3),Gibson,Ashcroft g:Pearce(3)	3rd	1,101
9/6/96	Hull KR(a)	L28-24	t:Gibson,Holliday,Birkett(2) g:Pearce(3),Holliday	3rd	1,721
16/6/96	York(h)	W64-0	t:Liava'a,Roach(2),McCabe,Riley(3),Wolfgramm(4) g:Pearce(10)	3rd	1,096
23/6/96	Leigh(h)	W30-14	t:Welsby(2),Roach,Wolfgramm,Riley g:Pearce(5)	3rd	1,848
30/6/96	Chorley(a)	W30-16	t:Wolfgramm(2),Gibson,Price-Jones,Roach g:Pearce(5)	3rd	600
7/7/96	Doncaster(a)	W25-4	t:Liava'a(2),Price-Jones,Roach g:Pearce(4) dg:Holliday	3rd	899
12/7/96	Barrow(a)	W32-18	t:Price-Jones,Pearce,Riley(2),Wolfgramm g:Pearce(6)	3rd	586
19/7/96	Hunslet(a)	W12-11	t:Liava'a g:Pearce(3) dg:Price-Jones,Holliday	2nd	1,318
28/7/96	Bramley(h)	W62-4	t:Roach(3),Wolfgramm,Sheals,Casey,Riley(2),Liava'a,Ashcroft,Gibson g:Pearce(9)	2nd	1,201
4/8/96	Carlisle(a)	W32-12	t:Holliday(2),Riley,Liava'a g:Pearce(8)	2nd	743
11/8/96	Prescot(h)	W90-0	t:Riley(6),Roach(5),Ashcroft(3),Pearce(2),Wolfgramm g:Pearce(11)	2nd	1,244
18/8/96	South Wales(h)	W26-16	t:Ashcroft(2),Roach,Riley,Holliday g:Pearce(3)	2nd	1,477
25/8/96	Hull KR(h)	L12-10	t:Roach g:Pearce(3)	2nd	2,292

SCORERS...League games only

	APP	T	G	DG	PTS
Simon Ashcroft	19	14	0	0	56
Tony Barrow	22	3	0	0	12
Martin Birkett	15(6)	6	8	0	40
Peter Cannon	16(4)	7	0	0	28
Leo Casey	19(2)	2	0	0	8
Steve Gibson	8(7)	5	0	0	20
John Gunning	1(2)	1	0	0	4
Les Holliday	19(3)	4	1	2	20
Talite Liava'a	11(5)	6	0	0	24
Carl McCabe	19	1	0	0	4
Tony Morrison	7	2	0	0	8
Greg Pearce	19	4	107	0	230
Gavin Price-Jones	12(8)	6	0	1	25
Mark Riley	15(7)	23	0	0	92
Jason Roach	22	24	3	0	102
Brett Rodger	(2)	1	0	0	4
Mark Sheals	19(1)	2	0	0	8
Ian Skeech	(5)	1	0	0	4
Mark Welsby	19	11	0	0	44
Willie Wolfgramm	15(4)	13	0	0	52

LEAGUE RECORD
P22-W18-D0-L4
(2nd, Div 2)
F785, A295, Diff +490
36 points.

ATTENDANCES
Best - v Hull KR (2,292)
Worst - v York (1,096)
Total - 16,570
Average - 1,506
(Up by 749 on
Centenary season)

Willie Wolfgramm -
13 tries in 15
full appearances

YORK

DATE	FIXTURE	RESULT	SCORERS	LGE	ATT
31/3/96	Swinton(h)	W23-18	t:Hill,Hopcutt,Laurence g:Precious(3),Smirk(2) dg:Precious	N/A	803
5/4/96	Hull KR(h)	L54-12	t:Laurence,Mountain g:Smirk(2)	7th	1,434
8/4/96	Doncaster(a)	L29-18	t:Hill,Pallister,Smirk g:Smirk(3)	9th	1,449
14/4/96	Carlisle(h)	W16-14	t:Pallister,Forsyth g:Cain(2),Ball dg:Smirk,C Brown	7th	575
21/4/96	Hunslet(a)	L48-18	t:Hopcutt,Cain,Laurence g:Smirk(3)	7th	1,105
3/5/96	Barrow(h)	W20-8	t:P Brown(2),Ball,Laurence g:Smirk,Ball	6th	462
12/5/96	Leigh(a)	L42-16	t:Mawer,Cain,Smith g:Smirk(2)	7th	968
19/5/96	South Wales(h)	W54-26	t:Smirk(3),Hopcutt(2),Cain(2),Laurence,Johnson,Judge g:Smirk(7)	7th	466
24/5/96	Chorley(h)	W32-4	t:Hopcutt(3),Ball,Smith,Johnson,P Brown g:Smirk(2)	5th	525
31/5/96	Prescot(h)	W30-10	t:Hopcutt,Ball,Laurence,Mawer,Smirk,Judge g:Smirk(3)	5th	533
9/6/96	Bramley(a)	W38-8	t:Mawer,Laurence(2),Hopcutt,Ball,Johnson g:Smirk(7)	4th	400
16/6/96	Swinton(a)	L64-0	No Scorers	5th	1,096
23/6/96	Hull KR(a)	L58-6	t:Mawer g:Precious	6th	1,546
28/6/96	Doncaster(h)	L18-14	t:Laurence,Smith g:Precious(3)	7th	832
7/7/96	Carlisle(a)	L20-19	t:Moore(2),Hopcutt g:Precious(3) dg:Precious	7th	589
12/7/96	Hunslet(h)	L34-12	t:Smith,Ball g:Precious dg:Precious,Smirk	8th	722
19/7/96	Barrow(a)	L35-18	t:Hopcutt,Smith g:Precious(4),Smirk	8th	611
26/7/96	Leigh(h)	L31-6	t:Smirk g:Precious	8th	503
4/8/96	South Wales(a)	L20-16	t:Smith(2),Ball g:Smirk(2)	8th	400
11/8/96	Chorley(a)	L19-14	t:Ball,Pallister g:Smirk(3)	8th	262
18/8/96	Prescot(a)	W44-24	t:Precious,Hopcutt,Knighton(2),Smirk,C Brown,Parry g:Smirk(7) dg:Precious(2)	8th	120
23/8/96	Bramley(h)	W27-19	t:Ball,Hayes,Forsyth,Cain g:Smirk(5) dg:C Brown	8th	501

SCORERS...League games only

	APP	T	G	DG	PTS
Damian Ball	21(1)	8	2	0	36
Colin Brown	3(9)	1	0	2	6
Paul Brown	7(4)	3	0	0	12
Mark Cain	15(6)	5	2	0	24
Craig Forsyth	21	2	0	0	8
Richard Hayes	20	1	0	0	4
Rod Hill	6	2	0	0	8
Chris Hopcutt	21	12	0	0	48
Mick Johnson	12	3	0	0	12
Chris Judge	4(6)	2	0	0	8
Adam Knighton	11(2)	2	0	0	8
Jason Laurence	14	9	0	0	36
Keith Mawer	9(1)	3	0	0	12
Craig Moore	8(3)	3	0	0	12
Gary Mountain	3	1	0	0	4
Alan Pallister	18(2)	3	0	0	12
Dave Parry	1	1	0	0	4
Andy Precious	8(6)	1	16	5	41
Terry Smirk	22	7	50	2	130
Dave Smith	12(6)	7	0	0	28

LEAGUE RECORD
P22-W9-D0-L13
(8th, Div 2)
F453, A603, Diff -150
18 points.

ATTENDANCES
Best - v Hull KR (1,434)
Worst - v Barrow (462)
Total - 7,356
Average - 669
(Up by 27 on
Centenary season)

Terry Smirk -
York's top scorer

TOP TRIES

SUPER LEAGUE
1. Paul Newlove 28
2. Jason Robinson ...24
3. John Bentley 21
4. Henry Paul 20
5. Danny Arnold 19
6. Robbie Paul 18
7. Keith Senior 17
   Richard Henare ..17
9. Greg Barwick 16
   Anthony Sullivan ...16
   Rob Smyth 16

DIVISION ONE
1. Jason Critchley 21
2. Nathan McAvoy ...16
   Darren Rogers ...16
4. Eddie Rombo 15
   Dean Hanger 15
   Fata Sini 15
   Brad Davis 15
8. Martin Pearson ..14
   Tevita Vaikona 14
   Andrew King 14
   Nick Pinkney 14

DIVISION TWO
1. Garry Atkins 26
   Stanley Gene 26
3. David Plange 25
4. Jason Roach 24
5. Mark Riley 23
6. David Ingram 21
7. Rob D'Arcy 19
8. Danny Russell ...17
   Mick Coult 17
10. Tane Manihera 14
    Andy Currier 14
    Shaun Marshall ..14
    Simon Ashcroft 14

OVERALL
1. Paul Newlove 28
2. Garry Atkins 26
   Stanley Gene 26
4. David Plange 25
5. Jason Roach 24
   Jason Robinson ...24
7. Mark Riley 23
8. John Bentley 21
   Jason Critchley ...21
   David Ingram 21

TOP GOALS

SUPER LEAGUE
1. Bobbie Goulding . .117
2. Andy Farrell 103
3. John Schuster ...101
4. Mark Aston 86
5. Frano Botica 84
6. Steve McNamara ..78
7. Graham Holroyd ..76
8. Iestyn Harris 63
9. Greg Barwick 50
10. Francis Maloney ..45

DIVISION ONE
1. Steve Blakeley 84
2. Martin Pearson ...81
3. Mark Hewitt 67
4. Brad Davis 62
5. Christian Tyrer ..54
6. Keith Dixon 46
7. Barry Eaton 42
8. Steve Booth 26
   Craig Booth 26
10. Greg Austin 25

DIVISION TWO
1. Mike Fletcher 143
2. Greg Pearce 107
3. Willie Richardson .100
4. Simon Wilson 93
5. Dean Purtill 90
6. Phil Atkinson 57
7. Tony Chappell ...52
8. Dean Creasser ...51
9. Terry Smirk 50
10. Ioan Bebb 45

OVERALL
1. Mike Fletcher 143
2. Bobbie Goulding ..117
3. Greg Pearce 107
4. Andy Farrell 103
5. John Schuster ...101
6. Willie Richardson .100
7. Simon Wilson 93
8. Dean Purtill 90
9. Mark Aston 86
10. Frano Botica 84
    Steve Blakeley 84

TOP POINTS

SUPER LEAGUE
1. Bobbie Goulding . .257
2. John Schuster ...236
3. Andy Farrell 226
4. Graham Holroyd ..198
5. Frano Botica 190
6. Mark Aston 181
7. Greg Barwick 166
8. Steve McNamara ..162
9. Iestyn Harris ...144
10. Francis Maloney ..114

DIVISION ONE
1. Martin Pearson ...219
2. Steve Blakeley 204
3. Brad Davis 187
4. Mark Hewitt 138
5. Christian Tyrer ...135
6. Keith Dixon 112
7. Barry Eaton 93
8. Greg Austin 90
9. Jason Critchley 84
10. Fata Sini 80

DIVISION TWO
1. Mike Fletcher 302
2. Willie Richardson .236
3. Greg Pearce 230
4. Dean Purtill 224
5. Simon Wilson 215
6. Phil Atkinson 159
7. Tony Chappell ...135
8. Terry Smirk 130
9. Ioan Bebb 118
10. Dean Creasser ...114

OVERALL
1. Mike Fletcher 302
2. Bobbie Goulding . .257
3. Willie Richardson .236
   John Schuster ...236
5. Greg Pearce 230
6. Andy Farrell 226
7. Dean Purtill 224
8. Martin Pearson ...219
9. Simon Wilson 215
10. Steve Blakeley ...204

ATTENDANCES

	'96 Avg	'95-'96 Avg	Diff
Bradford	10,346	4,593	+5,753
St Helens	10,221	7,143	+3,708
Wigan	10,152	11,947	-1,795
Leeds	8,581	11,594	-3,013
Paris	8,092	N/A	N/A
London	5,418	2,386	+3,032
Warrington	5,157	4,922	+235
Halifax	5,080	4,657	+423
Castleford	5,012	4,072	+940
Keighley	4,871	3,787	+1,084
Sheffield	4,534	3,106	+1,428
Oldham	3,629	3,187	+442
Salford	3,495	2,610	+885
Huddersfield	3,344	2,427	+917
Hull	3,008	2,824	+184
Widnes	2,528	2,908	-380
Workington	2,322	3,061	-739
Wakefield	2,109	1,824	+285
Featherstone	1,988	2,097	-109
Hull KR	1,699	1,638	+61
Swinton	1,506	757	+749
Dewsbury	1,402	1,324	+78
Batley	1,358	1,305	+53
South Wales	1,331	N/A	N/A
Rochdale	1,271	1,298	-27
Leigh	1,142	1,195	-53
Hunslet	1,098	870	+228
Whitehaven	1,081	1,205	-124
Doncaster	966	1,026	-60
York	669	642	+27
Barrow	630	666	-36
Carlisle	620	495	+125
Bramley	468	446	+22
Chorley	416	501	-85
Prescot	407	338	+69

Div One Total	264,542
Div One Average ('96)	2,405
Div One Average ('95-'96)	2,146
Difference	+259
Div Two Total	113,123
Div Two Average ('96)	857
Div Two Average ('95-'96)	780
Difference	+77
Super Lge Total	863,978
Super Lge Average ('96)	6,545
Super Lge Average ('95-'96)	5,515
Difference	+1,030

1996 FINAL TABLES

STONES SUPER LEAGUE

	P	W	D	L	F	A	D	PTS
St Helens	22	20	0	2	950	455	495	40
Wigan	22	19	1	2	902	326	576	39
Bradford	22	17	0	5	767	409	358	34
London	22	12	1	9	611	462	149	25
Warrington	22	12	0	10	569	565	4	24
Halifax	22	10	1	11	667	576	91	21
Sheffield	22	10	0	12	599	730	-131	20
Oldham	22	9	1	12	473	681	-208	19
Castleford	22	9	0	13	548	599	-51	18
Leeds	22	6	0	16	555	745	-190	12
Paris	22	3	1	18	398	795	-397	7
Workington	22	2	1	19	325	1021	-696	5

DIVISION ONE

	P	W	D	L	F	A	D	PTS
Salford	20	18	0	2	733	298	435	36
Keighley	20	14	2	4	558	333	225	30
Hull	20	14	0	6	565	392	173	28
Featherstone	20	12	2	6	557	371	186	26
Huddersfield	20	12	0	8	557	308	249	24
Wakefield	20	10	1	9	485	455	30	21
Widnes	20	9	1	10	413	447	-34	19
Dewsbury	20	6	1	13	264	618	-354	13
Whitehaven	20	5	1	14	328	546	-218	11
Rochdale	20	2	2	16	348	602	-254	6
Batley	20	2	2	16	230	668	-438	6

DIVISION TWO

	P	W	D	L	F	A	D	PTS
Hull KR	22	21	0	1	1009	294	715	42
Swinton	22	18	0	4	785	295	490	36
Hunslet	22	18	0	4	730	326	404	36
Carlisle	22	13	0	9	654	486	168	26
Doncaster	22	13	0	9	500	540	-40	26
South Wales	22	12	0	10	528	548	-20	24
Leigh	22	10	0	12	594	510	84	20
York	22	9	0	13	453	603	-150	18
Chorley	22	6	0	16	354	723	-369	12
Barrow	22	5	0	17	354	651	-297	10
Bramley	22	5	0	17	360	759	-399	10
Prescot	22	2	0	20	301	887	-586	4